WE ARE THE WORLD (CUP)

Also by Roger Bennett

*(Re)Born in the USA: An Englishman's
Love Letter to His Chosen Home*

WE ARE THE WORLD (CUP)

A Personal History of the World's Greatest Sporting Event

Roger Bennett

DEYST.

An Imprint of WILLIAM MORROW

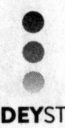

DEYST.

Without limiting the exclusive rights of any author, contributor or the publisher of this publication, any unauthorized use of this publication to train generative artificial intelligence (AI) technologies is expressly prohibited. HarperCollins also exercise their rights under Article 4(3) of the Digital Single Market Directive 2019/790 and expressly reserve this publication from the text and data mining exception.

Lyrics from "The Long Cut" written by Jeff Tweedy. © 1993 Words Ampersand Music (BMI). Used by permission of Universal Music Publishing Group.

Lyrics from "Don't Tread" written in collaboration with Clint Dempsey, John Edward Hawkins (Big Hawk), and Steven Molanders (XO) © 2006. Used by permission of Clint Dempsey.

WE ARE THE WORLD (CUP). Copyright © 2026 by In Loving Memory of the Recent Past 2 Inc. All rights reserved. Printed in the United States of America. No part of this book may be used or reproduced in any manner whatsoever without written permission except in the case of brief quotations embodied in critical articles and reviews. For information, address HarperCollins Publishers, 195 Broadway, New York, NY 10007. In Europe, HarperCollins Publishers, Macken House, 39/40 Mayor Street Upper, Dublin 1, D01 C9W8, Ireland.

HarperCollins books may be purchased for educational, business, or sales promotional use. For information, please email the Special Markets Department at SPsales@harpercollins.com.

hc.com

FIRST EDITION

Designed by Patrick Barry

Library of Congress Cataloging-in-Publication Data has been applied for.

ISBN 978-0-06-332077-2

26 27 28 29 30 LBC 5 4 3 2 1

To Vanessa, who always knew, believed when I did not, and saw it all. Big Love.

Football is a pleasure that hurts.
—Eduardo Galeano,
Football in Sun and Shadow

Oh, can you believe this? Go, go, USA! Certainly through! Oh, it's incredible! You could not write a script like this!
—Ian Darke, 91st minute,
USA 1 Algeria 0 2010

CONTENTS

Introduction xi

1: **1978 World Cup, Argentina** 1

2: **1982 World Cup, Spain** 22

3: **1986 World Cup, Mexico** 38

4: **1990 World Cup, Italy** 56

5: **1994 World Cup, USA** 72

6: **1998 World Cup, France** 94

7: **2002 World Cup, Korea/Japan** 119

8: **2006 World Cup, Germany** 145

9: **2010 World Cup, South Africa** 167

10: **2014 World Cup, Brazil** 196

11: **2018 World Cup, Russia** 238

12: **2022 World Cup, Qatar** 282

Afterword: **Soccer's Coming Home** 323

Acknowledgments 325

Introduction

A WORLD CUP has been compared to a solar eclipse that engulfs the entire planet simultaneously for its duration, though not in darkness but in football. I have always adored that image and believe it to be true. But for me, and millions of football mad fans around the world, the World Cup is far more powerful and personal than a mere cosmic lightshow. The tournament is both a history of moments and a shared text that creates the deepest connection to our own individual pasts as a biography of our childhoods, teenaged years, and beyond. It is the definitive mechanism through which we measure and mark the very passing of time.

The tournament's power is complex. Part of it lies in its every four-year pacing, a bassline rhythm which has made it the spine to my life. Allow me to explain this in practical terms. If I meet an aging relative, and they remind me that we last saw each other in 1997, my mind instantly relocates to the nearest World Cup year—in this case, 1998—to recollect where I was living and what I was feeling when I experienced the furious intensity of Zinedine Zidane's victorious France. Having then located myself via that bookmark I can then recalibrate and recall richer, more detailed memories of the time being referenced. I suppose it is akin to how music obsessives pin the moments of their lives to the songs and albums that formed the soundtrack of every era.

How has this come to pass? I am not a brain surgeon, but I would bet that if you cut open my central cortex, over 70 percent of it would consist of World Cup stories. The tournament has provided the greatest trove of my most powerful memories, both collective and personal. That is partially because the game of football moves me so deeply. I often joke that I am a gent who is dead inside. But when I watch football, I experience the all-consuming rollercoaster of human emotion—joy, agony, exaltation, stress—that most people feel in everyday life. For ninety minutes at a time, I feel truly alive.

The World Cup, then, is that reaction on steroids. When two teams take the field, their nation's histories, politics, and cultures take the field alongside them. It is that fusion of the sporting, cultural, and geopolitical aspects that makes the storytelling so epic, poetic, and multilayered. Like Walt Whitman, the tournament contains multitudes. With the games dripping out, one at a time, the entire planet is focused on a single match while it is being played, all the eyes of the world resting on twenty-two elite athletes acting out a sporting telenovela, live, making decisions without a script, under conditions of hysterical pressure. There may be other club tournaments where the quality of the actual football is better, with the Champions League the apex, but the World Cup reigns supreme in feeling. It delivers something far more precious than mere sport—global connectivity and shared emotion. There is no casual watching of a World Cup match. You, and every fan in the world, are fully present and invested, no matter who is on the pitch.

This then is a book about feelings. I may call myself dead inside, but I believe the true meaning of the World Cup lies in the joy the whole world shares. The national collective dreams invested passionately, but safely, not through war, but through matches. So, this is also a story of a boy whose life was defined by the power of football—the mystery of human beings, the geopolitics, the sense that somewhere within the game lies the magic of life. It is also about the evolution of the World Cup itself into a commercial juggernaut. An estimated one billion people watched the entirety of the 1978 World Cup. Over 1.5 billion people were blessed to have watched the final alone during the 2022 tournament. A testament to omnipresence of television and social media, which has made the World Cup feel like a single giant billboard visible from space.

The strand of storytelling I have found most personally meaningful in this recollection you are about to experience is the inexorable rise of the sport in the United States of America, which, as someone who loves both football and this nation, has been the dominant narrative of my life. There is also the subplot of how we fused the two to build the Men in Blazers Media Network, the biggest dedicated soccer-media company in the United States. MiB has become the first institution to wire together all the different football communities in our nation's history. As I like to say, no one had done that before us. Not George Washington, General Patton, or Neil Armstrong.

I write all of this in anticipation of the forthcoming 2026 World Cup, which will be played on North American shores and will act as a tidal wave, forever transforming the profile of soccer in this nation. The book is partially a personal history, but I also hope it will be used as a permission slip for the entire nation to cut work for a month. Let *We Are the World (Cup)* be encouragement for us to do what we do better than any other nation in the world: Savor the circus. After you read, I hope you are compelled to slink out of your office cubicles en masse, day drink, watch, revel, and inhale the World Cup in its full glory. Messi, Ronaldo, Erling Haaland, heroes, villains, echoes of wars past, dodgy haircuts, and ill-advised neck tattoos await.

This book is my life hymn, but, more than anything, I hope that it equips you, the reader, to add backstory to and heighten your own experience as a fan so you can write your own footballing story. To understand the layers, the subtext, the precedents of this tournament, and in so doing, to deepen the cross-generational memories you can make by opening your heart to what an event held every four years on the world stage can offer. That is ultimately all that matters. Life is very, very short. We do not have a moment to waste. Nothing should be taken for granted. Every moment, every game, every goal connects us to each other and gives us the opportunity to create collective memories that can last a lifetime. When you think about life and football this way, it becomes clear that we are witnessing fewer goals scored or matches played—and harnessing more meaning and memories. And we should savor each and every one while we can.

Courage,
Roger Bennett
New York City
December 2025

WE ARE THE WORLD (CUP)

Chapter 1

1978 World Cup, Argentina

I CAME OF age in Liverpool, a town whose very foundations feel like they have been sunk into the twin pillars of music and football. By the age of seven, I had been exposed to copious amounts of both. That was how old I was when I glimpsed my first live World Cup match broadcast. It was life-changing, transforming my sense of the planet, and challenging the foundation of beliefs I had clung to as self-evident bedrock truths.

The culture of football I had grown up with was grounded solely in the grim experiences of the English variety. A game played out by tubby, balding, unathletic men who looked like they were barely fit enough to kick each other around on a muddy pitch for forty-five minutes before retiring, exhausted, to the locker room at halftime for a hasty cigarette, a cup of tea, and a pie.

These were also the days in which a violent hooligan culture gripped England, so many of my fellow fans who were in attendance to support Everton, my local team, appeared to have bought a ticket just to fight each other rather than spend even a second watching the on-field endeavor. The carnage was so prevalent that when my father and I went to the games, we would routinely step over broken bodies scattered on the ground on the way from the car to the stadium without a second thought, as if the bodily harm was neither abnormal nor surprising. I say all that to explain that when I turned the television on to glimpse my first-ever World Cup game, broadcast live, on June 1, 1978, it was as remarkable to witness as glimpsing Clark Kent turn into Superman, or an innocuous moth turn into a tiger swallowtail butterfly.

Our family's lounge was a special room reserved for congregating only on the fanciest occasions: birthdays, Christmas Day, or Queen Elizabeth's Silver Jubilee. The opening broadcast of the 1978 World Cup was deemed one such special moment. My whole family was there crushed around our bulky television. Even my mum, whose interest in football was negligible—she preferred to live off a strict diet of daytime talk shows and dour British soap operas—sat upright in eager anticipation. She had spent the morning making a vanilla cake iced with sky blue and white stripes, the jersey colors of tournament hosts Argentina. My dad fired up the television. The screen always took a moment to crackle into life, but the instant it did, we were collectively transported from our home in dreary Liverpool to El Monumental Stadium in sunny Buenos Aires's Belgrano barrio. We were mesmerized. From that second on, the cake sat there sliced but untouched.

I had experienced the levels of exhilaration catalyzed upon first glimpsing the spectacle that greeted us live from Argentina but only once before. The previous year, while bored and serving a school detention, I had made the ill-advised decision to try and shatter the numbness by toying with a loose wire hanging from an electric socket. The current that ran through my body that day made my muscles spasm painfully, but it was also oddly enlivening. And I felt exactly the same the moment the next day the suave, shaggy-haired home team swaggered out onto the field before 72,000 of their adoring fans, as confetti and shredded newspaper exploded from all sides of the vertigo-inducing cauldron. Thousands of toilet rolls cascaded down alongside them—the crudest of ticker tape displays. A surreal assault, which created an ecstatic spectacle. A display of pride and delirious anticipation.

"Who would take a full toilet roll to a football game?" my mother mused quietly, as ever, caught up in the practical aspects of whatever we were experiencing. But I was lost in the thrall of this wondrous spectacle. The football I knew was parochial and fear-inducing. A violent game that smelt of bad breath, spilled ale, and police-horse turd. This was something else entirely. Football as an expression of collective joy and national passion. I had thought I knew everything about the game, trusting that the schoolboy comics I obsessively read about my English heroes taught me everything. But this was the revelation of a new side of the sport. Football didn't have to be war. Football could actually be fun.

Two things need to be made clear immediately, for context. The first is just how insular our football world was back then. The lens through which we lived our life on the island of 1970s Britain was very small and isolated. Rare was the occasion any sport was broadcast live on television. England is so tiny, just 50,301 square miles. Back then there were ninety-two professional clubs jammed into an area roughly the size of Georgia, and their owners were terrified that broadcasting even one game live would lead to an immediate and suicidal cannibalization of ticket sales. With very rare exceptions, the dominant way of watching a match was to go to the stadium in person and view proceedings with your own eyes. As a result, football fandom was hyper-local.

That carried through to the men who played the game. Most of the strikers, midfielders, and defenders in English football could trace their lineage back to the days Picts and Anglo-Saxons roamed ancient misty moors in the fifth century. The handful of Scottish, Welsh, and Irish players who plied their trade in England felt foreign and exotic in comparison. Also, the internet was still five years from its primitive early days of invention in 1978. So, while we knew other nations had their own universe of leagues and clubs, those felt more like theoretical concepts than real human beings. There was simply no information flow. We knew about these other clubs like we knew about the solar system. Yes, Jupiter and Uranus were out there somewhere, but that rarely affected our lives day to day. Instead, we clung to vague, stereotypical tropes: The Italians cheated. The French dived. The Brazilians could do things with the ball that British minds could barely conceive. A World Cup in which all the best teams from all these nations would assemble and play for twenty-four days—and we could follow along, watching every kick, goal, and unironic mullet—was as intoxicating as the thought of being handed a golden ticket to the Wonka Chocolate Factory.

The buildup to the tournament itself was an agonizingly slow boil that began three months before kickoff. It had been largely informed by the emergence of a new kids' card game named World Cup '78 Top Trumps, which spread throughout the nation's schools quicker than an infestation of head lice. At recess, whereas we typically played football, the balls became ignored, as clusters of boys played in a frenzy like the most experienced card sharps, in scattered huddles across the schoolyard. Top Trumps revolved around a pack of thirty-two cards, each bearing images of one of the world's best football players, replete with their stats, which would be read out in turn by those playing, in the hope of declaring the highest number, thereby leading to the acquisition of all the cards. The rules were rudimentary, and the game was less about skill than luck, but it was so much more than a game. To stare at those cards and begin matching the romantic, mysterious-sounding names—Roberto Bettega, Zé Maria, and Paulo Cézar—to their unique looks of untamed perms, furious lamb chops, and short, silky bulging shorts was to imbibe the sweet anticipation of the spectacle to come.

The other pretournament drumbeat was more sinister. When FIFA awarded the World Cup to Argentina in 1966, it had no way of foreseeing that by 1978 the country's two recent presidents, Juan Domingo Perón and his third wife, Isabel, would have been overthrown by a brutal military regime. That regime proceeded to wage a barbaric war against its own people, unwittingly leaving the World Cup to be used by a corrupt government as a golden lifeline of international legitimacy. At the 1934 World Cup in Italy, Mussolini had provided the blueprint for what would follow in Argentina, under generals—the junta, as they became known. The 1978 World Cup was held up by the hosts as a craven way to present a powerful and positive face to the larger world beyond its borders. For a true public relations coup, the home team had to win it all.

In the run-up to the tournament, the English news contained occasional harrowing glimpses of the reality in which the junta set about their task with sinister abandon. Naval admiral Carlos Alberto Lacoste was selected to prepare the nation for the tournament, inheriting the role after his predecessor was mysteriously assassinated en route to his first press conference. There were murmurs of Marxist terrorists possibly causing a frenzy throughout the tournament with a spate of planned attacks. Several renowned players talked vaguely about political protest, but the lure of playing in a World Cup meant little materialized in the way of action. Amnesty International managed to persuade German goalkeeper Sepp Maier and Italian striker Paolo Rossi to sign a petition against the torture of prisoners. The Dutch threatened to pull out of the tournament in its entirety. Indeed, their iconic captain, Johan Cruyff, did not participate, but at the time it was not clear why. Most of the football world's reactions were pragmatic. There were newspaper articles about how the English National Union of Journalists had provided its members with a Spanish-language handbook that included such handy phrases as "Please stop torturing me!"

The week before the tournament kicked off, there was a crackling sense in the English papers that *something* would happen. A protest. A boycott. A statement made. But as is so often with football, the rational thoughts—about corruption, geopolitical horror, or human rights abuse—were instantly overwhelmed by the emotional power of football once the whistle blew and the first ball was kicked. So, earlier in the evening, as my family marveled at a recording of the World Cup's opening ceremony, we watched General Jorge Videla, the mustachioed military leader of Argentina's ruling junta, proclaim to the 68,000 people in attendance that the tournament would "take place under a sign of peace." Nor did we pause to consider the irony as my mum said, "He looks like a little sparrow." We just wanted to feast on the football, sweet football.

Argentina were pretournament favorites, coached by manager César Luis Menotti, a gaunt Modigliani of a man who looked like a cigarette come to life, a resemblance he reinforced by puffing away on Marlboros on the sideline. Between drags, he had controversially omitted the nation's rising star, a seventeen-year-old named Diego Armando Maradona, from the squad. Menotti preferred to build his team around the more experienced Mario Alberto Kempes, a long-maned striker nicknamed "El Matador," and the guileful midfielder Osvaldo Ardiles. Ardiles played with a craftiness revered in Argentina as La Nuestra, or Our Way—a style of play that was physical yet skillful, combining movement, energy, and passion. I had never seen anything like it. A human being with the talent to dribble with the ball at his foot rather than just batter it as hard as he could like my English heroes. The other superpower the Argentinians possessed was a physics-defying ability to let any perceived touch force them to fall to the pitch in agony, whence they would proceed to roll over in a style ripped from vaudeville theater. It was as if their very molecules felt both gravity and pain, far more than mere normal human beings.

The array of sporting styles, stories, and haircuts I was instantly exposed to made the spectacle as startling as entering a Star Wars cantina of global football. There was the Dutch team in their bright orange jerseys, who played a style of collective football—Total Football—in which every player was capable of stealthily cropping up in any position on the field, like footballing ninjas. The Italians played a cynically defensive football named *Catenaccio*—or door bolt—in which they grimly feared losing as opposed to desiring to win. And then there was the circus style of the Brazilians, who played with an effervescence and frivolity in their golden yellow jerseys—purpose-made to gloriously shimmer across our technicolor television screens—as their players, in their tight shorts with thick golden chains bouncing flamboyantly, tossed the ball to each other as if it were a frisbee on the beach.

The one considerable blemish on proceedings was that my English heroes had, to my disbelief and dismay, somehow failed to qualify for the tournament, a moment akin to a theological crisis of faith for this seven-year-old. These were the men I worshipped. Their posters smothered the wall above my bed. Their failure to qualify, cemented by a botch job against the Italians, who beat us 2–0 in Rome, left me sobbing and inconsolable. An experience so searing and profound, I can trace roughly 70 percent of my lack of trust and deep pessimism right back to that moment. For the rest of England, the national team's failure was merely a collective humiliation. After all, we had invented the game of football and still possessed sufficient levels of self-deception to perceive ourselves as a superpower. In reality the national team's failure was merely the first of a great many moments in which I learned the harsh lesson all children experience at some point in their life: that even our gods—in this case a tightly permed midfield poet by the name of Kevin Keegan and a rugged Everton goal machine called Bob Latchford—were merely idols with clay feet.

Football fandom, like nature, abhors a vacuum. So, I had to root for the next best thing. My grandmother was born in Edinburgh, so I attached myself to the Scottish national team as a kind of footballing methadone. I was not alone. Scotland's departure for Argentina conjured the kind of spectacle Cecil B. DeMille would have dreamed up had he been born in Glasgow and partial to draining twelve cans of Tennent's Lager on the daily. Twenty-five thousand overserved Scottish fanatics congregated to watch their squad depart for a dramatic World Cup journey that began above Scotland's national football stadium, Hampden Park, and culminated upon arrival in Argentina with a welcome from "the massed pipe band of the St Andrew's Society of the River Plate Pipe Band."

Thousands of Scottish diehards traversed the roughly 7,000 miles along with their team, many unloading their life savings to watch their nation's finest seize this moment and attempt to drain Argentina clean out of lager in the process. A Glaswegian entrepreneur appeared on the evening news talking proudly about his unhinged plans to charter a Tartan Army submarine to travel to South America. Rumors spread of Scotsmen flying to New York, taking a Greyhound bus to the Mexican border, and attempting to cycle the rest of the way. This fanaticism was so intoxicating, even the English tabloids, typically the last institutions one would expect to respect anything with the merest Scottish whiff, became swept up in the hysteria. They were soon touting Scotland as dark horses to win it all across their pages.

As a kid, the spotlight on this sudden Scottish strut and bluster was enthralling, particularly because it existed in the face of all evidence to the contrary. An early and important introduction to the infinite and renewable power of misplaced hope in football. The Scottish national football team had a proud history, but it was of passionate self-sabotaging failure, not of valorous victory. And yet, that failure is just what their fans embraced. This squad though was chock-full of perms and fearsome mustaches, and felt capable of playing with fiery flair.

Led by Kenny Dalglish, one of the most artistic British players of all time, and Graeme Souness, a gent who played as if the football field was a pool hall into which he had entered with the sole intention of starting a bar fight. I admired their hardiness, which remained undented, even as the British Foreign Office tried to warn of the potential dangers between well-libated Scottish fans and armed Argentinian police, issuing a press release in which they reminded British visitors that "the Argentine army can open fire at unexpected moments."

The Scottish manager, an extroverted cheerleader named Ally MacLeod, did little to dampen the ecstatic levels of pre-tournament frenzy surrounding his team, quipping, "You can mark down twenty-five of June, nineteen-seventy-eight, as the day Scottish football conquers the world." Perhaps because of his uncharacteristic British optimism and self-confidence, MacLeod's face was plastered on everything in the weeks before the tournament. His agent clearly and shamelessly brokered one commercial deal after another, as MacLeod was even willing to lend his name to carpet sales in a commercial in which he sat on a rug dressed as a pistol-wielding Argentinian gaucho. The Scottish "Battle Fever" even had a soundtrack. Both Rod Stewart and second-tier comedian Andy Cameron recorded celebratory Top 10 singles; Cameron's "Ally's Tartan Army" compared the Scottish manager to Muhammad Ali, while declaring:

> *When we reach the Argentine we're really gonna show*
> *The world a brand of football that they could never know*

It would turn out there was a hidden prophecy buried deep in these lyrics. One noticed by a lone dissenting voice at the outset, Jock Stein, another leading Scottish manager, who portentously cautioned that Scottish confidence was born merely of succeeded in qualifying when their dread rivals England had failed, warning mournfully, "There's a big world out there and the English aren't the only people who live in it."

Yet, before their first game, I would not have been more certain of Scottish Glory if Robert the Bruce, Rob Roy, and William Wallace had themselves laced up their boots and been part of the starting lineup. Indeed, it only took fourteen minutes for the Scots to take the lead in their opening game against Peru, fulfilling our expectations with a goal slotted home from a tight angle by the fearsome giant Joe Jordan. However, Peru was tenacious and equalized on the stroke of halftime via a clinical finish from César Cueto, the shock and pain of which was mitigated slightly by the discovery that the goal scorer's charming nickname was "El Poeta de la Zurda" (The Left-footed Poet), which, as a bookish child, moved me on account of fusing all of my passions.

The Scots were gifted a penalty with which to restore order, but midfielder Don Masson stepped up to take the kick and spanked it at a savable height for Peru goalkeeper Ramón Quiroga, who swatted the ball away. A moment that spawned a freefall of turmoil and disarray. Fueled then by a sense of reprieve, the Peruvians proceeded to romp away with the game.

I watched in shock and horror as the ecstatic Teófilo Cubillas used his guile and trickery to render the Scottish defenders impotent, slamming home a thunderous free kick that left his teammates skipping around the field in wonder. We had been promised the defiance of Bannockburn. We were given only surrender, as we discovered the Scottish were capable of playing with spite and fight, but only when they faced England. Other nations, it turned out, did not quake in fear like the English did the moment a Scottish accent graced their ears. A truth that was reinforced when matters became worse in the next game as the Scots somehow only managed to draw with unfancied Imperial State of Iran.

The sense of spiraling sorrow radiating from the Scottish players as they trudged off shamefaced in disbelief after the 1–1 draw in Córdoba was palpable through the television screen. The Tartan Army had traveled afar to witness historic glory. Instead, they had been forced to watch national humiliation, their team incapable of linking the most basic passes. You could hear the bedraggled chants of "What a load of rubbish" in thick Scottish brogue aimed at their own players.

Scotland now had to win their final group stage game by three goals to stay alive. The problem was they would have to do that against the Netherlands. The mighty Oranje, who had been defeated in World Cup finals four years earlier, were widely considered to be Europe's strongest team. Although they were without the avant-garde creativity of absent, gaunt genius Johan Cruyff, they still had Ruud Krol, Johan Neeskens, and Johnny Rep on the field—men who could switch positions, conjure angles, and see space like Piet Mondrian in cleats.

I watched this game on my own. Both my dad and my brother Nigel, two years my elder, had given up on the novelty idea of Scottish potency. Mum had signed off after the opener. Despite the waning support from the Bennett family, the Scots charged into the game with the ferocity of a feuding border clan. They proceeded to hit the crossbar, had a handful of credible penalty shouts ignored, and even prodded the ball into the back of their opponent's net twice, only for the goals to be ruled off for infringements. But Scotland was still alive.

In the 34th minute, a sucker punch. The Dutch took the lead from the penalty spot, a strike that felt like it extinguished all hope. Our numbing worst-case scenario had occurred. However, King Kenny Dalglish equalized for Scotland in the 45th minute. One minute into the second half, a lifeline. Graeme Souness was brought down in the penalty area and Scotland was awarded a spot kick, which Archie Gemmill, a squat, balding stump of a winger, converted.

What was it that Emily Dickinson wrote? "Hope is the thing with thinning patches of hair"? I found myself involuntarily leaning forward and gnawing on my fingers in the 68th minute, as Gemmill took possession on the right of the penalty area, then unleashed an ingenious moment worthy of being woven in tapestries or celebrated in ballads. A miraculous run, cut from centuries of wounded defiance and his countrymen's drunkest dreams. The thirty-one-year-old from the Scottish Lowlands surged forward, dribbling the ball with murderous intent, with just ten touches, jigged past two astonished Dutch defenders before nutmegging a third and mischievously clipping the ball crisply past stunned goalkeeper Jan Jongbloed. I was on my feet dancing a highland fling of my own as Scotland roared to a 3–1 lead and were now just a single goal away from achieving the unfathomable. Hope was ours once again.

For one hundred and eighty sweet seconds, I, along with five million Scots, dared to dream. Then the Dutch sniper Johnny Rep casually, coolly, callously lashed a cruel blast from thirty yards, which was still rising as it smashed into the net, serving as a harsh life lesson: There can be no romance in football. Scotland was out. Yes, Gemmill had delivered a flickering moment of pride to his nation, but in its own way, it only served to deliver more pain. Just as the BBC commentator declared, "Scotland can at least go home and look people in the face."

Despite Scotland's self-immolation, I was by now truly, madly, deeply hooked on the World Cup as a global spectacle in its own right. The sheer scope and impact of the tournament was evident as it made headlines on the sporting back pages of every newspaper—while also dominating the headlines. One day, the world's newspapers were filled with reports that the revolutionary Montoneros guerrillas had proposed a truce with the Argentine dictators with whom they had warred for nearly eight years, so they too could watch the football. Next, we learned that a nun had been arrested in Frankfurt when she tried to strangle a man who had been cheering too loudly for Austria during their 3–2 win over West Germany. It seemed I was not alone in my World Cup fever.

What I was experiencing watching these games was more profound than what happened on the field. The realization that the spectacle we were all witnessing forged a sense of global connection, which far outstripped the local storylines propelling the English football I had been reared on. This realization, that football was about more than football, was intensified by the dominant storyline which now gripped the tournament: that to deliver the glory the Argentine junta craved for their nation, the hosts had to win it all. A challenge they set about by all means necessary, uncoiling a style of roguish football, startling for its commitment to both the beautiful and the dark arts of the game. Head coach Menotti, nicknamed "El Flaco" (The Thin One), cut a rakish figure as he chain-smoked his way through his team's often unconvincing performances. Striker Mario Kempes had been the team's savior, finding his goalscoring rhythm once he shaved off his mustache, at Menotti's suggestion it turned out. Though undoubtedly skill-soaked, the Argentines too often had to rely on a pragmatic brutality in line with their manager's mantra, "Efficacy is not divorced from beauty."

In the second round of games, which would determine the

tournament's two finalists, the Argentinians were neck and neck with their dread rival and neighbors, Brazil. Their fate came down to this: In the last game, whichever team had a better result would make the final. Brazil was controversially scheduled to face Poland in the blazing afternoon sun, after which Argentina would play Peru in the cooler evening climes. An astonishingly unfair arrangement that conveniently gifted the hosts an enormous advantage as they could take the field armed with the knowledge of the exact score they would need to make their World Cup final Shangri-La.

After Brazil dumped Poland 3–1 in Mendoza, there were reports of mourning across Buenos Aires as the Argentines had struggled to score all tournament. They would now need to win by four goals to qualify. I tuned in to the game with the thrill of a rubbernecker, truly believing we would all soon experience the singular schadenfreude-tinged pleasure of witnessing this Argentine team of rogues and their junta overlords experience their comeuppance.

As the tournament built, I had warmed to the audacious Peruvians, led by the dynamically creative Teófilo Cubillas in his bright white kit slashed by a proud red sash. What my naive young mind had not yet conceived was that the Argentine government would later transfer 35,000 tons of free grain to Peru, and release $50 million in unfrozen bank credit. Hence, Peru opened strongly, but after fifteen minutes transformed into a zombielike state. As their defenders inexplicably ducked under goal-bound shots, and goalkeeper, Ramón Quiroga, who had been born in Argentina, played like a lunatic. I watched wide-eyed as this curly-haired rogue, already nicknamed "The Crazy one," inexplicably elected to charge out past the halfway line to make reckless tackles and leave his goal invitingly unguarded.

The Argentines ran up the score, dancing on the field in Rosario, finishing with a 6–0 win that left no doubt that they had made their final.

The Brazilians were left convinced that quid pro quos had been exchanged, awarding themselves the title of "moral victor" as they departed a tournament from which they had somehow been eliminated despite remaining unbeaten. Their coach, Claudio Coutinho, predicted, "I do not think they will hear their national anthem at the World Cup with pride again." Indeed, they were greeted by a mob of their own fans who threw coins at them in disgust after they arrived back in Lima.

The Netherlands were now all that stood between Argentina and their Promised Land at the vertigo-inducing, steep-banked El Monumental. Mum came back into the fold, as this was another World Cup event that passed her high bar for the family's use of our lounge to watch the evening spectacle broadcast live. The Dutch were appearing in their second successive World Cup final and, yet again, they faced the home team. The Netherlands had lost, 2–1, to West Germany in the 1974 final at Munich's Olympiastadion, a game in which they had taken the lead quickly and let arrogance be their undoing by attempting to humiliate the Germans with their dominant possession rather than kill off the game. Now they were a more experienced and savvier team, which made them slight favorites, despite the fact not a single European nation had ever won the Cup on South American soil.

I loved the Dutch. It had been the thrill of the tournament watching them play themselves into form, game by game. This gang of languidly cool men had the demeanor of great jazz improvisers, passing the ball with a mesmerizing sense of space and time, sucking opponents into their midfield whirlpool and charging forward with ferocity and flourish into crevices only they could see. I spent the days running up to the final in the family lounge, kicking a balloon around the room without letting it touch the floor, pretending I was Johan Neeskens, unleashing flicks and tricks with his flared mullet that made him look more like a beat poet than a world-class creative midfielder.

The whole family watched on in horror as the game began in controversial fashion. The Argentinians had done nothing to erase the stench of skullduggery that cloaked them after the Peru game. In fact, they embraced it during the hour before the final. In a supremely premeditated act of gamesmanship, they shucked protocol by staying behind in their dressing room, forcing the Dutch team to walk out alone onto the field, then kept them waiting there for five agonizingly long minutes to be confronted by the frightening noise and intimidation of a hostile home crowd, who howled and whistled with a curdling ferocity. Finally, the Argentinians brazenly strolled out before their adoring fans, who erupted with that battery of toilet rolls and confetti blizzard, which only served to reinforce the sense of broiling tension and anxiety.

There was further delay as the Argentinians elected to object to one of their opponents, winger René van de Kerkhof, wearing a plaster cast on his arm, which the confused Dutchman had been wearing all tournament to protect a broken hand. The British commentator foamed about the lack of sportsmanship and how these Argentinian dark arts were designed to roil up the crowd and rattle the Dutch, making them lose their focus. Indeed, the Oranje fleetingly considered walking off the pitch before the kickoff, giving the outset of this global spectacle the stink of farce, until the panicked referee, sensing he was losing control, withdrew his objection to Van de Kerkhof's cast and brought the game to order.

In England, football was still played under a general rubric of fair play. Despite the general mayhem that occurred in the stands, a sense of decency prevailed on the field. My father rarely swore, but even he could not help himself from mouthing the word "Fucker" at the goings-on from the safety of his rocking chair. What we were witnessing was just not right. And so, the World Cup now introduced me to football in a way I had never experienced before. It had previously all felt low stakes. Win some. Lose others. Shake hands. Drink a pint. Maybe have a quick fight. This game felt like it was about something altogether more elemental. A battle between the force of good and the force of evil. As I watched my dad rock back and forth furiously upon kickoff, it felt as if whatever innate sense of justice that existed in the world could be bolstered or shattered, pending the result.

The game itself was also a clash of footballing ideologies. Argentine virtuoso passion against Dutch collective logic. Of sorcery against imagination. I was not Dutch. I had never been to the Netherlands, but once the ball was finally kicked off, ten minutes late, I cheered for them with all my heart as if I had been born into a multi-generational dynasty of cheesemakers in Gouda.

During the opening exchanges, the field was still covered in flecks of confetti, which gave the pitch a sense of chaos that was reflected in the play. The game moved with a howling fury, both because of what was at stake and because these humans truly did not seem to like each other. This was a grudge-filled street brawl, in which the players vented their anger toward each other, unleashing reckless tackles that made it a game played on the cusp of a brawl, fueled by spite as much as tactics. A game played with sly elbows to the ribs, as much as via the feet. In which Dutch ingenuity flickered episodically as the Argentinians countered it with their passion, speed, and willingness to fake injuries with vaudevillian dives. Masters of physical comedy. Rolling over and over and over to ensure the referee saw the agony they were experiencing.

In the 37th minute, some football broke out. The clinical Argentine star Mario Kempes received the ball on the edge of the area; his first touch was that of a lethal assassin as he set himself up to poke home. Kempes charged away with arms outstretched to a howling scream of release from the fans that felt like it could be faintly heard through the window of my family home in Liverpool, seven thousand miles away.

That goal felt so debilitating and final in the moment. Like it would shatter most teams—most human beings. Yet, the Netherlands only seemed to become more determined, focused, and collectively intense. And so, the Argentine defense was under immense pressure throughout the second half yet appeared resolute until eight minutes from time. René van de Kerkhof lofted an arcing cross that was emphatically headed home by Dutch forward Dick Nanninga with a thunderously theatrical snap of his neck. So dominant were the Dutch, they almost summoned a winner in the last moment of regulation as a shot prodded by Rob Rensenbrink beat the goalkeeper, only to bounce off the crossbar. The crowd audibly gasped. A moment of fate. An inch of difference, and the outcome of this game could have been so different. An agonizing lesson that football is a game which is won and lost by the most minute of fractions.

Then, it was into thirty minutes of extra time in which

sound and color now seemed to collide. The Argentine coach gave his players a rousing team talk in which he urged them to win the game for the butchers and teachers of Argentina, not for the generals in the presidential palace. They responded decisively. Again, it was Kempes who made an explosive burst into the penalty area which saw him steam clean through two defenders. The goalkeeper parried his advance, but the ball spun away into a scramble in which a pair of exhausted Dutchmen desperately attempted to smother the ball as if it were a grenade with the pin pulled out, but Kempes reacted faster and with deadlier force, pushing the ball into the net. This goal unmoored the Dutch, who instantly lost any semblance of self-control. The same went for my father, who started screaming impotently as if his words could go through the television screen and impact proceedings in the Estadio Monumental.

The Dutch now had no option but to swarm forward in search of an equalizer, which left them vulnerable at the back. Kempes was yet again the exploiter, unleashing another signature dazzling charge to feed Daniel Bertoni and secure the World Cup for his nation, a moment that felt both intensely dazzling in its sense of theater, yet excruciating in terms of fairness. As the giddily triumphant General Jorge Rafael Videla, his deputy Emilio Eduardo Massera, and commander-in-chief of the airforce Orlando Ramón Agosti handed over the World Cup trophy they coveted to the Argentine captain Daniel Passarella, I felt dual emotions. A sense of fury and the awareness that time is not infinite. I grabbed the balloon with which I had practiced the Dutch stylings of my own game over the course of the last week of the tournament. Exiting the lounge, I headed for the sanctuary of the hall, where I promptly stomped on it, ushering a satisfying sharp pop that filled the darkness of the room around me. I stood there, in silence. I was a changed boy. My first World Cup taught me an important life truth: As a football fan, wherever there is hope, there is almost always soon to be shattered hope.

Chapter 2

1982 World Cup, Spain

ALTHOUGH THE 1982 World Cup was played in Spain, I spent almost all of it in France. I was eleven years old and my parents had elected to devote the summer to driving around the small towns of Brittany and Normandy in my father's big old brown Audi. We had neither a destination in mind nor any kind of plan. This was fortunate as my dad could not read a map. That never stopped him from pretending he could, however. We spent hours marooned by the side of French farm-country backroads, with my father spreading out an impressively large roadmap across the hood of our car whenever we were lost, which was often. He obstinately refused to ask locals for directions, and we ended up just rolling lazily, and circuitously, from village to village.

My poor, game mother was heavily pregnant with what would turn out to be my little sister. Mum was understandably, deeply uncomfortable, armed only with a small arsenal of compression socks and her natural willingness to suffer. Yet, at a certain point in the afternoon it would always become too much, at which point she would inevitably sigh, snap, and inform my father she was at her breaking point. This was the sign for him to pull over in whichever village was nearest, then march into the lobby of a random sleepy, dusty guesthouse and demand two rooms in his finest pidgin French. Despite the fact we had not booked, there was always space. Indeed, we were often the only guests in the place. My father would stride back outside proudly, often accompanied by several puzzled porters in his slipstream, confused because my dad had asked for help fetching "les fauteuils" (armchairs) from the trunk, instead of "les valises" (the suitcases).

As a Liverpool kid, who had barely traveled outside of Britain up to then, I found rural French life to be invigorating. This was Northern France out of central casting. Quiet, still, timeless towns in which the only action was a cluster of old beret-wearing men lazily playing boules in the town square, while sipping on calvados. I was tickled by the custom of having a public urinal in the center of each, with the day's newspaper pinned up so you could speed-read the news as you went about your business.

All of this, *and* nightly World Cup action. Much of which we would watch over the course of dinner in some French inn with its dazzling array of delicacies. Liver pâtés. Horse meats. Tripe sausages. Each one a conceptual terror for my limited and English-trained palette but inarguably ravishing to the taste buds. Then, dessert, which would involve some patisserie-action, unleashing dizzyingly intricate, delicate fruit-filled pastries in an infinite number of glazed shapes and sizes.

For the World Cup, it felt as if every French restaurateur had the same idea of jerry-rigging some kind of public television-watching contraption set up in their establishment. To watch football abroad—even with a restaurant full of strangers and as foreigners to boot—added another dimension to the experience. I was used to encountering football live in stadia with English people, for whom the act of watching the game was inseparable from draining six-packs of beers. In France, the experience was far quieter, yet far more intense. Lots of men sitting and seething in silence, furiously drinking tiny coffees while chain-smoking Gitanes. They largely followed along mutely, and if they had to speak, did so only in conspiratorial whispered tones in which we could pick up the odd word—about "le football," "les tacles," and "le ballon."

The French restaurateurs would fill the silence by blasting the broadcast commentary out of their improvised speaker system, many of which looked like they had been requisitioned straight from the restaurant owner's home record player. Loud Gallic goal-accompanying squeals of "Ouiiiii!" were the soundtrack to our summer. My ear had been attuned to English commentators, who favored a subdued, subtle unemotional style no doubt born of centuries of repression. The French commentators evidently had very different ideas, screaming over the game as if it were merely the supporting act to their frothy stream of consciousness. The fact I did not speak French and could not understand a word did not prevent me from reveling in it. The commentary was a stark contrast to the stoicism of the fans watching the broadcast alongside us. A patter so electric it made every game feel like twice the number of goals had been scored. Even the most mundane 0–0 draws felt like ecstatic 10–10 affairs when you had watched them play out on French television.

One night, my dad uncovered the difference between English fandom and French during a late postgame Bénédictine shared with a sad-eyed restaurant proprietor named Alain.

We English fans always believed our team were on a march of destiny, headed for inevitable glory, even though all evidence pointed to the opposite outcome. The French, according to Alain, felt the opposite. Victory was neither possible nor the point. His reasoning was admittedly roundabout, romantic, and hard to follow. Alain told us a story of a conflict in 1863 that, from the emotion with which he recounted it, felt as if it had happened yesterday. It involved the Battle of Camarón during which sixty-five men from the French Foreign Legion held two thousand Mexican soldiers at bay until they ran out of ammunition. With five men remaining and not a bullet among them, the Frenchmen swore to fight to the death, fixing bayonets, and attempting a futile charge. It took Alain time to explain the next point, but he was at great pains to tell us that the wooden prosthetic hand of the deceased platoon commander was recovered. Every year it is solemnly sent out on parade, a reminder of his death, the nobility of defeat, and the Legion's motto, "March or Die." "This is French glory," Alain told us solemnly looking down at his Bénédictine as he swirled it around in his glass. "Understand it and you will appreciate the essence of French soccer—it is better to lose with honor than to win without style."

"Defeat with dignity" were Alain's last words that night before he drained his glass. My dad muttered, "Damned Inferiority Complex," as he strode off with slightly drunken steps toward the car. I found Alain's portrayal of the French team as a small, gallant, fighting force for whom defeat was inevitable to be poetic but unrealistic. The French national team, though inexperienced, was one of the most elegant in the world, propelled by Michel Platini, a scrawny, mop-topped, and heavily stubbled creative genius, who looked more like a 1980s

Madison Avenue account executive than a world-class athlete. Alongside Alain Giresse, Jean Tigana, and later Luis Fernández as "Le Carré Magique," Platini was the transcendent heart of one of the most creative midfields to ever play the game.

All of this felt trivial to me at the tournament's outset, however. The only storyline I cared about was this: For the first time in twelve long years and, indeed, the first time in my viewing lifetime, ENGLAND HAD QUALIFIED FOR THE WORLD CUP.

Yes, their arrival had been fortunate. The team had favored chaos over organization, barely surviving a kind qualifying group—despite losing to Switzerland, Romania, and a bunch of amateurs and semiprofessionals from Norway along the way. Win or lose, the English fans made their mark, rioting and fighting their way across Europe, leading some French politicians to call for them to be banned from the tournament for their violent threat. None of this mattered to me. All I cared about was that my heroes had made it. To watch the iconic English stars I worshipped on a weekly basis unite to form a super team was akin to witnessing a band of superhero Avengers Assemble while wearing cleats.

Ahead of the tournament, the England team went into the recording studio to croon the then prerequisite World Cup single, "This Time (We'll Get It Right)." The song was a jaunty yet bold number that dominated the radio airwaves and fired up my imagination with images of glory conjured by the promise-filled chorus: "This time, more than any other time, this time, we're going to find a way . . . To win them all." In the run-up to the tournament, I spent a solid month in my bedroom playing that single endlessly on repeat to kill the boredom until the World Cup kicked off. I would stare at the players on the record cover, running my fingers over them, telling myself these men were warrior-heroes whose vows of song I would be wise to treat as prophecy. I was a fanciful lad.

That summer, my pride and joy was a knockoff kit I had coveted at first sight after seeing it hanging on a stall at the local street market, then saved up seven months' worth of pocket money to buy. The jersey was bright white, the shorts were blue, and a proud bulldog wearing the very same colored kit had been placed where the official England badge was supposed to be. I adored that shirt, and although its polyester was itchy to the skin, I wore it nonstop, or at least, until my mother told me to put it in the laundry for hygiene-related reasons. To wear it felt empowering. Like I could run faster and kick harder. And like my English National Team heroes, *get it right*.

On vacation in France, I wore the kit for the entirety of the first week as we made our way through Normandy and Brittany. England experienced a promising start to their World Cup campaign, and though I kept this feeling to myself, I sincerely believed that my lucky shirt was at least partially responsible. In their opening game, the English shaggy-haired midfield talisman Bryan Robson needed just twenty-seven seconds to ghost in at the back post and acrobatically stab home before punching the air with a shocked fist of wonder. That the goal was scored against France both doubled the pleasure but halved my ability to scream out in celebration as I stifled a high-pitched squeal of delight at the back of the cellar-like restaurant outside of Rennes, in which we found ourselves eating along with three dozen seething Frenchmen. My mum had wisely insisted I wear a sweatshirt to cover my bulldog pride, and that decision was probably for the best as England ran out 3–1 winners.

A routine 2–0 win over Czechoslovakia followed. An opening goal from Trevor Francis meant that England became the first European team to qualify for the second round with a game still to play. Their final group stage game against lowly Kuwait was now a formality, which was a relief as England labored in the Bilbao heat, conjuring just a single goal to maintain a perfect record and advance to play Spain and West Germany in this tournament's format in which teams progressed to play a "second group stage."

England's football had been cautious and conservative, yet I could not have cared less about the quality of play. "It's a results business," my father insisted as he ordered a celebratory cognac after the final whistle of the Kuwait game. Our team's perfect record fueled my dreams of an invincible World Cup journey. I had "This Time (We'll Get It Right)" taped on a TDK cassette and filled much of the time, until their next game against dread rivals West Germans, playing it in the back of the car, on repeat, on the radio-cassette player my brother had been gifted for his bar mitzvah. Without headphones.

The English always feared *and* loathed the West Germans but rarely more than in 1982. That year, the Germans' World Cup run had been achieved with conniving stealth and trickery that was extreme even by their standards. In their opening game, the Germans, then European champions, faced tiny minnows Algeria. African sides were not taken at all seriously, and the Germans swaggered into the game with extreme hubris. One of their players said before kickoff, "We will dedicate our seventh goal to our wives, and the eighth to our dogs."

Algeria emerged as 2–1 winners, one of the greatest shocks in World Cup history. I did not see the game, but I do remember the Frenchmen in the small town we happened to have chanced upon that night toasting German defeat as heartily as if it were their own nation's victory. The subsequent results however left West Germany in their final group stage game to face Teutonic neighbors Austria, knowing that a 1–0 German victory would enable both teams to progress at Algeria's expense. To no one's shock, the Austrians leaked a goal ten minutes in and then both teams played as if they had signed a nonaggression treaty. In a macabre noncompetitive spectacle, the players conspired to ensure the ball rarely made it out of midfield for the remainder of the game, tapping it around aimlessly, without intent to wound. As outraged yet impotent Algerians waved banknotes from the terraces, one German fan, disgusted at what his own team had been reduced to, set fire to his own flag in protest. German coach Jupp Derwall only fanned the flames when he shrugged, "We wanted to progress, not play football."

I remember watching this game, and the cruelty of the injustice perpetrated on the Algerians was palpable. They had played audaciously without fear, only to be shafted by the collusion of two traditional European teams. I felt the agony of their fans, and a sense that there was a developing world of football that would not be long in coming. However, it was also an introduction to another theme that would dominate much of my footballing life: German inevitability. Watching this game was the first time I understood the Germans were a sinister footballing power for whom winning was all that mattered. Any which way. Negativity. Cynicism. Dullness. Neutralizing opponents. The outcome was assured.

The England–West Germany game was actually a dull one. Both sides played to avoid defeat, and both were successful in a physical grinding battle that each nation was delighted to emerge from intact, with a 0–0 draw. Germany then proceeded to clip host Spain 2–1, which meant that England had to beat the hosts by two goals or more to proceed. On the day of the big game, I could not slap on that lucky kit early enough as we headed out to tour Dunkirk, spending a rainy afternoon walking around the harbor and beaches from which nearly 340,000 Allied forces had been evacuated during World War II. I don't know if it was the dodgy mussels I had gobbled down for lunch, or simply extremely elevated pre-match nerves, but my body was abruptly overwhelmed by the sudden need to go to the bathroom. Immediately. To my relief, the search for a public toilet was both frantic and brief. We were by the waterfront, and down some stone stairs I located the men's bathroom through a rusting gate. The place was dark and dank. It smelled sour, of urinal cakes and decay. But as Shakespeare wrote in *All's Well That Ends Well*, "he must needs go that the devil drives." I slushed my way through a layer of water coating the floor, kicking open the door to the toilet stall, with not a second to spare, before yanking down my shorts and experiencing the thrill of instant and explosive release the second my bum hit the seatless piss-covered rim.

The experience of immediate relief I felt morphed into a growing disgust as I sat there, and my eyes adjusted to the darkness of the space. It appeared as if this toilet had last been given a deep clean sometime around the dying embers of the Napoleonic Empire. The heavy stonework was damp, ancient, and moss covered. A mysterious stream of water trickled down the wall opposite me. The silence of the room was interrupted by my mother's voice from the real world outside, inquiring if I was okay. My work felt like it was done, so I replied in the affirmative and looked around for some toilet paper. A pang of horror gripped me as I realized there was none. In fact, this bathroom seemed like it had most probably been "sans papier toilette" since 1873.

Another voice from outside. My dad's this time, commanding me in vexed tones to hurry up. Desperate now, I waddled out of the cubicle in vain hope of discovering some hand towels with which I could improvise. There were, of course, no hand towels. There was not even a sink. My dad's voice rang out again, this time as an order. I was caught between a rock and an extremely angry parent. That was never a choice. I did what I had to do. Reaching down to my precious England National Team shorts, raising them slowly, sadly, from around my ankles, back to full mast.

It was a sickening feeling, experiencing the single item of clothing I most cherished becoming tarnished by my own hand. I waddled outside and was greeted by a look on my mother's face, which quickly turned from concern to empathetic shame. My dad was slightly less empathetic, bellowing "Have you *shat* your pants, Roger?" I tried to explain the technical realities of the lack of toilet paper in situ, but to no avail. It was widely assumed by my family that I had indeed shat myself. My mother quickly flagged down a French taxi, and I guiltily tried not to press my bum cheeks on the unwitting driver's backseat as we hurtled toward the sanctuary of our hotel. As I soaked, humiliated, in a warm bath, I watched my mother stare at my prized England shorts, now lying as a scrunched-up ball, the once proud blue stained beyond belief. She picked them up between her thumb and forefinger and dropped them into a plastic bag. "Well, these are going straight into the bin," she said, and before I could protest, they had been tossed into the bathroom garbage can, as I slowly lowered my body deeper into the now lukewarm water and looked up at the ceiling and realized that without my lucky shorts, my beloved England National Team were almost certainly done.

That is called foreshadowing, and the agony I felt in that moment proved to be nothing compared to the thousandfold torment I experienced actually watching the game that night over dinner. England needed a victory by those two precious goals to progress. As they toiled against Spain in cauldron-like conditions at the Santiago Bernabéu in Madrid, my mother was legitimately worried the English players might melt in the 91-degree heat. As the minutes ticked away, England threw nearly every player forward in an ever more desperate attempt to score. The best chance of the night fell to Kevin Keegan, one of England's most prolific finishers. Exactly the man we would have chosen in that moment of national need, yet he got the mechanics all wrong, heading the ball meekly straight to a relieved goalkeeper. "If he didn't have a woman's perm, that would have been a goal," my father shrieked, suggesting that Keegan's thick, long-haired hairstyle, which was de rigueur for footballers in those times, softened contact between the player and the ball. England was out of the World Cup, and I had been reintroduced to the notion of national failure as a fundamental part of my British identity.

After the final whistle, our waiter smirked as he came to clear our plates postgame, muttering, "Angleterre sont un petit chien qui pense il est un grand chien." My father took about five minutes to translate that sentence using the mini English-French dictionary he carried around for these very interactions. "England . . . are . . . a . . . small . . . dog . . . that . . . thinks . . . it's . . . a . . . big . . . dog," he said in a voice that became ever more a whisper.

I felt a mix of shock, and personal guilt as I anger-ate an intricate apple pâtisserie for dessert. My team, this English team of destiny, who had promised us they would "find a way . . . to win them all"—had been proven liars. However, they were leaving the tournament an unbeaten side, having conceded just one goal in the five games they played. Would they have won if I had not shat my shorts? Did that squalid incident cause the team euphemistically to do the same? The fact that the world will never know the answer to those hypothetical questions made the pain feel more personal. However, part of me embraced a very hard truth that night: Never trust the English National Team again.

Predictably, the Germans emerged from the group into the semifinals where they faced our gallant vacation host France, who had summoned some of the most beautiful football in the tournament, propelled by the creativity, flair, and elegance of the deceptively athletic Michel Platini. I used my father's dictionary to translate the headline of the French newspaper *L'Équipe*, which hung over the public toilet in the village we were touring on the day of the game. "You can find three million French people who run faster than him, who can jump higher than him, but you could not find a man who can play football better than him."

We watched the game in a bistro in Calais, which had classily hired a bugler to toot out a raspy version of "La Marseillaise" pregame. This was the night I realized that World Cup rivalries take on their nation's histories. And France and Germany have more than a little history. Touring Calais during the day, we saw old buildings pockmarked by shelling from Allied bombing, reminders that the city had only been liberated from Nazi occupation thirty-eight years earlier. Looking at the craggy faces of many of our fellow diners that night, it was impossible not to wonder what emotions they were experiencing as their plucky players took the field in a game that had been billed a battle between the French "artistes" and German "automatons."

If England had made a World Cup semifinal, the combined roars from every pub would have been vaguely audible around the world. The atmosphere in this French restaurant was tense to the point of silence. No one was eating. Everyone was smoking, and there was barely any celebration, even as Platini converted a penalty to equalize after the Germans had taken an early lead. The French, playing with freedom and verve, became ascendant, which only seemed to ratchet up the anxiety amongst my fellow diners and the bombast of the French commentator.

As I tucked into some liver pâté, Platini carved the German backline open with a poem of a pass. His teammate Patrick Battiston raced onto the ball, outrunning the defenders, charging in alone on a dash toward glory. The German goalkeeper Harald "Toni" Schumacher had other ideas. He sped out like an NFL safety, ignoring the ball, locked on only to his opponent, before launching himself into the air and exploding into the man with a sickening and brutal thud. With every subsequent replay of this sporting assault, the restaurant became ever more airless. A woman at the table next to me screamed and quietly began to sob as cameras zoomed into the poleaxed Battiston who lay lifeless on the field. Platini would later tell the French media he thought his teammate was dead. Medics ran out to administer oxygen to the unconscious man, and when he was finally stretchered off—with spinal cord injuries, concussion, and without two of his teeth—there would be further French agony. Everyone in the restaurant waited for the goalkeeper to be red-carded for his attack, forcing Germany to play with ten men the rest of the game. When the Dutch referee refused so much as to award a foul, never mind issue a card, the collective sense of injustice felt like it was at levels of pain familiar only to poor Battiston in his moment of injury.

At the end of regulation, the score remained 1–1, so the game agonizingly hurtled into thirty minutes of extra time. Somehow the French summoned the focus to smash home two astonishing goals with a ferocity that felt like a venting of collective pent-up national anger. But instead of bunkering in defensively to kill off the game, France continued to will themselves forward, as if hell-bent not only on winning but humiliating their German opponents in the process. An enormously naive mistake. France was about to discover a sporting truth: Germany is at their most dangerous when two goals down.

Upon substituting in Karl-Heinz Rummenigge, a talisman who was returning from an injury, the momentum of the game changed. The Germans began to counterattack with an unerring, clinical ruthlessness. Rummenigge himself cut the lead to 3–2, causing someone behind us to shout "Sangfroid," which I honestly did not know was a French word. Almost immediately after the restart, it was Rummenigge again who was instrumental as Germany leveled the score on an audacious bicycle kick by the acrobatic Klaus Fischer. What was shocking to witness was the lack of mourning from the French in this second. The Germans scoring two goals in six minutes was less an agony, more a reassuring fulfillment of their national self-image of predestined French doom. A moment which set up the World Cup's first-ever penalty shoot-out, and the subsequent inevitability of Gallic vulnerability and German superiority.

Penalty kicks are always an agony to live through for any

football fan. An individual battle of nerves between shooter and goalkeeper more akin to Russian roulette than the collective game of football that preceded it. Worse for the French shooters was that they would have to face the very goalkeeper, Schumacher,* who had just callously hospitalized their friend and teammate. France shot first. The teams missed one penalty kick apiece through five rounds. The game became sudden death. Maxime Bossis, the brave anchor of the French defense, drilled his shot toward the left corner, only to have Schumacher hurl himself across the goal to save it, raising his fist as a symbol of indestructible indomitability in the heat of the Seville night. When Horst Hrubesch scored to finish the game, the Germans mobbed their goalkeeper, who shouldn't have even been on the field.

This match had just delivered every single human emotion inside little more than 120 minutes. The French team had been mugged. They had come within twelve minutes of a World Cup final appearance. Yet the atmosphere around us from our fellow diners was oddly spirited. It was as if losing again, and being cheated by Germany in the process, was reassuringly familiar. That was who they were, and what they did as Frenchmen. I thought back to the stories Alain, the cognac-swilling restaurant proprietor, had regaled us with earlier in the trip. The narrative of the Battle of Camarón, the legionnaires, and that wooden prosthetic hand. "Defeat with dignity" were his words, and that was what we had just witnessed. The agony and injustice of defeat to the Germans was the perfect apogee of French glory. Platini and his team had lost with honor as tragic

---

* Schumacher would later beat Adolf Hitler in a French newspaper's poll of the nation's most hated historical figure.

heroes. As the tables in the restaurant were pushed to the side, and the diners started to sing and dance, they embraced the team, which had confirmed the nation's destiny: to come up short but always to delight.

The French could draw solace from the fact that they had exhausted their opponents. The Germans faced Italy and were picked off 3–1, in a one-sided final, the defining memory of which was Italian midfielder Marco Tardelli sprinting away and roaring after netting Italy's second goal, as if releasing a lifetime of sacrifice and aspiration in that moment. I did not see it as we were on the ferry back to England. The last moment of World Cup action I glimpsed was in the window of a Calais sport shop I forced my parents to take me to on our last day whilst hunting for a replica French kit to replace the English one I had soiled earlier on the trip. The store was predictably sold out, but I marveled at its window display, which consisted of a small television set and a VCR that had been set up to play the moment of Battiston being crushed by Schumacher on a loop. The television had been dressed in a black scarf of mourning, and there was a small crowd of French people who stood staring at it in silence, nodding at each other with appreciation.

Chapter 3

1986 World Cup, Mexico

WHEN THE 1986 World Cup rolled around, I was a fifteen-year-old high school student preparing to face one of the most future-defining sets of exams of my life. My "O levels." The kind of tests that are a crucible in which you are meant to live a yearlong monastic existence, studying obsessively day and night.

As June approached, my parents determined they were sufficiently impressed by the depths of my academic rigor to trust me while they took my three-year-old sister away on a ten-day summer vacation. My brother, Nigel, was away at university. With doe-eyed obedience, all I asked for in return was for my best friend, Jamie, to be allowed to move into our home during their absence, so I had both company and study partner. A request my parents quickly approved, believing that Jamie's diligence and maturity would reinforce my intellectual dedication. The ten days my parents were away conveniently overlapped with the beginning of the World Cup in Mexico. Neither Jamie nor I did a lick of work amidst that fiesta of total freedom, feeding ourselves a steady diet of football, delicious football. Yes, our academic futures were important, we reasoned, but the World Cup was more so.

Those ten days were ones lived in a delirious fever dream of football-filled recklessness. In truth, Jamie and I barely knew how to look after ourselves. We were capable of mustering just one recipe to cook between us, which meant every meal consisted of steaming bowls of pasta upon which we had melted an entire bag of shredded cheese in the microwave oven. A brand-new technology my mum was so proud of. We then charged outside to kick an orange plastic "Wembley Trophy" ball around my back garden, in serious, sweaty one-on-one games in which I made-believe I was Socrates, the bearded luscious-locked Brazilian with a medical degree and side gig in revolutionary politics, while Jamie attempted to channel the finishing skills of Emilio Butragueño, the Spanish striker whom we feared, mostly on account of his awesome nickname, "El Buitre" (The Vulture).

We would kill off the final hours before each night's kick-off by poring over the newspaper back pages, which mentally prepared us for the forthcoming action to be beamed live from exotic cities such as Guadalajara, Irapuato, or Nezahualcóyotl. By the time the evening's television coverage burst to life, signaled by the tinny crescendo of "Aztec Gold," the pseudo-sophisticated theme tune one of the British broadcasters had elected to match our notions of Mexico, we were both guaranteed to be salivating more than Pavlov's dogs in the proximity of a ringing dinner bell.

By virtue of hosting in 1986, Mexico became the first nation to hold the tournament twice. They had inherited the duties from the original selection, Colombia, whose own efforts had collapsed under financial weight. It was hardly the most obvious option. Just eight months before, Mexico City had experienced a brutal earthquake with the equivalent power of over a thousand atomic bombs, which had left more than ten thousand dead, a quarter of a million homeless, and $4 billion worth of damage. The Mexican economy was tanking. In the run-up to the tournament, British newspapers had been filled with incessant coverage of the resulting runaway inflation that had caused the value of the peso to plummet, yet somehow Mexican broadcaster Televisa was able to cobble together an enormous financial bid that even beat out the United States. Still, it was impossible to ignore the reality that all was not well in the country. When the Mexican president, Miguel de la Madrid, spoke on the opening day, every word was drowned out by boos from his own citizens who packed the Azteca stadium. Before a ball had been kicked, the world's sports press remained bemused. Rather than talk of goals and footballing glory, the subjects of corruption and conflict of interest filled their airwaves. Even after Mexico opened their tournament with a 2–1 victory over Belgium, the home fans' postmatch celebrations quickly degenerated into a seething nightlong riot, battling police.

The choice of Mexico as host was also a practical challenge. Many games were played in the thin air and lofty altitude of venues 7,000 feet above sea level. To make matters worse, kickoffs were scheduled for the convenience of prime-time television audiences in Europe, forcing players to endure midday temperatures that approached 100 degrees. The searing heat elicited complaints from many of the players that the search for profits had become more important than the competitive quality of the tournament itself. There was truth to that. When the World Cup was first televised in 1954 there had been fewer than forty million television sets in the world, the vast majority of which were in the soccer-averse United States. In 1980, the entire continent of Africa boasted barely a million televisions.

By 1986, however, there were nearly a billion sets across the world—most tuned to the World Cup, which had become the world's most visible billboard. All eyes were upon it, including mine and Jamie's.

The tournament was played by twenty-four teams, in twelve stadia, during fifty-two games sprinkled over thirty days, but from the very beginning, it centered around one man: the Argentinian icon Diego Armando Maradona. Squat and impudent, part urchin, part prince. A gent known as "El Pibe de Oro" (The Golden Boy). I had never seen anyone take the field with such nonchalant arrogance. My English heroes were all large, lumpy men. Cut from granite and fueled by stout ale. Maradona was just 5'5", his very being proof that one need not be a muscle-rippled titan to be a world-class soccer player. He seemed to be 73 percent composed of thigh muscle and glutes, a physical combination that caused my father to marvel, "You could rest a pint glass on that behind," the first time we had watched him play back in 1982. That ass was Maradona's gift, giving him a low center of gravity with which he defined himself as one of the most mesmerizing dribblers the game had ever seen.

Maradona had been just seventeen years of age during the 1978 World Cup, played on home turf in Argentina. Though already a rising star, the manager César Luis Menotti had controversially omitted Diego, explaining he felt he was too young "for such a confrontation." Four years later, the 1982 World Cup was played just two months after Argentina's military junta had invaded the Falkland Islands, a South Atlantic vestige of the British Empire, in an ultimately futile effort to divert attention from their flailing domestic economic woes. The national team, by now reinforced by the twenty-one-year-old Maradona, descended into Spain confident of glory, emboldened by the state-run media's reporting that the Argentinian military was on the brink of winning a majestic Falkland victory. The team arrived in Europe, read the free press for the first time, and discovered the awful truth—their ramshackle, ill-trained army had suffered shattering losses and were on the verge of surrender. With their locker room morale broken, the team limped out in the second round. The nadir saw a frustrated Maradona sent off the pitch for chopping down Brazilian substitute Batista with a kung fu kick to the midriff—his red card the coup de grâce in their 3–1 loss to their neighbors and archrivals.

The 1986 World Cup came when Maradona was at the peak of his powers. When the Argentinian team underperformed as they prepared for the tournament, his coach, the pragmatic Carlos Bilardo, elected to go all in, deciding to make the oft-undisciplined player his captain, emphasizing that this was Diego's tournament to win or lose. Maradona swaggered into Mexico, with his curly black hair, a diamond earring, and a singular braggadocio, poking the organizers in the eye for the sweltering conditions by declaring that the noon kickoffs were "ravioli time, not soccer time." A World Cup can be an unforgiving cauldron of pressure, but El Diego appeared utterly unfazed. Argentina was the first foreign team to arrive in Mexico City, and they were met by a thronging mob, triggering a riot quelled only by security forces using their rifle butts to press fans back. Maradona strolled right through the noise, unbothered.

The mania around the Argentinian team bordered on the surreal. To prepare for the tournament, the Argentines had undergone high-altitude training in the northern part of the country, where a twenty-eight-year-old fan shot himself because he was unable to gain access to a training game and experience

Diego in the flesh. That frenzy off the field carried through to the football played on it. In 1978, Argentina had won the World Cup under César Luis Menotti, who fostered a buccaneering tactical philosophy. Current coach Bilardo was a stark contrast to his predecessor, favoring a negative, defensive, cynically physical style that had led to faltering performances and left many Argentines feeling pessimistic in the run-up to the tournament. Furthermore, bar Maradona, the Argentinian squad was considered short on talent. One player, José Luis Brown, had been so poor of form he had been unable to attract a club team to offer him a contract. He had trained on his own in a local park to be ready for World Cup action.

In truth, Jamie and I watched all of this out of our peripheral vision, as the early days of the tournament were viewed purely through the prism of England. Led by charmingly avuncular gentleman manager Bobby Robson, and goal-poacher-extraordinaire Gary Lineker, an instinctive finisher with boyish good looks who appeared capable of compelling the ball to come to him in and around the opponent's goal. That Lineker played for Everton, the Liverpool-based club side Jamie and I both obsessively supported, made us adore him all the more. Jamie and I were besotted. Lineker wore his football shorts snug and tight, so we wore our football shorts snug and tight. Like the rest of the nation, we believed his skills would deliver World Cup glory with a quasi-religious fervor. The English had arrived in Mexico on a tabloid media-hype train, the result of an eleven-match unbeaten run and an undefeated record in qualification. Yet, it was impossible to ignore one nagging concern: Our players were used to the rain and cold of Britain's football's muddy pitches. How would they fare under the kind of savage sun that would fry most Englishmen into a sunburnt crisp?

I did not want to hear about the players' moaning though. We fans had to make our own sacrifices—many of the opening-round games kicked off at the ghastly late hour of 11 p.m., which caused Jamie and me to burn through our adrenaline long before kickoff, then muster a second wind by mainlining a family-sized Toblerone bar just to stay awake. The tepid football our heroes summoned did not help at all. The first game, a shocking 1-0 loss to a middling Portugal, was a humbling reality check, played under a cloudless, stiflingly scorching sky. England conspired to miss chance after chance, then dropped their guard and let the Portuguese score late. One of the English commentators undiplomatically compared the feeling of defeat to the emotions the Mexicans must have experienced during their earthquakes. Jamie and I sat at home in bewildered disbelief watching our heroes be incinerated in the Monterrey sun. We could not speak a word to each other, our ears still ringing from the whistles of seething derision cascading down from the three thousand English fans who had traveled all that way to Mexico.

The English press pack quickly had their knives out and sharpened. Many of them aimed in Lineker's direction. A man of whom much was expected after he had stabbed home 30 league goals to finish as the English football's top scorer. Three days later, after a second desperately flat performance, the media's agony tipped toward meltdown settings. An insecure England delivered a damp squib 0-0 draw with rank outsider Morocco, an opponent whom the English media had described as a "third world team" before kickoff. Worse, captain Bryan Robson limped off the field and out of the tournament after popping his shoulder out on the fields. His World Cup was over, and the way his teammates had labored made it feel like theirs would soon be also.

With one group game left, England was now in must-win territory. They had to beat Poland to remain in the tournament. The media were unrelenting in their embrace of their doom-narrative, venting their disbelief and fury by screaming accusations at the avuncular and ambassadorial English manager Bobby Robson, begging him to bench Lineker. Robson stood by his man, but we knew injuries and Wilkins's red card would necessitate changes in personnel. When the starting lineup was announced, Jamie and I were astonished to see Lineker had been joined by three other players from Everton. The bar-brawling midfielder Peter Reid, and the overlapping right side tandem Gary Stevens and Trevor Steven. That an all-or-nothing game rested on our club-heroes' shoulders made us both proud and fearful.

We need not have worried. The familiarity the Everton quartet had forged from the repetition of club games played together gave England a sense of the collective verve and movement, which had been lacking. Indeed, Steven and Stevens were both involved in the buildup to the first goal, the former rolling the ball out wide so the latter could sweep in a weighted cross, which Gary Lineker flashed in to prod home from close range, charging away heroically with his left arm in a cast raised high. The emotional release this goal unleashed was unparalleled. It had taken 188 minutes of the World Cup to witness an England goal, and as Jamie and I hugged and jigged around the glass-topped coffee table in my otherwise empty house, we shared a burst of joy and relief in equal measure. Even the traditionally objective BBC commentator struggled to muffle the quavering emotion in his voice.

Something had suddenly clicked for our England. A reality Lineker emphasized by quickly rattling home two more goals inside the opening thirty-six minutes to complete a sizzlingly epic first-half hattrick—the first scored by an Englishman since Sir Geoff Hurst netted three times in the 1966 final. It was a late, hot night in Liverpool, and through the open windows of our lounge, we could hear cheers emerging from every neighboring home, which made it feel as if the entire nation was experiencing a simultaneous, communal mood swing from despair to sudden surging confidence. Jamie and I toasted the final whistle with a shot of Baileys Irish Cream I had liberated from my old man's drinks cabinet. The next morning's papers afforded Lineker's hattrick treatment on par with Alan Turing cracking the Enigma Code in 1941, or Sir Roger Bannister breaking the Four-Minute Mile. It was an immense historic achievement the nation would remember forever.

The good news was England was still alive and had qualified for the knockout round against Paraguay. The bad news was my parents returned home the night before the game, and so I watched our team cruise through with my ecstatically enthusiastic father, who poured us both a celebratory scotch with a heavy hand to accompany the second half of a 3–0 win, courtesy of two more close-range finishes from the now-unstoppably potent Lineker. I tipsily extricated myself from my dad's protracted postmatch analysis to share a moment with Jamie on the telephone. This was the first time in our lives we had ever experienced England truly soaring in World Cup play, and we marveled as if we had just witnessed Dumbo the elephant take flight. Everything now felt possible.

The entire country surged in unison behind our buoyant England team, even as the fates pitched them into the narrative-overload of a quarterfinal clash against Diego Maradona and Argentina. A nation with whom, according to our opponents at least, we were still at war. Within minutes of beating Paraguay, England manager Bobby Robson was asked to address the sudden significance of the first footballing clash between the two countries since the 1982 Falkland Islands War. "I am a football manager, not a politician. Don't ask me that kind of question," he declared, eliciting a spontaneous burst of applause from the British journalists, who surrounded him.

That kind of commonsense approach was signature Bobby Robson. But football is a hysterical beast, so it was never going to be permitted to last. First, even before the Falklands, our two nations shared a footballing rivalry bordering on blood feud. The roots of the enmity dated back to the 1966 World Cup quarterfinals, which England won 1–0 amidst scenes of violent carnage that peaked with Argentine captain Antonio Rattín being sent off for insulting the match officials, then exiting the field after fiendishly and theatrically wiping his hands on a Union Jack corner flag. Postgame, an incandescent England manager Alf Ramsey unwisely labeled the Argentine players "animals," a slur that the South Americans neither forgave nor forgot.

The open wound that was the Falklands Conflict—or the "Guerra de las Malvinas" as it was known in Argentina—turned the simmering tension to a rolling boil. To be honest, the Falklands were tiny, remote islands in the South Atlantic Ocean no one had even heard of in Britain, before the Argentinians had gone and invaded them in a desperate attempt to prove they were still a regional power. That turned out to be a devastating miscalculation as the British struck back to demonstrate that the embers of the British Empire still smoldered. Prime Minister Margaret Thatcher dispatched 127 troop-carrying ships over

8,000 miles to defend our honor. The battle that ensued lasted 74 days as 649 Argentinians and 255 Britons lost their lives.

This World Cup quarterfinal was a chance for Maradona to exact revenge. Even though his nation had been humiliated on the military battlefield, the football pitch remained the last arena in which Argentina could announce itself as a true global superpower. A month before the tournament, Diego had been asked about what then felt like a remote possibility of facing England. Diplomatically, he elected to declare, "Politics has nothing to do with soccer. When we take the field, we do not bring bombs and machine guns with us." Yet, it was clear to anyone watching him training in the run-up to the game that he was preparing with a dedicated focus which belied those words.

As the drumbeat to kickoff began, this clash felt like the ultimate grudge match—one which would prove that in football, as in life, spite and revenge are the rocket fuel of motivations. Fans from both sides coalesced behind the moniker "The Malvinas II" as the Argentine and English media worked themselves into mutually reinforcing levels of hysteria. Published reports out of Argentina described in delicious detail the nightly burning of British flags on the streets of Buenos Aires. Drunk English fans were broadcast pregaming outside Azteca Stadium, while chanting with jingoist glee,

> *In '82, it was a rout,*
> *In '86, we'll drink our stout,*
> *We'll take no lives, we'll use no tanks,*
> *But the gauchos again will give no thanks.*

The game itself was to be held in one of the most theatrical and daunting venues in all of world sports: Mexico City's historic Estadio Azteca—less a football stadium, more a fortress. A smoggy, steep-banked stronghold perched 7,200 feet above sea level, built out of 100 tons of concrete laid on top of volcanic rock. Nearly 115,000 fans packed the steeply banked stadium as temperatures simmered to over 100 degrees.

"That place looks about as far from Sheffield, Luton, or Coventry as you can get," quipped my uncle Eric, part of the Manchester side of the family whom my mother had invited over to watch the game. One of the British broadcasters proudly boasted of the English game plan, "The nearest man to Maradona kills him. And if he doesn't, the next one does. It is as simple as that." My uncle could not help himself from shouting, "We are going to do these Argies." I attempted to match his optimism but could only feign a confidence I did not feel. While it was true, player for player, the Argentinian team were no match for our boys. Yet, they had Maradona. This strange mystical man, who even during warm-ups projected a godly power, like a footballing Joan of Arc, that left me in the grip of a gnawing terror.

The English executed their game plan from the whistle, blatantly hacking down Maradona with blunt force at every opportunity. Yet, the little man remained almost impossible to knock off the ball. When another player managed to kick him off the field, he would quickly dust himself off and demand the ball again, drawing strength as he drained defenders of their energy. Though the first half remained goalless, the Azteca surged with energy, especially that of the Argentine fans, whose white and light blue flags greatly outnumbered the Union Jacks and Crosses of St. George.

At fifty-one minutes the cagey stalemate was broken in the most jarring fashion. An England midfielder lofted an ill-judged back pass to his goalkeeper, Peter Shilton. The ball floated in the smoggy Mexican city air, and the tiny Maradona followed it and elected to use his entire 5'5" being to challenge the 6' Englishman to an aerial battle. By all rights, this should have been a routine ball for the keeper to pluck. Yet, it happened so fast that all we saw in real time was the Argentinian wheeling away in delight as the ball, in some science- and rationale-defying fashion, bobbled into the net. The English players were incensed and surrounded Ali Bin Nasser, the Tunisian referee, screaming for handball. The immediate replays revealed the throat-constricting truth: As Shilton jumped, at light speed, Maradona had used his left fist to punch the ball into the net. Everyone in the world could see the illegal use of a hand, apart from the one guy who mattered, the referee, who had awarded the goal, and later blamed his error on a hemorrhoid treatment he was taking that affected his sight. "It's not cricket," moaned Uncle Eric softly. "What is this, volleyball?" snorted my father as the replays rolled and rolled, each one adding to the waves of trauma that were washing over me.

In the postmatch press conferences, Maradona would quite brilliantly proclaim the goal to have been scored "a little with the head of Diego and a little with the hand of God," a phrasing which captured both the impudence and immorality of the goal as well as the sense of impotence I experienced in the face of it and the injustice that it conjured, which was utterly debilitating. Four minutes later, while the English were still reeling, Maradona proceeded to score a spectacular solo goal that even God would have had difficulty replicating. With searing acceleration, poise, and balance, he launched a spectacular 60-yard dash, a brilliant display of the *Gambeta*, the Argentinian art of dribbling, weaving delicately past five England players, the last two of whom desperately tried to take out the man rather than the ball, then simply rolled the ball into the net. One of the single-handedly most emasculating goals I have ever witnessed scored against my team. The audacity and execution were so divine, my mother could not help but clap on the couch beside me. Both goals were a reflection of the different sides of Maradona's persona: The first required the stealth and pluck of the pickpocket; the second, the daring and polish of Thomas Crown.

God bless England. This particular duet of goals—one cruel, the other glorious—would have finished off lesser squads, yet they summoned the tenacity to force themselves back into the game, flinging on attacking players and asserting themselves with valor. Nine minutes from time, Lineker struck his signature close range goal to give us hope and life. In the dying seconds of the game, he was inches away from connecting with a cross on the goal line. The Englishman somehow ended up in the net, but the ball did not. Just like that, the game was up. England was out, and our place in the last four evaporated.

The final whistle felt like a release. For ninety minutes, I had been nearly incapacitated by fear. That fear had been realized in the most extreme way possible, by means foul and flair. One goal borderline evil. The second almost divine. Now, there was an intense grief welling up deep inside me. I ran out into the back garden and started to dribble that plastic Wembley Trophy football Jamie and I had spent the first ten days of the tournament training with. Picking up pace, I chipped the ball up in the center of the garden, and then with a primal roar, vented every trace of anger inside me, by blasting it straight through the front window of our lounge. There was a crash, then silence. A ball-shaped hole now stood between me and my astonished family, who stared back through the shattered glass, splinters of which continued to tinkle to the floor. My father, who could be quick to anger at the best of times, simply nodded calmly at me, as I doubled over and clutched my thighs, now bereft of energy, sobbing and utterly spent. My dad then let himself outside and after wiping the tears of anger stinging my cheeks, solemnly hugged me, letting me know he shared my pain. "I understand, son," he said. "I understand."

Yet, World Cups do not stop for your feelings. After scoring his second goal in the England game, Diego modestly claimed he could only deliver a run like that against the English because they were "the only players noble enough not to knock me down," but then promptly repeated his magic act by scoring an almost identical slaloming run against Belgium in the semifinals. By now, even the English papers had to admire his guile, slapping the now classic image from the semifinal in which Diego had six Belgian players around him. I cut the photograph out and put it above my bed and would kill off afternoons waiting for Argentina to play again by staring at it. You could almost smell his opponent's fear through the newspaper's fibers. You also could tell that even against six opponents, Maradona fancied his odds.

In the final, Argentina returned to the Azteca to face the West Germans who had, once again, played their favorite role of tournament heels, scraping by tournament underdog darlings Morocco and clipping hosts Mexico before facing France once more. The team the Germans had eliminated in such cruel circumstance on penalty kicks four years before. Both Patrick Battiston and Harald Schumacher took the field again, the latter steadfastly refusing to discuss their previous confrontation.

This time around the game was not close. Michel Platini was neutralized, and the French were oddly meek and dead-legged, as the ruthless Germans rolled their way into a second successive final 2–0.

The final was what the World Cup should be. A battle of continents, tactical philosophies, and opposing ideas of football. Argentina, unpredictable yet explosive. The Germans, organized, disciplined, and relentless. My family watched in the dim light of our boarded-up window. From the off, the West Germans were so spooked and preoccupied by Maradona, they decided to shadow him with their best player, the domineering Lothar Matthäus. However, in nullifying the Argentinian superstar, Matthäus, the creative hub of the German attack, essentially took himself out of the game as well, as Maradona reveled in the role of cunning decoy, dragging the Germans out of position to create space for his teammates. When Matthäus chopped down Maradona, Argentina's Jorge Burruchaga lofted the resulting free kick into the box. It was fitting that José Luis Brown—the player who had steadfastly trained on his own in a Buenos Aires park to make the tournament—was the man who met with a run he would have practiced alone hundreds of times. As Burruchaga's cross split the air, he ghosted toward the far post, met the ball perfectly to open the scoring, and collapsed in a joyous, sweaty heap on top of Maradona.

It was the only international goal that José Luis Brown would ever score. A reminder of the power of the World Cup—that it can turn journeymen into global heroes. Jorge Valdano made it 2–0, but the Germans were ferociously determined, clawing their way back with two goals in six minutes. In his nation's time of need, Maradona stepped up. Six minutes from time, he stopped being a mischievous distraction, unleashing a poem of a pass to split the German defense and set up Jorge Burruchaga to score the winner. Argentina had won their second World Cup in three tournaments and it was clear to all, this man had delivered the single greatest individual performance the World Cup had ever seen, scoring or assisting on 10 of his team's 14 goals on the path to glory. Maradona clung possessively on to the trophy, even as his teammates lifted him into the air, just as Maradona had lifted the hopes and dreams of an entire nation on his own shoulders.

As a postscript, I should note that over time, my perspective on football—like that on beer, Camembert cheese, and leafy greens—evolved. I have come to realize that football's greatest gift is its ability to make you feel. No one made me feel more alive than Maradona in that moment, and I am not alone. Throughout his career, Maradona made entire cities, regions, and nations come together and share some of the most profound, empowering, joyful experiences of their lives.

I corresponded with the late Uruguayan writer Eduardo Galeano before his death and asked him about his warning in relation to Maradona: "When humans become gods, there is only one ultimate outcome, they have to become fallen gods." Anyone who watched Maradona flail during the embers of his career will know this is true. A sordid downfall marred by cocaine addiction, organized crime ties, and doping bans. Even more so throughout his peripatetic retirement in which he often cut a beleaguered, corpulent figure in search of sanctuary.

Galeano explained, "Maradona became a kind of dirty God, the most human of the gods. That perhaps explains the universal veneration he conquered, more than any other player." I love that framing. The most human of gods. A gent who experienced extremes of ecstasy and misery, veneration and loneliness in a way that encapsulates life itself. Shortly after the conversation with Galeano, I came into possession of a signed photograph of Maradona punching the ball over Shilton, the bewildered England goalkeeper. I framed the image and hung it on the wall opposite my desk, where it remains. A moment that traumatized me so deeply as a kid is now the one thing I look at every single day. A reminder of Diego's memory, power, and the singular ability he had to make the world feel alive.

Chapter 4

1990 World Cup, Italy

DESPITE MY PROPENSITY to be distracted by anything and everything, I somehow made it to university. Even my own parents were barely able to mask their surprise as I was accepted to study at Leeds, in the north of England. An academic institution I had chosen on account of the fact it was the only university I had actually bothered to visit. I use the word "visit" very loosely. In our final year of high school, the careers officer gave us a single afternoon off to experience life on a campus of our choosing. I took the train northeast with my friend James Kay. We swaggered off at the station, found the nearest pub, aptly named the Railway Arms, and merrily drank the afternoon away, before catching the return train home. I neither set foot on nor glimpsed the actual university but determined I had experienced enough of the city to be sure I wanted to spend the next three years there studying law. As a fresher, I honestly majored in drinking and promptly proceeded to fail each and every one of my first-year exams.

One of the greatest contributions to my failure was that the criminal law and torts finals overlapped with the first two weeks of the 1990 World Cup. Watching elite football descend upon the land of AC Milan, Juventus, and Inter—then the world's greatest club teams—completely destroyed whatever dwindling interest I had in immersing myself in the differences between the actus reus and the mens rea of criminal intent.

I lived in Bodington, a sprawling hall of residence. A dreary mini-town of identikit student mid-rises, perched on the edge of the city. A place where the 1989 Stone Roses debut album felt like it was faintly audible at all hours, and the boredom born of being miles from nowhere was not quite enough of a motivator to encourage us to make the effort to schlepp downtown and reconnect with human civilization. So, wall-to-wall coverage of the World Cup, which coincided with the last two weeks of our term, felt like more than a sporting event. It was the first good reason approximately 90 percent of us had to get out of bed before dark all year. A motley crew of my fellow hallmates would congregate in the shabby student lounge, late afternoon, some actually dressed, but those more seriously hungover electing to sidle in wearing boxer shorts and bathrobes. We would arrange ourselves around a giant primitive rear-projection big box television as it warmed up and began to cast its fuzzy images, live from Italy, across the screen.

The widely shared rumor about Bodington Hall was that its original design had been knocked off from a Swedish prison, and the lounge did have a grim, institutional feel to it. Light brown peeling paint. Cigarette-burned carpet. A well-worn pool table rendered unusable by the fact all the cues had long since been snapped. The shabby atmosphere was in stark contrast to the shiny, modernist aesthetics now beamed live on television straight from Italia. To welcome the world, the Italian nation had undergone a building boom that had seen avant-garde stadiums, like the rebuilt San Siro in Milan with its concrete-brutalist beauty and signature spiral towers, rise across the nation. Yes, government investigators would discover after the tournament that this appetite for construction was stimulated by corruption and kickbacks rather than a true love of postmodern architecture. That was lost on us at the time. The English papers simply served up reports of the zealous levels of Italian fan passion. I read about one such fan, convicted of hooliganism at an Italian League game in Genoa, who was not just fined but ordered to refrain from speaking to anyone else about soccer for the entire month of the World Cup. This honestly seemed like such cruel and unusual punishment, I felt that Amnesty International should have looked into it.

The beauty of the stadium architecture was the antithesis of the actual football, which was played throughout the tournament. The 1990 World Cup was tactically combative, often bordering on the cynical, plagued by fouls, in which many of the big games were decided by penalty shoot-outs. This physical tone was set in the opening game when the "Indomitable Lions" of Cameroon faced up to the reigning champions, Argentina. Cameroon was considered patsies when they took the field. African teams were traditionally filler at the World Cup, like extras in the background of movie scenes. Argentina's iconic Diego Maradona felt so disdainfully confident before kickoff that during the pre-match captains' handshakes, he dapped up his opposite number, Stephen Tataw, then brazenly flicked up the ball from its spot on the center circle and walked back, deep into his own half, bouncing it off his shoulder with the flourish of a performing seal.

Tuning in from Leeds, we all expected the game to have a "gladiators fed to the Lions vibe." It did. Just not in the way we expected. Cameroon lived up to their "Indomitable" nickname from the opening whistle, unleashing a barrage of brutal tackles, and managing to have two men red-carded before the ninety minutes were up. Yet, the end justified the means. In the 67th minute, their attacker, François Omam-Biyik, leaped into the air, and with the hang time worthy of any NBA highlight reel, nodded the ball downward, as a quaking Argentinian goalkeeper muffed the catch. Cue a delirious frenzy of drumbeat and goat bells from a euphoric Cameroonian fanbase. Their traditional costumes—one man was wearing a splendid custom fabric emblazoned with lions and footballs—reflected the pride and joy they were experiencing in that moment. This was an extreme juxtaposition to the angry violence I was used to from England games. A point reinforced at the final whistle when two of my fellow students, who had downed at least a dozen pints, were so moved by Cameroon's achievements, they took off their shirts and had a bare-knuckle brawl in the corner of the lounge.

The game instantly became the stuff of legend, known around the world as "The Miracle of Milan." By defanging Maradona's Argentina, Cameroon announced themselves to the world as the first African nation to be truly feared on the football field. Before kickoff, I could not have pointed to their nation on a map. Now, a fairytale run had begun. The Lions became global darlings, and in Leeds nightclubs, their resplendent green Adidas jersey became the de rigueur shirt for any discerning ravers to wear for the rest of the summer.

Argentina was not the only giant to flounder initially. Hosts Italy were a squad stuffed with handsome hair-gelled footballers. Demigods as if painted by Botticelli. Yet, they struggled in their opening game against a lightly regarded Austrian side.

Desperate for a goal, fourth string striker Totò Schillaci was inserted on a hunch in the 74th minute. Schillaci, a twenty-five-year-old journeyman, had grabbed the last place on the host's squad, having played with them only once before the tournament kicked off. With his bedraggled, thinning hair and heavily weathered face, he looked like a shelter dog surrounded by pedigree alphas. Yet, within four minutes, it was Totò who broke the deadlock and headed in the winner to deliver a 1–0 victory. This was the beginning of a scoring streak that never stopped. In a tournament in which Italy won six of its seven games, on the way to a third-place finish, Schillaci netted the winning goal a remarkable five times, charging off, arms outstretched, bald patch glowing in the breeze, eyes bulging in surprised elation. He became the face of his nation, changing the course of his own life in that four-week scoring spree, and setting off a baby-naming flurry across Italy in the process. A statement, again, to the true power of the World Cup: that it could take a player who was little known and turn him into a global superstar, less in the blink of an eye, more in the heading of a ball.

Slightly less ecstatically, England was back in the World Cup. With them came their massed band of hooligan fans, who had honed their aggressive craft since the 1970s, a product of English football's dizzying array of local rivalries, combined with large crowds and copious amounts of alcohol, which incubated the perfect conditions for massed incendiary violence. The Italian police feared the English supporters to such an extent, they forced them to play all their opening-round games in isolated conditions on the island of Sardinia, where a security force of up to 10,000 police could relentlessly monitor them. One of England's most feared hooligans, a gent named Paul Scarrott, was sophisticated enough to hold his own press tour upon arriving in Italy, during which he gloated, "The police are afraid of me." A boast which proved not to be true. Within twenty-four hours, an extremely intoxicated Scarrott was arrested and deported back to mainland Europe, still wearing the Union Jack that had been tied around his neck when he had been located.

Expectations for the English National Team were muted. Led again by gentleman-coach Bobby Robson, they had qualified as runners-up in their group, surviving by mere inches—one Polish long-range shot hitting the English crossbar instead of floating into the net—from not making it all. No doubt, the Italian police were the lead amongst those who had wished that the Polish shot had gone in and England had not qualified. The team were accompanied by that much-feared hooligan fanbase, who were the dark side of any English football journey. Yet, there were hints of joyous narrative surrounding the squad, thanks to their bold decision to record their World Cup anthem with Manchester electro-dance pioneers New Order, a hedonistic quartet who, predictably, proceeded to pack as many nudge-nudge drug double entendres as is humanly possible into a four-and-a-half-minute track. "World in Motion" is honestly a surreally perfect pop tune. Footballers singing over Balearic beats and breezy synth riffs—and maverick winger John Barnes even laying down a rap, in which New Order persuaded him to talk about "get to the line" in a style that both football fans and cocaine enthusiasts would appreciate in equal measure.

The track was a banger, and its positive themes of love and celebration made it a harbinger of English football culture's transformation from one pockmarked by relentless violence to blissed-out passion. A metamorphosis that was a by-product of the surge in ecstasy consumption amongst young working-class males, who became obsessed with raving in place of fighting. A transformation that tempered hooliganism almost overnight. In turn, New Order's involvement fused football with pop culture, taking the sport from the dingy terraces to places it had never really gone. Once the single was released, there was not a nightclub in Leeds in which the track was not played at least three times in any self-respecting DJ's set. Each spin inevitably ending with the dance floor packed full of hot, sweaty bodies, bellowing the song's final refrain.

Despite all those cozy vibes, England's first game was a politically fraught affair against the Republic of Ireland. A boisterous mob who had qualified for their first-ever World Cup, fielding a team that joyfully played a physical style of "agricultural" football. I hitchhiked to Scotland to watch the game with my childhood friend Jamie, who was by now studying in Edinburgh. We watched it in a cavernous beer hall packed with hundreds of students. The game was a crude affair. A battle of resilience, lacking all imagination, in which England were heavy favorites. When that impish striker Gary Lineker opened the scoring early on, I impulsively jumped up to celebrate, naively oblivious to the extent Scottish people detested the English. I quickly found out as a fusillade of lager cans—most of them still full—were angrily flung in my direction. A second salvo of cans was sent airborne sixty-four minutes later—but one born of delight—when Irish midfielder Kevin Sheedy pounced on some English slop, charged into the box, and rifled a delicious shot past the stunned English goalkeeper, Peter Shilton. To the Scots who packed the bar, the game ending 1–1 felt as good as an English loss. The result was an excuse for the entire city to attempt to drink itself out of beer. I watched on in wonder at the night of infinite debauchery. Not to mark a national victory, but to revel in the failure of their neighbor. A reminder that pettiness and spite are two of the greatest human motivators.

A second English draw, 0–0 against the favored European champions, the Netherlands, was hard-earned, but not as hard fought as the pitched battles between huge rival hooligan groups before and after the game in which rocks were launched at riot police. Once the tear-gas clouds cleared, the English were left clinging to their World Cup existence. The third and final group stage game against Egypt was a must-win. Victory came by the narrowest of margins. A 1–0 squeaker delivered by the tantalizing creativity of jester-maverick Paul Gascoigne, and a second-half goal from defender Mark Wright, which was enough to break down the Africans' resolute defending. No sooner had the final whistle blown than the English press, who had delighted in eviscerating their team on the back pages of its tabloids, underwent a 180-degree collective mood change. Writers who had spent the previous week deriding the team began to speculate wildly about the ease with which England would now stroll all the way into the semifinal.

The English World Cup would continue. But in many ways, this also marked the moment I was prepared for mine to end. I was headed off to spend the summer in the United States as a camp counselor in the backwoods of Maine, to become one of the vast battalion of British students who descend upon that great American institution, with their pasty limbs and cut-off denim shorts. I knew in the moment that leaving Leeds was to risk cutting myself off from football. The United States was renowned, like space to Captain Kirk, as the sport's final frontier. The one final location on earth that has remained stubbornly immune to the lure of the game. I say that even though the United States had qualified for the tournament for the first time in forty-long years, their stay was short and unmemorable. The team, a ragtag mix of college kids and indoor football players, was dispatched quickly without making any real mark. The only true memory they etched during their fleeting cameo was the hype hip-hop track the squad had released to celebrate qualification, which the English broadcasters played on repeat during the tournament, in the spirit of laughing at, not with, them.

Imaginatively entitled "Victory," the video that accompanied the tune featured America's finest footballers, soullessly rapping, on a beach, inexplicably topless, whilst doing keepie-uppies with a bizarro world assortment of celebrities, including O.J. Simpson, a tennis-playing actress named Cathy Lee Crosby, and one of the swole dudes from *American Gladiators*. That strange confection proved to be the only form of victory the team were connected to. Once they arrived at the tournament, they were quickly smashed by Czechoslovakia, then clipped by Italy and Austria, departing with a modicum of World Cup bona fides, which was important as they had been selected to host the next tournament and so needed to create some level of "optics." In truth, global football fans paid no more attention to the United States than the United Arab Emirates, a team who made their tournament debut that year and arrived accompanied by ten camels for good luck. Those dromedaries were regrettably held up in customs, and the UAE were subsequently obliterated three times.

I landed at JFK on June 20, which was coincidentally the same day my university law exam results came out. I collect-called my mum from baggage claim to find out how I had performed. The anguish and disappointment in her voice as she spoke to the operator and accepted the phone charges told me all I needed to know: that I had failed them all and would have to replace my plans to end the summer by traveling across the United States with a speedy return to Leeds to retake them. That reality felt so inevitable that in the moment, I was honestly more pained by my inability to find a bar at the airport playing the final round of World Cup group stage games.

I hightailed my way into New York City. The summer camp where I was to be working had arranged for a one-night stay at the YMCA in midtown Manhattan. Back then, New York City was still a thrilling human circus. The sign over the front door of the Y greeting any new arrival set the tone, warning, "Do not turn left, you will be shot."

My room was tiny and spartan. A bed, a chest of drawers, and a tiny television. I flicked through the channels hungrily hoping to find a broadcast of Brazil and Scotland's opening-round clash to no avail. It was as if the World Cup did not exist. Indeed, almost every channel broadcast the same thing: competing with each other to carry breathless live reports covering the latest sensational attack by a citywide phenom named "Dartman," who had terrorized women in midtown Manhattan by using a makeshift blowgun to shoot tiny darts into their buttocks as they passed by him on the crowded streets. Looking out of my window, I saw to my horror below, those camera teams were actually broadcasting in a scrum, live, on the streets directly outside of my hostel. I immediately abandoned any fanciful notions of spending a night out on the town, putting the chain across the door in my room, before hopping on a Greyhound at a grimy Port Authority Bus Terminal to Maine at first light.

The summer camp experience turned out to be one of the

most fulfilling of my life. A parallel universe filled with bunk mates, appropriated Native American terminology, competitive sports, libido-soaked socials, and snugly fitted velour shorts. All of it topped off with tube socks. Yet, knowing I was living in this American Fantasy Island, whilst the World Cup was unraveling its storylines without me being able to watch them, made it feel like a luxury prison. This was an era before cell phones and the internet. The only football news I received came a week late courtesy of the news clippings my mother faithfully cut from *The Daily Telegraph* and airmailed to me on the daily to keep me abreast of the tournament's progress. Even though the events depicted had happened a week earlier, I ripped open every envelope with the hunger of a death row prisoner awaiting commutation of their sentence from the governor's office.

On July 1, England was to face the Cameroonians, who had blazed a fairytale pathway all the way to the quarterfinals, deeper into the tournament than any African team had ever ventured. They had been propelled by the goals of a remarkable man: thirty-eight-year-old Roger Milla.

While it is true, some are born great, some achieve greatness, and some have greatness thrust upon them, the World Cup teaches us that still others do it by walking onto the field of play as a substitute with fifteen minutes to go, and scoring late, critical goals, just as Milla had spent his summer doing. Quite a feat for any man, never mind one who was probably even older than his reported age of thirty-eight, and who, until the World Cup, had been playing part-time football on the remote Indian Ocean island of Réunion, having retired from a career spent predominantly in the French leagues.

In Cameroon's first knockout game against Colombia, Milla had scored twice, barreling through to drive the ball home for the first, and then humiliated the goalkeeper by grinning ear to ear as he sauntered past him close to the midfield and slotted the ball into an open goal. Joy was a critical component of Milla's game. He had the foresight to brand all his goals with a trademark celebration, first running along the goal line to dry-hump the corner flag, then gyrating with the exuberance of Barney the Dinosaur. The move became the signature highlight of the tournament as the Indomitable Lions, with their organized displays—physical at the back and relying on Milla to score a goal or two up front—shattered every cliché previously attributed to African soccer.

In the quarterfinals, England became Cameroon's toughest test yet. This was a battle of the big cats. The Indomitable Lions against the Three Lions. The game fortunately fell on my day off from camp, and I drove down to Boston in the bright yellow convertible Camaro of Phil, a fellow camp counselor with whom I was not particularly close but who pitied me sufficiently to offer me the chance to sleep overnight at his family home in Brookline and watch the game. The broadcast on TNT was my first experience of watching a live soccer game in the United States of America. A reality which was immediately apparent, because, for several times a half, the game would be interrupted, by a commercial break, which was ridiculous, bewildering, and possibly the most American-soccer thing ever.

Despite his generous hospitality, Phil was, by nature, a dour kid. As I screamed at his family's living room television screen, he sat alongside me on the couch, blank-faced, lazily leafing through a copy of *Sports Illustrated* he had picked up from the coffee table. Even with his disinterest, the game was an emotionally cacophonous drama. England's team may have been stuffed with globally revered household names and scored inside twenty-six minutes, yet even after Cameroon conceded on the stroke of halftime, they remained undaunted. They knew Milla's time was still to come, and my fellow Roger did not disappoint, swaggering onto the field and tearing my heroes to pieces before my helpless eyes. First Milla won a penalty, then to my horror, he set up the second goal by storming through the English gut and dishing a pass to fellow substitute Eugène Ekéké, who flicked the ball home.

Phil did not so much as look up from his magazine, but my heart felt like it was constricting in medically dangerous ways. England manager Bobby Robson looked like a mourner at a funeral as the commentator giddily wondered aloud, "Are England on the next plane home?" I could not help myself from picking fretfully at the tassels on Phil's mother's couch, which began to fray between my anxious fingers. Cameroon was eight minutes away from securing the most improbable semifinal slot in World Cup history. Phil was unfazed. I was in pain.

There were only two random cuts to commercial break in that last eight minutes, but one managed to miss England winning a penalty in the 83rd minute to draw level. I lived and died until the final whistle, and also saw commercials for Coke and Eggo Waffles in the process. Extra time was electric. I had been forced to turn up the volume as Phil, extremely bored, and no doubt regretting the kindness of inviting me to his home, spent the entire half hour talking very loudly on the phone in an attempt to track down a pair of Red Sox tickets. A conversation he did not even break from when England took the lead courtesy of a second penalty and I leapt onto his back in a smothering, relief-filled embrace. England held on and scraped by. We indeed went to watch the Red Sox that night. It rained. Boston sports fans proved themselves to be a decent bunch. Unlike at an English football match, no one elected to spend the night fighting fellow supporters. I sat there and thought only about the postmatch interview with England's coach Bobby Robson when he was asked if he had been guilty of not taking the Cameroonian challenge seriously enough. "We didn't underestimate them," he said, "but they were a lot better than we thought."

Despite the slight drizzle, I forced Phil to keep the top of his Camaro down as we drove back to camp, so I could live out my *Miami Vice*-infected fantasies. I spent the entire ride flicking through Maine's hearty abundance of classic rock stations, all of which seemed to alternate between blasting one of two tracks. America's "Sister Golden Hair" and the Allman Brothers Band's "Blue Sky," both of which seemed perfect echoes of the joy that consumed me. Yet, somewhere close to the border between Massachusetts and Maine, it dawned on me that England's success had created a problem. The semifinal against archnemesis Germany now loomed in just three days' time. One which would require me to beg the camp for another day off. A mission at which I was successful, mostly by swallowing any sense of shame, as I forced myself to break down in tears and then hyperventilate while explaining to a bemused camp director just how crucial this, the most important England game of my lifetime, was to the future of human civilization. Three days later—on the Fourth of July no less—I left camp, this time accompanied by Jeff, a South African sports counselor and fellow passionate football fan.

The day, which, in my heart, I had hoped would be one of my greatest ever as a football fan (and by extension, as a human being) turned out to be the single most frustrating. Jeff and I spent an entire afternoon driving around the backroads of Maine, charging into one sleepy, stale-aired, rural dive bar to another. We would park the car and run inside. The scene was always the same. One or two daytime drinkers lazily propping up an otherwise empty bar. Patsy Cline or Skynyrd blaring out of some tinny jukebox. A baseball game crackling across the little television perched high up in a corner of the bar. Feigning a confidence we did not feel, we would order two bottles of Bud and ask the barkeep if he was willing to change the channel to the England-Germany game. "Nope," we would inevitably be told, with extra emphasis on the letter *P* to underline the relish of the rejection. "Pittsfield Mets are playin'," we were advised, as if the broadcast of some minor league baseball game was sufficient reason to explain away the bar's refusal to employ the giant satellite dish they had perched precariously on the roof of their shack-like building to pull in the World Cup semifinal.

As kickoff time neared, then passed, our mission became ever more desperate. We must have tried twelve to fifteen bars to no avail. As the clock ticked, and the laws of time and space made clear we had missed the entire game, a day that had begun with the effervescent giddiness of a big matchday in which anything felt possible ended in something even worse than defeat: the impotence of not being able to watch at all. A numbing, shattering blow I had never been dealt before. The most important football experience of my lifetime had just taken place a continent away, and I was unable to witness it or forge emotional memories around it. By the time we drove back to camp, under cover of darkness, I was seething. Any one of those barmen could have let us watch the football with a flick of their remote control. The spiteful delight they drew from denying us that pleasure summed up America's full-throated rejection of the game we loved.

I had to wait for the next day's *Boston Globe* to be delivered to discover the result. The camp director read it out aloud at flag raising, tacking it onto his customary report of the latest Boston Red Sox score. "England 1, Germany 1," he boomed, in the tone of a man clearly not understanding the meaning of the words he was reading. "Germans Win 4–3 on Penalty Kicks." My legs buckled slightly, for a second, as I began to process this news, which felt like an obsidian blade to the heart.

    Once I processed the cruelty of the way England had lost to the eventual champions, that emotion was replaced by surging gratitude. Yes, that experience had forced me to come face-to-face with the reality that Americans were not just indifferent to the sport I loved, they actively hated it and furthermore, enjoyed the misery they could inflict upon those who found it meaningful. Yet, missing the match—and the ultimate torment that is the treacherous lottery of penalty kicks, as well as Paul Gascoigne's instantly iconic in-game tears—felt almost like a mercy. Perhaps it was for the best that America was so cruel. Football was more so.

Chapter 5

1994 World Cup, USA

THE 1994 WORLD Cup brought football to the United States of America. And also me. Straight after university, I moved to Chicago, finally completing a three-generational odyssey. According to our family myth, my "great-grandfather the butcher" had originally intended to move to Chicago, the great "Hog Capital of the World," when he boarded a boat in Odessa and headed for the promised land at the turn of the twentieth century. When that boat docked to refuel in Liverpool, he, and several hundred of the other, clearly lower IQ travelers, saw the three tall buildings on the Merseyside skyline, believed they were in New York City and disembarked.

Eighty years and two generations later, I completed my family's journey. When the plane landed at O'Hare Airport, I felt the urge to mark the weight of the moment and dropped to my knees dramatically on the tarmac, a move I had seen Pope John Paul II execute many times upon arrival in a foreign land. I was momentarily overcome by a surge of adrenaline but, unsure what to do next, quickly became self-conscious as the other passengers pushed their way impatiently around me with their carry-ons. I peeled myself up and tried to play it cool as I joined them on the shuttle bus, attempting to ignore the fact I now had acquired a sticky oil stain on the left knee of my jeans that I could never quite remove.

It is one thing to land at an airport as a tourist ready to tear up the city for a time-bound period. It is an entirely different feeling to arrive in a place with no return ticket, and the hope and fear that accompanies any leap into the unknown. I was a twenty-two-year-old quasi-man landing with big dreams in the American Midwest. An area I was largely unfamiliar with and in which I lacked any kind of support network of family or friends. The only things I had brought with me were a law degree I had miraculously managed to secure, a vague grasp on rudimentary life skills, an enormous 'fro, and little in the way of financial resources. My father had been unimpressed by the woeful lack of direction I had demonstrated after graduation and became irritated at my vague talk of signing up to be an air steward or doing a postgraduate degree in peace studies. Late one night after I had come back inebriated from the local pub in Liverpool, he informed me that he was cutting me off. "A man can think and think in life, Roger," he said with equal measures of exasperation and contempt, "but sometimes he simply has to learn to do." That decision forced my hand and spurred me into "doing." Picking up my life and heading to Chicago, then overstaying my tourist visa was the sum total of my plan.

Upon arrival, I looked at a map of the city, saw there was a neighborhood in the far northside named Rogers Park, and, based solely on its name echoing my own, elected to set up shop there. My immediate challenge was to make some money. Lacking a work visa, I hustled like Tony Montana in the early scenes of *Scarface*, throwing myself into any opportunity that would pay me illegally under the table and off the books. For the first year, I made just enough to live, as a truly clueless yet enthusiastic baker on the early morning shift in a local French pâtisserie and a well-meaning but utterly bewildered waiter at a soul food restaurant at night. In between, I picked up shifts restocking books in a local library, which really meant me sleeping in the stacks. I cobbled together just enough to rent my small, totally empty apartment. If I scrounged food from the restaurant, I could occasionally put my surplus tip money toward treating myself to a $4 bottle of Kentucky Gentleman bourbon whiskey.

The soul food restaurant—Orly's in Hyde Park on the South Side of the city—provided an eye-opening initial glimpse of America. The cooks were all elderly African American South Siders, the busboys young Latinos from the West Side, the barman and manager were a pair of white suburban bros who ruled the place and largely spent their nights crassly hitting on the other servers who, besides me, were all attractive young female students at the University of Chicago. I bonded most of all with the kindly Mexican busboys, who loved to talk football while poking fun at my long, curly hair and round spectacles, alternating between two nicknames they quickly coined for me: "lady" and "Juan Lennon." Two of the dishwashers were a pair of brothers from Mexico, and they took time to show me how to game the system and set up the basics any illegal alien needs to survive: a black market Social Security number, healthcare, and a bank account; teaching me how to furnish an empty apartment for free by scavenging for couches, desks, and kitchen tables dumped in alleyways across the city on the last day of any month, aka moving day.

The extent to which I missed my family back in Liverpool

surprised me. This was before AOL became omnipresent and when long-distance phone calls were still prohibitively expensive, so we corresponded like Victorians, by letter. I would stay late at night, alone, in the library's office, typing out long letters to my parents with just my pointer fingers, determined to convey the minutiae of my work and the details of America that exhilarated me. The celestial taste of Arby's; the intensity of the bruising NBA playoff series between the Michael Jordan–less Chicago Bulls and the boastful New York Knicks of Patrick Ewing, which felt like a high-stakes collision in which the future of good and evil were at stake; the thrill of driving down Lake Shore Drive in a cab at night, and speeding past illuminated skyscraper after skyscraper, an experience which made me feel like I was living on the set of a sci-fi movie.

The mundanity of the letters they mailed back to me in return, 90 percent of which revolved around complaints about the perpetually damp, rainy weather, reinforced my confidence that the journey I was on was the right one. The only thing I truly and achingly missed was football. Soccer. As thrilling as it was for me to be able to immerse myself in the new American sporting traditions of Bears, Blackhawks, White Sox, and Notre Dame gamedays, English football was my foundational text. It was how I understood and made sense of the world. My ballast in life's stormy sea. I was well aware that the sport had outsider status in the United States. Yet, I was still shocked by just how hard it was to follow in my new home. This game that thrilled the rest of the world, had stopped wars, and spurred revolutions barely made a dent on the American sporting subconscious. In a national survey of favorite spectator sports released shortly after my arrival, it ranked 67th. Tractor-pulling was 66th.

To be clear, Americans were not just apathetic toward the

game I loved. They seemed to take a perverse delight in actively and openly despising it in the 1990s. Most nations would have announced a national holiday if FIFA awarded them the hosting rights to the tournament. Yet, when the United States was given the honors, their decision was received with a general tenor of bewilderment. On the floor of Congress, Representative Jack Kemp, a former professional quarterback, felt the need to defend his nation's honor by saying, "I think it is important for all those young men out there who someday hope to play real football, where you throw it and kick it and run with it and put it in your hands, that a distinction should be made that football is democratic capitalism whereas soccer is a European socialist sport."

One journalist compared the honor of hosting the biggest sports event in the world to "holding a major skiing competition in an African country." A sense of contempt reinforced by rumors that began to abound that FIFA were attempting to "Americanize" the sport by splitting the game into four quarters rather than two halves to increase the amount of advertising they could jam into the broadcast. I was baffled by the lack of noise around the whole affair. The World Cup was something I had always counted down to, with a sense of joyous anticipation, but that sense began to be replaced by a gnawing feeling of unease that the Americans were going to blow this—to transform the most celebrated event in the world into the equivalent of a Weird Al cover song. The tournament draw, which took place in December 1993, live from Caesars Palace on the Las Vegas Strip, dialed my sense of disquiet up to eleven.

The football world had never seen the likes of a veritable night of a thousand stars including Barry Manilow, Julio Iglesias, and Faye Dunaway. Few seemed to know what they were doing there. ESPN's host, that veritable broadcasting legend Bob Ley, declared the spectacle to be akin to "Salvador Dalí producing a state lottery." Fittingly for such a surreal occasion, it was Robin Williams who stole the spotlight. First, the comedian described the draw bracket as "the world's biggest Keno game," then proceeded to refer repeatedly to FIFA's General Secretary, Sepp Blatter, as "Sepp Bladder" even after the Swiss administrator testily corrected him, insisting, "This is not a comedy!"

Beneath the pizzazz, the significance for the future of the sport could not have been higher. US midfield star Tab Ramos was one of the pitifully few American players who had managed to find a pathway to play club football in Europe, and he worried aloud, "I think this will be the last chance, the last go-round for soccer to make it big here." If those were the stakes, it did not seem to be going very well. *New York Times* columnist George Vecsey noted: "The United States was chosen, by the way, because of all the money to be made here, not because of our soccer prowess. Our country has been rented as a giant stadium and hotel and television studio for the next thirty-one days." Panic truly kicked in when a national poll undertaken three weeks before the tournament's kickoff discovered that 71 percent of Americans were still not aware it was about to be played in their country. The prospect of empty stadiums felt very real. In the weeks running up to the kickoff, a late flurry of marketing materials featuring images of Reggie Jackson and Michael Jordan pretending to juggle the football were unfurled in a last-ditch effort to create excitement. That did not exactly inspire confidence, as if athletes from other sports were needed to give heartland Americans permission to watch the foreigners' game.

The moment of truth came June 17, 1994, when the opening match was held, by chance, at Soldier Field in my adopted hometown of Chicago. The night before the tournament began, my mood ricocheted between the dizzying sense of childish anticipation I always experienced on World Cup eve, and an unshakable terror that America was throwing a party for the sport I loved, and that no one would turn up. In my destitute state, there was no chance I could afford a ticket for the opener, which featured reigning World Cup champions Germany against Bolivia, yet I felt a need—more than that, a responsibility—to travel down to the stadium to pay witness to the scene. Partially to respect the moment and come as close to this tournament in the flesh as I had ever been. But mostly to help fill in as an extra, and create the sense of a crowd, hoping to build the fiction of America caring in the worst-case scenario, as so many doomsayers were saying, that the venue was deserted.

I need not have worried. With a searing sense of relief, I found Soldier Field to be as overwhelmed as if the Bears were playing the Packers. Yes, it felt like half of Baden-Württemberg had traveled to cheer on Germany, and every Bolivian in the vicinity of Chicago had massed by Lake Michigan. But there were also thousands of families, congregating around the ticket gates, with the kind of crackling sense of anticipation emitted when entering the circus. In truth, this was unlike any football crowd I had experienced before. There was little noise. No audible chanting. Few team colors. Yet I soaked in the scene with relief and wonder. America had turned up. The fact that many of those in attendance seemed to know little about what was about to happen felt like nitpicking. This emotion was reinforced by a big-screen television near the gate broadcasting a short video in which iconic baseball manager Tommy Lasorda of the Los Angeles Dodgers declared his unshakable belief that even if the country had no idea what the World Cup was, America would win it.

Ticketless, I raced home on the L to catch the razzamatazz-filled opening ceremony on my television, which, like the rest of my furniture, had been rescued from the alleyway behind my apartment. I had jerry-rigged an antenna out of a clothes hanger, so the picture was scratchy, but visible enough to witness the spectacle that managed to blend a message of American good intentions, celebrity pageantry, and gesturing at heartfelt passion for soccer.

A nearly sold-out crowd, including President Clinton, was privy to a ceremony that began with emcee hometown hero Oprah Winfrey screaming, "Let's celebrate!" before tripping off the stage and seemingly maiming herself just seconds after welcoming a worldwide television audience of a billion. That slapstick opening set a tone the rest of the celebrity guests then strove to one-up. Singer Jon Secada suffered a dislocated shoulder when a trapdoor from which he was meant to emerge onto the stage misbehaved, forcing him to sing with just his head and shoulders protruding from a hole in the floor. Richard Marx, a Chicago native with a spectacular mullet, sang the national anthem. Diana Ross added to the surreal display by prancing around and lip-syncing, "I'm Coming Out," a performance capped by her slicing a penalty quite wide of a goal from less than five yards out. Nonetheless, the crossbar still split into two, as if she had shot with accuracy and potency. A clumsy piece of footballing choreography gone wrong amidst glamor and glitz, which felt like a cruel metaphor for all that was to come.

The psychedelic out-of-place, out-of-body celebrity moment was echoed, and eclipsed, later that night, by the breaking news of O.J. Simpson's infamous white Bronco chase. An earth-shattering celebrity cultural moment, which even preempted the NBA final and easily overshadowed the day's football, the personal highlight of which came just a minute into the opener when the ball flew into the stands, and the game was held up while the fan who caught it was ordered to throw it back, after being told this was not Wrigley Field and you were not allowed to keep that ball as a memento.

It took twenty-four hours before the fuse was truly lit on the World Cup, driving it straight to the front of America's sporting cortex. A game billed as "the Showdown in the Swamp" pitched Italy against Ireland in the crackling heat of Giants Stadium in New Jersey. A confluence of time and context. Thirty-two million Americans claim Irish descent, roughly half have Italian roots, and the greater New York area had largely been built by their ancestors and thus overflows with both hyphenated identities. This game felt like the type of Peroni- and Guinness-fueled epic gang rumble Scorsese would have directed in one of his early movies. A fight for pride born of echoed pasts taking place in the swamplands near the Hudson.

The Italian team had long been a traditional footballing superpower. Handsome, slick-haired footballers like the iconic Roberto Baggio and Paolo Maldini played for the biggest clubs in the world. Ireland was a mob of scrappy, bar-brawling upstarts in comparison. A Dirty Dozen–esque mob—many of whom were English-born but had chosen to represent Ireland because of their own familial lineage. They were managed by a charismatic, beer-drinking, straight-talking former English World Cup winner, Jack Charlton, who was so beloved, he achieved honorary Irishman status and was christened "St. Jack." The English National Team had yet again failed to qualify, so a lot of

English fans spent the early days of the tournament desperately trying to discover secret Irish roots of their own.

I watched this game in a packed bar in Rogers Park, stuffed with Irish Americans and a ton of non-Irish Americans who just felt a vicarious kinship courtesy of their Notre Dame fandom. As I entered, a large old man dressed as a leprechaun kissed me on the top of my head while screaming to no one in particular, "Our boys are on the craic with it!"

As Jameson-inflected as these words smelled, they turned out to be prophetic. My leprechaun friend may have passed out before kickoff, but had he been conscious, he would have loved what he saw. The fearless Irish snatched the lead with a euphoric strike from midfielder Ray Houghton, a Glasgow-born son of an Irishman, who audaciously clipped the ball past the despairing fingers of the Italian goalkeeper. The collective defensive intensity Charlton had instilled did the rest, as a green-and-white-cloaked Giants Stadium rocked to the sound of bagpipes and the thump of bodhráns as a chant of "You'll never beat the Irish!" resounded. The final scoreline, chaotic energy of the occasion, and medical miracle that 75,000 Irish fans somehow survived nasty cases of sunburn drove the event into the hearts of the American viewing public. This tournament had kicked off for real.

This being a World Cup, Diego Maradona of course grabbed center stage. The golden street urchin had been the hero of the 1986 win. He played the role of villain in this one. Having worn out his welcome in Italian football, "El Pibe de Oro" fled Europe with his career imploding and personal life in meltdown. A fifteen-month ban earned in 1991 for testing positive for cocaine was the least of his problems. Maradona had been charged with smuggling $840,000 worth of blow into Rome's Fiumicino

Airport in 1990, and his reputation was further pockmarked by rumors of paternity suits, tax charges, and intimate connections to Naples's Camorra crime family.

A beleaguered, overweight Maradona returned home to Buenos Aires in search of sanctuary. As he arrived, the notion the player was physically or mentally ready to lead the national team to the 1994 World Cup appeared as believable as a storyline from a Philip K. Dick fantasy. Yet, the star resurfaced sensationally on the eve of the tournament, having somehow shed twenty-six pounds in a month. His message was one of redemption. "I am tired of all those who said I was fat and no longer the great Maradona," he proclaimed. "They will see the real Diego at the World Cup." The icon did not know how true those words would prove to be.

Aged thirty-three, the little warhorse prepared to drag his tattered body into battle one more time. His fourth World Cup would begin against Greece at Foxboro Stadium in Foxborough, Massachusetts. A light aircraft buzzed above the field pulling a banner that proclaimed "Maradona–Prima Dona" ahead of the game, and the star lived up to his billing. In the 60th minute of the 4–0 victory, Diego received the ball in the box, jinked to his left, and rifled the ball into the top corner, then celebrated the achievement in hopped-up style, charging a sideline television camera and flashing his maniacal mug toward it. Tight-lipped after the game, Maradona would only declare, "I'm letting my actions speak for themselves."

Four days later, the player was selected for random drug testing after a 2–1 win against Nigeria. FIFA quickly announced the Argentine had tested positive for five variants of ephedrine. *The Guardian* would later note the way Maradona had celebrated his goal against Greece was as conclusive as any drug test: "Broadcast around the world, his contorted features made him look like a lunatic, flying on a cocktail of adrenalin and every recreational drug known to man."

Faced with the disgrace of being expelled from the tournament, Maradona first sought pity from Argentinian television. "They killed me," he said. "They have retired me from soccer. I don't think I want another revenge, my soul is broken." He then proceeded to appeal to his nation's easily fired-up paranoia, adamantly declaring, "They didn't beat us on the pitch. We were beaten off the pitch and that is what hurts my soul."

As his team moved on to meet Bulgaria in the Cotton Bowl, Maradona loyalists in the Argentine media seized on Dallas's reputation as the cradle of conspiracy theories. "In this city, where thirty years before Kennedy was assassinated, the theories surrounding footballer Maradona will now be explained. Was he 'randomly' selected for a drug test?" they asked.

FIFA dispatched Sepp Blatter to smother any doubts. "The king is dead, we play on," he declared. A shattered Argentinian squad mustered the requisite sound bites about "winning it for Diego." But leaderless and disoriented, they proceeded to wilt against Bulgaria and were finally sent home by Gheorghe Hagi, Ilie Dumitrescu, and the elegant Romanians in the Round of 16.

Even Maradona's fall from grace could not dampen the American energy now building up around the tournament. The stadiums were packed, never more than when the US team first strolled onto the field in Detroit's Pontiac Silverdome. I knew so little about the team. Few Americans did to be honest. Hosting duties meant their qualification had been automatic, a mixed blessing as a woefully inexperienced squad faced four long years in which it had been deprived of the one thing that could battle-harden the players: competitive matches that mattered. This challenge was reinforced by the reality that only a handful of American soccer players had found professional opportunities in Europe. American soccer players had as much credibility in the eyes of European scouts as aspirational English quarterbacks would have received in the NFL. A couple of players including the cocky gunslinger John Harkes and physically gifted striker Eric Wynalda had gained the attention of minor clubs in England, Spain, and Germany. The rest were left struggling to make a living playing indoors or on a local team, which provided the salary equivalent of an internship.

The personal stakes could not have been higher for these men. The focus was on not embarrassing themselves. They were not just playing for their nation; they were fighting for the very future of their sport. Desperate to avoid the humiliation of becoming the first home team in history unable to emerge from the World Cup's opening round, the United States Soccer Federation had undertaken a bold experiment, establishing a residential training center for its team to live together, essentially living off a tiny stipend and their enormous shared dreams, for eighteen months in Mission Viejo, California. Crap the bed, and the profile of soccer in the United States would never recover. The mission was simple. They had to get out of the group stages.

Their draw had been tough. In the opening round, they would face a robust Switzerland, dark horse Romania, and sandwiched in between, the truly fearsome Colombians, who had just whipped Argentina 5–0 in qualifying and whom Pelé himself had picked to win the entire tournament.

First up were the Swiss, who had drawn and beaten Italy in qualifying. I watched from the futon on the floor of my boxy Rogers Park apartment, nervously adjusting the wire hanger to try and coax a clearer signal. The blurry images on my television made it look like the US team were swaggering onto the field wearing a faux stonewashed denim jersey. Then the commentator mentioned that the US team were indeed wearing faux stonewashed denim jerseys and that was the very second I fell in love with this team of goatee- and mullet-sporting risk-takers, dreamers, and pioneers.

Tellingly, kickoff was slated for 11:30 a.m. so that broadcasters ABC did not have to cut into their coverage of the US Open, an event they deemed to be far more important. At that time, Midwest temperatures topped 106 degrees, and so this, the World Cup's first-ever indoor game, was played in sweatbox conditions. I felt enormous empathy for the players as I could not afford air-conditioning in my Chicago apartment and was sweating up a storm myself as I watched in just my underpants and T-shirt. The Swiss looked like they were poised to melt. In contrast, the American players looked utterly amped. So few of them had ever played before a truly large crowd—never mind one that was 100 percent pro-American. As the cameraman panned their eyes during the national anthem, they looked like a group of men who knew this was their time to show the world that American football was about something more than a bold choice in football jersey design. That carried through once the opening whistle blew. The Americans were not the most sophisticated in tactic or touch. But what they clearly lacked as footballers, they compensated for with collective fitness, ferocity of tackle, and an unshakable team spirit embodied by the sheer number of high fives they doled out to each other in-game.

A beanpole ginger center back, Alexi Lalas, caught my eye. A gangly mix of lanky leg and flowing red hair. He looked less like a footballer and more like a guy who worked behind the counter at a record store in some suburban Detroit mall, turning kids on to Van Halen's latest album one sale at a time. But on the field, in the global spotlight that day, Lalas appeared as if he embodied America itself. All rock 'n' roll hustle, idiosyncratic style, and can-do spirit wrapped in frosted denim. As if David Lee Roth had taken the World Cup stage. Both shirt and athlete unlike anything I had seen play football before.

When Switzerland opened the scoring off a free kick, it fleetingly felt like the sum of the American players' fears was about to become real. But just five minutes later, the US won a free kick of their own, 28 yards out. Up stepped Eric Wynalda, the maverick, hotheaded striker who looked like an extra ripped from a beach scene in *Baywatch*. Wynalda composed himself, then swung his foot to strike as casually as if he were on the Californian fields in which he had mastered the game as a kid in Orange County. That ball seemed to be in the air forever, silencing the stadium as it flew, spinning away from the goalkeeper's panicked dive straight into the corner, greeted with a crescendo of noise like that experienced by a diver breaking the waterline and resurfacing. Wynalda was as shocked as anyone watching at home.

The goal was a relief. It not only enabled the US to hold on for a draw and a point, but it also validated the sense that their quest to qualify was in the realms of the possible. The fearsome Colombians awaited four days later in the Rose Bowl, Pasadena, California. Again, I watched alone in my apartment, cowering as the South Americans in their ecstatic yellow attempted to blow their opponents away from the opening kickoff, attacking with hunger and intensity. It felt like a borderline miracle when the game was still scoreless five minutes in. The Colombians hit the post, and American defender Fernando Clavijo scooped the ball off the line in a way which defied science.

But football—especially World Cup football, with its international squads who are essentially as practiced as All-Star teams—is a game of moments. And in the 35th minute, the United States forayed upfield. John Harkes, the cocksure son of Kearny, New Jersey, who had played in England for four years and had instantly adopted a fake Cockney accent, whipped in a cross. Colombian defender Andrés Escobar, a fine man widely known as "The Gentleman of Football," made the unfortunate decision to stretch out a leg and block it, but he only succeeded in redirecting the ball past his own flat-footed goalkeeper into his own net.

Escobar's own goal is what is remembered from the game. Ten days later, he would return home and was shot to death while leaving a Medellín nightclub in the early morning hours. The assassin fired half a dozen times, yelling "Goal!" after every shot. But in the moment, when that ball bobbled off his foot into the back of the net, the American players felt only ecstasy. Even though I was watching alone in my apartment, I was moved to shake up a bottle of Budweiser and spray it around the room, creating a beer puddle that sat in the middle of the floor long after the tournament was a memory. I was to housekeeping what Diego Maradona was to legal weight loss.

Emboldened, the United States conjured a second goal right after halftime, a stunning moment of real counterattacking football, finished off by the speed freak Earnie Stewart, a Dutch-born dual-national with an American serviceman father. The celebrations were an astonishing moment for the team. You could tell by their rapturous reactions; this was a group of men proving themselves to themselves with the world watching. Now they knew, as American footballers, they could face a big team in a big game and win. To me it all felt transcendent. An epiphany akin to witnessing a baby being born, only with 90,000 people in the delivery room.

At the final whistle, the Americans soaked in their moment, walking around the Rose Bowl—the historic American sporting shrine—shirts off, American flags draped round their shoulders, with the delirious crowd bellowing, "USA! USA! USA!" After all their work and sacrifice, these men had just shown that American footballers could belong in the game with the rest of the world. The next day, headline writers gave the performance the ultimate sports accolade, hailing the victory as a "Miracle on Grass!"

Miracle or not, the third game did not go as planned. A 1–0 loss to the canny Romanians. The United States finished third in their group with four points, scraping into the knockout stages by virtue of being one of four third-placed teams who advanced into the sixteen-team second round. Next, they would face Brazil, the fiercest of opponents and number 1 team in the world. The match was to be played in Stanford, California, on July Fourth to boot. Could they do it? I watched the players' interviews, and it was clear by listening that having qualified from the group and achieved their goal—avoiding humiliation—all the pressure was off. Anything felt possible.

Once again, I watched the game alone in my apartment. I did not have a lot of money and, in reality, I did not have a lot of friends. In truth, I felt immensely lonely, but I loved this team of try-hards. I connected with them. When I watched them, they seemed to embody a sense of hope that I needed in my own life at the time. If a group of footballing duffers in stonewash shirts could take on the powerful Brazilians in the World

Cup and win . . . I too might find my way to glory. Or at least a television without a coat hanger for an antenna.

However, there was no way to mask the gulf in class between these two teams. It was evident the moment they walked side by side onto the pitch. Brazil's deadly striking duo Romário and Bebeto, feared around the world, took the field alongside Cobi Jones, a twenty-four-year-old legal student from California.

This Brazil team were different from past iterations. The battering they had received from the European teams over the past decade had forced them to add defensive steel to their offensive flamboyance. Their jerseys were still the traditional golden yellow, but this was a pragmatic, functional, almost soulless squad who advanced on the strength of their physicality, which peaked on the stroke of halftime. American midfielder Tab Ramos attempted to nutmeg his opponent, Leonardo, who retorted by headhunting, with cruel, blunt application of his elbow to Ramos's skull. A shocking moment of violence that earned the Brazilian a red card and left the American in agony on the ground, knocking him out of the game with a fractured skull.

Theoretically, the Americans now had a one-man advantage, but you could not tell from the way they responded. Their players' focus was utterly broken by that moment of savagery, which had knocked out their creative heartbeat. The Brazilians became relentless. In the bright sunlight that would melt lesser men, they glimmered like a shoal of fighting fish sensing the weakness of their prey. The Brazilian goal, when it came in the 74th minute, was almost a relief. A precise Bebeto shot driven low, callously and cruelly through the desperate legs of Alexi Lalas and past a despairing goalkeeper into the corner of the net.

Despite the loss, the US mood at the final whistle was far from despondent. Even in defeat, this young, raw team of American nobodies had earned a moral victory. They had not soiled themselves with the nation watching. Television ratings were high. The US boys had proven they could go toe-to-toe with the world's best by harnessing a collective spirit, exiting with millions of T-shirts and celebratory tchotchkes sold, and the feeling of a match lit and something powerful loosened deep in the nation's consciousness. Sitting in my shit Chicago apartment, I thought of all the American icons that had drawn me to the United States in the first place, patriots who glowed with bold self-confidence. Ferris Bueller, the Super Bowl–winning Chicago Bears, the Beastie Boys. This American football team now fit in that pantheon. They were the rare US sporting entity who were scrappy underdogs. A gaggle who acted as if they willed themselves to believe something, it was no fantasy.

Brazil's spiritless football became a symbol of the entire tournament. Below the celebrity glitz and American naivete, the play was mediocre, and the games pockmarked by overzealous refereeing that broke up play. Fittingly, the final was one of the most soul-crushing the tournament has ever witnessed. I had not wanted to watch alone and went out solo to take it in, draining a generous stranger's pitchers of beer, at a packed Hyde Park bar, Jimmy's Woodlawn Tap. The energy, which was at Mardi Gras levels at kickoff, soon burned off as the Brazilians' cocked fist was negated by Italy's smothering play. As the two teams conspired to provide every soccer cynic's worst nightmare—the first goalless final, 120 minutes of dreary soccer followed by penalties—the bar became quieter and emptier. I could almost imagine the teeth-gnashing of every investor who had just stepped up to own a team in the soon-to-be-launched American club league: Major League Soccer.

One of the reasons I love football is that even in the dullest of spectacles, a moment of human revelation can occur on an almost biblical scale. Italy had been carried to the final by the wizardry of one man: Roberto Baggio, an almost mystical figure, known for his signature "Divine ponytail" (*Il Divin Codino*), his conversion to Buddhism, and the way he seemed to float just above play, beyond the grasp of the mere mortals with whom he was sharing the field. Baggio's five goals in the tournament had propelled his team to the final. In the fifth and final round of penalties, with Brazil leading 3–2 and Italy needing to score to keep hope alive, it was Baggio who stepped to the spot. It had been his tournament. Now, the hopes of all Italy rested on his shoulders. With just the goalkeeper to beat from a mere 12 yards, he proceeded to sky the ball 3 feet over the crossbar. At the pub I was in, it felt like we had just witnessed a human tragedy. Screams accompanied the replays of the ball soaring into the Pasadena sky, as Baggio, that quasi-holy man, doubled over in astonished agony, hands on knees in private mourning. A hallowed figure who so often appeared to rise above the limits of what was humanly possible, frozen in a moment of mortality. It was fitting that two diabolical penalties bookended the tournament. Diana Ross's showbiz miss opened it, and Baggio's elegiac catastrophe brought it to an emotional close and handed Brazil a fourth World Cup win, at last. Their first in twenty-four long years.

Many Americans had their lives changed by the tournament. European teams deigned to welcome a handful into their teams, most noticeably Alexi Lalas, who played fleetingly in Italy, a cameo in which his greatest achievement may have happened off the field when he was invited to strum his guitar as a support act on a leg of a Hootie & the Blowfish tour. Most of the players were reduced to jester-like side-hustles with Tony Meola accepting a chance to try out as a kicker for the New York Jets, which reeked of a PR stunt, as did his being attacked by "soccer-playing pitbulls" on Jay Leno.

In the end, the legacy of this World Cup was mixed. Records had been broken in terms of attendance, but those who expected American fans' sporting appetites to be transformed instantly and forever by the tournament would be disappointed. The spike in interest in football soon burned off as if the World Cup had been a giant circus, which momentarily thrilled before leaving town. A year later, when my beloved club team Everton reached the semifinal of a major tournament, I was unable to find a single cable channel that could summon a broadcast, despite a frantic search of Chicagoland sports bars. Utterly defeated, I ended up calling my father in Liverpool and persuaded him to hold his telephone against the radio so I could hear the local broadcast and follow the action. A long-distance connection that was worth every cent, even though the bill was so eye-bulgingly expensive, it took me seven months to pay off in installments. Each time I chipped away at my football-induced telecom debt, I felt a numbing angst as if the World Cup in America had never happened.

Deprived of my football fix, my American life continued to progress, relying on hustle, grind, and the kindness of strangers. Professionally, I astonished myself by finding utility in the law degree I had somehow earned. I gained work as a welfare rights advocate. This was the height of the Clinton Welfare debate in which the safety net had been shredded. Working with a nonprofit who agreed to apply for a visa for me, I trained homeless men to talk to the media, telling the story of their descent into the streets and highlighting the vast number of hidden challenges that existed between them and job security.

The homeless guys I worked with were sweet and earnest. They lived on the streets south of the city in the area around Robert Taylor Homes. A vast, bleak public housing project that consisted of dozens of identical, hulking buildings spread out in a line for two miles. Having grown up in Liverpool, I thought I was used to grim neighborhoods awash with hopelessness. The Robert Taylor Homes were another level altogether. This was a heart-wrenching island of abject poverty. The work was fulfilling and soul-destroying in equal measure. Lacking football in my life, I threw myself into the Chicago music scene for solace. Uncle Tupelo's album *Anodyne* had just been released. I saved up enough to watch the band play gigs at the legendary Lounge Ax. Their track "The Long Cut" was my anthem, and I listened to its message of struggle and eventual promise on repeat on my Discman:

> *Come on let's take the long cut*
> *I think that's what we need*
> *If you wanna take the long cut*
> *We'll get there eventually.*

The lead singer, Jeff Tweedy, was singing about his fraught relationships with his bandmates, but the lyrics always held a double meaning for me, reflecting the journey I hoped soccer had just begun in my chosen home.

Chapter 6

1998 World Cup, France

BY THE TIME the 1998 World Cup rolled around, the US football tidal wave, which was the legacy the organizers dreamed of in the wake of 1994, had petered out into backwash. While Americans had relished the opportunity to host, the sport's grip on popular imagination appeared to have all the staying power of the pogo stick or hula hoop. A fad that burned brightly then reduced to a simmer. Football fandom largely returned to the shadowy crevices.

In January 1996, I packed my scant belongings into the back of a small U-Haul truck and drove from Chicago through the teeth of a Category 5 blizzard to arrive in our nation's capital, Washington, DC. Somehow, I had blagged my way into both a visa and a job in a human rights nonprofit on K Street. I loved my work, but the undoubted highlight of my week occurred at 7:30 every Saturday morning when I would rise earlier than I would on a workday and stumble from my home in Adams Morgan down to a bar in Dupont Circle named Planet Fred. The English Premier League had just begun a global broadcast of a single live game via an obscure Irish pay-per-view start-up named Setanta. In DC, Planet Fred, run by a Welshman who was a Manchester United fanatic, became one of the earliest and possibly only subscribers.

Saturday mornings, a small but motley crew of a dozen or so expat regulars would assemble, awaiting kickoff in collective hungover silence. The only words exchanged were muttered orders for a hair-of-the-dog pint or Full English Breakfast. I knew every one of these men—and they were *all* men—so well, though for reasons that made sense at the time, none of us knew each other's names. Perhaps because of the ungodly hour at which we congregated, we never went through the social niceties of introducing ourselves, and once that reality had set in, it could never be undone. There was a hulking line chef at the Mayflower Hotel, a giant Northerner with two tattoo sleeves, who would suck his knuckles when Manchester United conceded a goal. A short, sullen Australian skinhead who screamed obscenities whenever his beloved Aston Villa scored. A gaunt, acne-ridden attaché who did something vague at the British Embassy and showed no emotion but would never let go of his briefcase, even when drinking a pint or polishing off a bacon buttie with the other hand.

The second the game kicked off, our collective energy levels rocketed, as we all locked on to the action more than three thousand miles away. The fact that the broadcaster, Setanta, was a low-rent operation and had somehow only secured the rights to the single worst game of the weekend did not diminish the exhilaration. After years of famine in which we had all struggled to find any kind of English football available on American cable, we were hungry to come together and feast, treating a mediocre fixture like Sheffield Wednesday against Coventry City as if it were the Super Bowl. As I quickly came to experience, football had a remarkable ability to transport you. Not just emotionally but also spiritually. For ninety minutes, we were no longer in northwest DC. Together, we teleported back to Liverpool, London, or whatever corner of the nation was beamed into one of the three small televisions hung over the bar.

This eccentric fraternity came in all shapes and sizes, yet I was also painfully aware who was not there. Not a single American was in our midst. One Saturday, about a year into my watching, the doors of the bar crashed open mid-game in a way they never had before. For all us regulars, football was akin to worship, and we could never bear to miss a minute of the game. So each of our heads instantly snapped from the action on the screen to see who would have the temerity to arrive unfashionably late, clocking a gent standing before us in the doorframe wearing a Baltimore Orioles cap. Feeling a dozen sudden unwelcoming eyes upon him, the interloper attempted to bond in a jaunty American accent, stammering, "Hey guys, what time is Fulham playing?" A club which the Orioles cap wearer, like so many other Americans, insisted on mispronouncing by drawing out the second syllable as "Full-HAMMMM" in a way no Englishman would.

The hat. The accent. The ill-judged attempt to demonstrate bona fides by dropping knowledge. All of it made this interruption as out of place as a hardcore vegan at a barbecue joint. There was a prolonged moment of awkward silence, which was probably measurable in seconds but felt like hours because of the extent to which the initial confidence of the stranger shriveled away. Then the lumbering chef seized the initiative, launching himself from his traditional seat in the corner of the bar with admirable speed for a big man. He intercepted the stranger at the door and with arms outstretched, proceeded to pat him on the cheek twice whilst uttering, "Stroll on, mate, stroll on," a phrase known to every Englishman as an invitation to back down, or start a fight. The American may not have been able to pronounce Fulham, but he understood exactly what was being said in this moment. To my relief, he silently turned round and slunk out of the bar, defeated.

"Fucking Plastic," the big chef seethed, shaking his head, as he retook his seat and we all attempted to re-engage on the football. It felt like that scene in a Western movie, in which the piano player roars back into action after a shoot-out in a bar. That term "Fucking Plastic" chilled me, though. A derogatory slur English football fans used to denigrate those they deem to be fake or clueless supporters—those who had not traveled home and away to watch their teams in their formative years and thus did not truly understand the culture. I realized in that moment that as much as I loved America and yearned to make my childhood dream of living here come true, if football was to break out of the secret subculture that was furiously gatekept in this bar, it would need a wider embrace, less judgment, and much more love. How could Americans embrace the game if it was being held so tightly by those who didn't want to share it?

And so, the 1998 World Cup felt significant. Unlike 1994, there would be no inspirational games hosted on American shores for fans to attend in person. I was genuinely fascinated to discover how much interest there would really be. The US team had been an ephemeral presence in our lives in the wake of their respectable 1994 performance, appearing fleetingly on the front of cereal boxes, and in meager numbers, on European rosters. An American league, Major League Soccer, had sprung up after the tournament. Its roots were still shallow. So much depended on the 1998 team's success—though you wouldn't know it from the bravado of the players. Their interviews were unlike any I had seen before in the sport. Englishmen are fully aware just how hard it is to win the World Cup. The US players gave out bombastic hot takes, where they were certain about their chances. Alexi Lalas quipped, "Nineteen-ninety we showed the world we belonged. Nineteen ninety-four we could compete. This year we are going to win the damn thing."

Win. What Americans do, in every sport, apart from soccer. In fact, men's soccer was the one sport that felt like the rest of the world reveled in our lack of skill. More than that, they knew that we knew that they knew we were woeful, and it drove us crazy. It was the one thing in which America just could not compete on the global stage, and it filled us with a sense of shame and self-loathing. I knew in my soul this had to change. We had to show the world we could compete. We also had to demonstrate to the widest possible American audience that our boys were worth any emotional investment. The 1998 French World Cup had to be that moment.

The draw unfolded onstage at a packed stadium in Marseilles and gave us a brutal gauntlet to confront. The United States found themselves in Group F alongside reigning European champions Germany (think Darth Vader in cleats), a nation against whom we had fought two world wars. Also, Yugoslavia, a very strong European team whose nation the United States was about to bomb on behalf of NATO. But it gets worse. The third team the US draw would face was the Islamic Republic of Iran. A country who saw us as the "Great Satan" after their 1979 revolution in which the US Embassy was occupied, and 66 citizens held hostage for 444 days, leading to a severing of diplomatic relations. As one US Soccer official quipped, "The only way it could have been more of a challenge was if there were Iraqi referees for every game."

The US team were a strange beast at this point. They were coached by a raw telegenic novice, Steve Sampson. A gent who had been plucked from obscurity as a college coach, making a sum total of $1,250 for the season while living on a friend's couch until fortune led him to be appointed as an interim national team manager. A freakish run of good results meant that interim appointment became full-time, despite every indicator Sampson was hopelessly out of his depth. Handing the national team job to a bloke who had never head-coached a single pro-game before was quite a gambit. Even I, a gent who had grown up watching American movies like *Rocky*, *Rudy*, *The Karate Kid*, found the idea of Steve Sampson leading a team to the World Cup insane. America loves an underdog. But this was extreme.

Sampson's shtick was to bluster about bringing "American values" to his football team. He talked about his desire to take risks and bring the fight to the opponent, emphasizing a buccaneering all-in style of football he nicknamed "forward-mindedness." When given the chance to babble on about his vision, he would often describe it as "the American way." I adored the United States as deeply as Bruce Springsteen loves America, but to hear football discussed in such a way made me feel queasy. The idea of an American trying to invent new ways to play soccer sounded about as naive and unreliable as an English basketball coach claiming to have pioneered new hoops strategies.

From a football perspective at least, the United States faced their strongest opponent in the first game. The Germans were Teutonic robots with big thighs and mighty foreheads. There is an old English quote that "football is a simple game, twenty-two men kick a football for ninety minutes, and at the end the Germans always win." To be clear, the United States weren't expected to emerge as victors here, but if they were thumped, it would make the games against Iran and Yugoslavia that much harder. I ran down to Planet Fred to watch this match with my expat mates. We were shocked to see the Americans, who had talked with such cockiness about attack and fight, open in a formation rarely used in football. A 3-6-1. That is football born of fear. A cautious, negative defensive tactic that the US team had barely practiced. A style designed to keep players behind the ball, committing just one man into attack, thwarting the worst outcome of defeat and hoping the team could emerge intact with a draw, relatively unscathed.

Right before kickoff, ABC's studio host Brent Musburger reinforced just how lowly football's status remained in the United States, as he was forced to explain to viewers why they were being subjected to football in the first place. "Some of you folks have turned on expecting to see *General Hospital*. Don't despair." He then told them when that show would air, and I was suddenly overwhelmed by the deflating image of an angry nation exclaiming "WTF! No GH?!"

Soap opera or no soap opera, the United States needed a strong start. They did not summon one. In the very first minute, the German midfielder Jens Jeremies set a tone by giving the United States key midfielder Claudio Reyna a sneaky shot to his kidney, sending a message and knocking the US's best player off the game. Eight minutes later, off a German corner, there were jitters across the American backline. A German midfielder, Andreas Möller, rose up to nod the ball goalward. It somehow crept past Mike Burns, the American defender who had been positioned on the line for the sole purpose of repelling that very kind of attack.

The US response was confused and timid. They looked like a team who had never played together before. Eric Wynalda, so strong and cocky in 1994, was left alone up top struggling like a man on a desert island. There was a brief flurry when Frankie Hejduk, the Bob Marley–loving Californian who talked about his true love, surfing, whenever given the chance in interviews, took the field fearlessly as a halftime substitute. Hejduk played with the frenzy of a man who had just downed five or ten double espressos, which he later admitted was exactly what he had done. He grabbed an opponent by the foot to stop one breakaway, then launched a diving header that forced a magnificent save from Andreas Köpke, the German goalkeeper.

For a moment, even the neutral French in the crowd got behind the Americans, bellowing "Olé" to encourage and accompany every pass they made. But in their desperation for a goal, the US naively overcommitted, leaving themselves utterly exposed at the back. The Germans are the one team in football hardwired at birth to exploit these very moments of vulnerability. In the 65th minute, striker Oliver Bierhoff floated a high, lofted, yet precise pass to his bleach-blond counterpart, Jürgen Klinsmann, who utterly bamboozled the American captain, Thomas Dooley, with his balletic control. The German calmly yet ruthlessly caressed the ball into the single part of the net where the flailing American goalkeeper Kasey Keller couldn't hope to reach it.

It was a remarkable moment to witness. Sometimes a goal is born of such an elite combination of vision, ability, and clinicality. You cannot help but admire it, even when it has just been struck against you. Indeed, this was the kind of goal that hurt all the more because it was utterly apparent to all who were watching at that moment, it could never have been summoned by an American foot. The truth was, the three-time world champions were stronger, smarter, and savvier and barely had to break sweat to swat us aside 2–0. A defeat that seemed to signal an alarm bell that while our ambition was first-rate, our football level appeared more third tier.

That alarm rang louder when several American veterans whom Steve Sampson had benched elected to vent to the media. Alexi Lalas, one of the US stars of the last World Cup, played the role of willful saboteur in this one, blaming the team's remote chateau home base for their poor form. "We were isolated in the middle of France, then plopped down in the middle of Paris where it's like a circus," he moaned. Another veteran, Roy Wegerle, lambasted the 3-6-1, as "twice the work and half the help"; and Eric Wynalda called out the inexperience of his own teammates, "You could tell some of us were playing for the first time in a World Cup." I watched the sniping and the feuding and was confused and numbed by it. It was not a normal response to a first-game defeat. An ugly and strange overreaction to a gutting loss that bordered on mutiny. The Americans had been outplayed by Germany. Lots of teams lost to Germany. And America still had two games—two games that still felt winnable to save their World Cup and save football in this nation.

None of this seemed impossible. In a World Cup, collective spirit and tenacity can always propel a dark horse team to giddy heights. Nigerians the world over celebrated a come-from-behind 3–2 victory for the ages against the heavily favored Spaniards. Their unrelenting attacking style overwhelming the Spanish, despite the fact they had been able to draw on players from two of the biggest clubs in the world, Real Madrid and Barcelona. When I watched the next game, I prayed that the US would be similarly inspired to rise up. But our players appeared too busy bickering to notice.

Next up was Iran. Less football rivals, more mortal sworn enemies. You could not match two more geopolitically charged opponents if you tried. For their part, the Iranians did not shy away from the theater of the game during a buildup, which felt more PBS News Hour than ESPN. The US State Department had just labeled Iran the world's "most active" state sponsor of terrorism. Khodadad Azizi, the Iranian attacker, countered by speaking to the press about how he believed the United States had fueled the eight-year Iran-Iraq war for its own purposes, in which 1,000,000 Iranians had been killed or injured during the conflict. "We will not lose the game," he promised. "Many families of martyrs are expecting us to win. We will win for their sake."

I was driving to the Jersey Shore on the day of the game, only to have my car break down on the highway. I found myself at kickoff stranded at a repair shop somewhere off the Garden State Parkway. I joined three mechanics—a father, son, and silent assistant—who closed their garage to watch the game. It was quickly evident to me these men were not soccer fans by any stretch of the imagination. "This is Jets country!" one kept insisting. Despite that, I have rarely experienced human beings more deliriously amped to watch their country in World Cup play. They invited me to their office to watch the match with them on an old television. The buildup to the game was filled with archive footage of Iranians burning American flags, but I doubted you could find an Iranian who hated the United States more than these garage hands detested Iran. "Fuck the Ayatollah!" the oldest guy told me while ripping open the first of several six-packs of Bud. "I wanna see a beatdown."

As I opened my first beer, I said a silent prayer that America would indeed open a can of whoop-ass on their opponents, less for political reasons than footballing ones. The US needed a win at the Stade de Lyon to stay alive in the World Cup, and, to be honest, I felt pretty confident before kickoff. This was the first World Cup game I had ever witnessed in which the United States was not the underdog. In fact, they were the favorites. These Iranians had never won a World Cup match. Nineteen of their twenty-two players were still based in Iran, a remote footballing hinterland where they had grown up kicking soccer balls on the postrevolution streets with little in the way of formal elite coaching.

And so, the most momentous game—or at the very least the strangest—in US soccer history began. A pressure-filled match with geopolitical repercussions meant that every single American was watching the United States play, even if only for jingoistic reasons. Not a time for experimentation, unless you were US coach Steve Sampson, who decided this was the right time to make five changes to his starting lineup—half the team—also completely switching their style of play again. If his team had been too cautious in the first game, they were going to be the exact opposite in this one, playing not only with two attackers but also maniacally inserting another forward at a key defensive midfield role, which was akin to flinging one of your best wide receivers into the offensive line. Sure, Americans would have difficulty preventing Iranian counterattacks. But the whole point of Steve's new strategy was to attack first—and keep attacking. Most of the grousing veterans were left on the bench, and the whole system was suddenly designed around twenty-six-year-old Brian McBride, a tall, active, physically dominant target player in his first World Cup ever.

Seeing the lineup sent me into a cold sweat. Luckily the switch was a tactical subtlety that was lost on my new garage friends, who were caught up in the pregame pageantry. There had been a lot of talk in the buildup about how the teams would navigate the new tradition of the pre-match handshake. The US State Department and the UN became involved as neither Iran nor the US could agree as to who would initiate for fear of seeming politically weak in front of a global audience. So, at an emergency meeting held in the run-up to the game, an alternative solution was offered. The players would exchange pennants and flowers and assemble for a joint photograph. An attempt to show the world's children that even countries that are political adversaries, through sportsmanship, can be friends. My garage buddies did not like this. "Fuck that flower shit," one screamed, jumping to his feet and howling at the screen. The game had not even kicked off yet. He was up again just three minutes into the action as a young raw and hungry McBride crashed a header off the crossbar. "That dude looks like he is headbanging to some Judas Priest or some shit," he shouted, miming the way the player had snapped his neck.

I was encouraged by this all-business start. The Americans hit the post again in the 33rd minute. Indeed, for forty minutes the US team absolutely dominated Iran, and we watched and cheered as a third six-pack of beer started flowing at the same rate as the American players' confidence. The United States was playing the kind of battering-ram football carved from my dreams. McBride was indeed physically dominant. A highly caffeinated Frankie Hejduk ran at will, tormenting all-comers. But the thing about soccer is, you can be so dominant, so strong, outpass, outpossess, outshoot your opponent, but then one single mistake, careless oversight, and the tides, they just turn. And the only stat that truly matters, in the end, is the score.

Remember, the team had been set up without a true defensive midfielder, the one player used to prevent counterattacks. With five minutes to go until halftime, Iran broke down the right, floated a cross in from deep, which was quite brilliantly met with by Hamid Reza Estili, who calculated flight and angle to loop the ball into the net. Charging away in his moment of glory, the Iranian broke down in tears to reflect the epic nature of his achievement, but the garage guys were reeling as if they had all simultaneously taken a full volley to their nether regions. This was not just a goal. This was an affront to their American morals and identities. When the halftime whistle blew, the US was a goal down and the mood had completely soured in the garage. All the pre-match adrenaline had evaporated. The cameras panned the surreal scenes in the stadium in which both Iranian dissidents and supporters of the Islamic regime waved their respective T-shirts and banners jubilantly at halftime as the public-address system randomly played the Macarena, a stadium standard in the '90s. I tried to talk myself into maintaining belief. The way we were playing and creating all those goal-scoring chances, we could come back.

It was essential that the US summon an equalizer. They attacked relentlessly and recklessly as if it were a national mission to muster the tying goal—the longer the game went on, the more the American side of the field was left unguarded and vulnerable. In the 84th minute, the inevitable happened. Iran's Mehdi Mahdavikia launched a one-man counterattack, bearing in on goal and lashing home before reeling away, speeding the breadth of the field in glorious celebration, arms swinging, eyes wide open. The US grabbed a consolation goal but that was all they could manage. Bob Ley, that great American broadcaster, summed up the enormity of the moment with the sudden solemnity of Walter Cronkite, "More than just a win for the Islamic Republic of Iran. Ninety minutes of faith in action tonight for these men. What this result will do around the world where American soccer has fought for respect, it will frankly take steps backward."

I was living out those steps backward in real time. The garage bros simmered with anger. The silent assistant smashed a beer bottle against the garage floor. "We got beat by Iran!" said the old man, pronouncing the nation's name with a long drawn out "eye-ran" sounding like an American howl. "Fag game anyway," the son grumbled as he went to reopen his garage. This was my worst nightmare. As the garage guys stormed out, to fix my tire, I hoped, they took time to debate what the score would be if the US played Iran at a real men's game like the Jets played. I was left there in front of the television screen watching the deflated American players walking around the field, feeling the deep pain of something I loved. I had watched England be eliminated from countless World Cups as a kid, but this felt far darker and more harrowing, because even when the English were beaten, I did not have to worry how that would impact the overall popularity of this game in the nation. The sun would still come up, and the world would still spin. But this felt like a footballing death. Millions of Americans, like my mechanic friends, had put their faith in American soccer players to do the right thing—the American thing—and win. Instead, the best men's soccer players our nation could field had humiliated themselves against our greatest enemy with the whole world watching. It was as if the entire sport of soccer had died and the players themselves had killed it. All the pride and joy built in 1994 had been fritted away to be replaced by a darker narrative. One that was still very American, but less *Karate Kid* and more *Apocalypse Now*.

By virtue of this being a World Cup, England also raised their nation's pulses, gave them reason to believe, then shattered hearts in excruciating fashion. Despite the presence of eighteen-year-old, fleet-footed, attacking prodigy Michael Owen and the still boy-band-esque World Cup first-timer David Beckham, their early games were marred by cautious football on the field and shattering fan violence off it. English hooligans turned up, less to support their team, more to fight tear-gas-tinged battles against youths of North African origin on the streets of Marseille. Brutality filled the group stage experience with an apocalyptic dread. England actually lost to Romania in the group stage but progressed to the knockout round courtesy of a 2–0 defeat of Colombia in which Beckham scored. The team's lackluster form meant they had to face a powerhouse in the first knockout game: Argentina. Of course.

This would be the third time the two historic foes had faced each other in knockout play. The previous two, in 1966 and 1986, had been historic traumas. One a bloodbath won by the English. The second, that Maradona-fueled Hand of God, which still felt so raw. The game happened to coincide with my first-ever professional work trip. I had inconveniently been dispatched to Chicago to solicit a potential donor. Inevitably, the time of the meeting and kickoff overlapped exactly. So, in what was probably not my sagest professional decision, I persuaded the donor to meet me for an afternoon drink at an Irish bar in the Loop I knew would be playing the game. Trust me, I knew at the time this was a rogue judgment that might come back to haunt me, but prayed my English accent would somehow allow me to charm my way through it all like a poor man's Hugh Grant. After all, how many times would England play Argentina in my life? Alright, probably a lot. But what is a successful career compared to the ability to make World Cup memories that last forever?

The potential donor walked into the bar just before kickoff and judging by his astonished reaction, this was not his kind of place, and he was no football fan. While the bar was not packed, its clientele consisted exclusively of highly intoxicated expats in England jerseys. The way my guest was dressed screamed Four Seasons lobby gentility rather than Kilkenny dive bar. I tried to seize the initiative by ordering a Guinness for us both. Mine was half finished before a ball had been kicked; his untouched as he began to pontificate on the intricacies of the shifting power balance in the Middle East. I attempted to feign interest while keeping one eye on the television, stifling a scream as the game opened in a frenzy that almost saw England score inside the first two minutes. My stealth strategy lasted roughly five minutes until England's goalkeeper brought down an Argentinian player, Diego Simeone, conceding a penalty. An agonizing moment in which I could not mask my feelings, involuntarily leaping to my feet and cursing at the television screen.

While the divine-looking Argentinian striker Gabriel Batistuta went about blasting the subsequent penalty through the English goalkeeper's hands, I was coming clean with my guest as to why I had asked him to meet me in such dingy circumstances. He turned around to look at the screen just as David Beckham appeared in closeup. This was twenty-three-year-old David Beckham, a shimmering sight. As if Michelangelo had carved a cherub who was very, very good at football. A cherub with Brad Pitt–esque blond, gelled curtains. In the pantheon of Beckham looks, still definitely top five. To this he said, "OK. I will watch your 'match' for ten minutes."

Freed from the constriction of pretending to be professional, we both turned to face the action. And what mesmeric action it was. A clash of attacking styles. Argentina, so canny, so capable of suffering, then attacking with the flow known only to the greatest dancers. England responded with a hard-running frenzy. Robust tackles flying in. Limbs flailing. Beckham's hair flouncing and bouncing as he attempted to control the energy of the game. Suddenly the ball was played in behind a momentarily confused Argentinian backline and teenage prodigy Michael Owen sped to it like the fleet-footed Greek hunter Atalanta made human. The boy was a blur, a blur that was tripped in the area, and England had a penalty of their own.

One of the English fans in the bar threw his beer in the air to mark the moment. The fear I always experience that England will miss a forthcoming penalty merged with my relief that my guest was sitting just outside of the airborne beer's blast zone. English captain Alan Shearer played the role of nerveless hero, battering the ball home, and the bar was suddenly bouncing with everything to play for again at 1–1.

The game now existed in an almost airless, breathless state. Even my guest was utterly sucked in. The Argentinians attempted to pass themselves into control. England flickered between caution and risk, with nothing in between. On the 16th minute, a passage of play that felt like witnessing a biblical revelation. Beckham sprang Michael Owen in the center circle. A kid too young to be afraid, he freed himself from his defender with a mischievous flick of the heel and charged onto the ball at full pelt. Owen was no longer a human being, more a speeding comet headed goalbound, determined to flame everything that stands in its way. His twisting half-field run was one of those mythic sporting moments when the outcome is clear to all before it happens. All we lesser mortals had to do was prepare to pay witness. As Owen charged into the box, the goalkeeper's fear was palpable through the television screen. Fear that was justified. The English attacker pulled his foot back and unleashed on the ball like a master archer, compelling it to fly into the corner of the net.

Moments like these are what you dream of. They are why you watch hours of football. The dull parts. The mistakes. The goalless games. For moments like these, when something otherworldly occurs that is so mystical, it feels like a glimpse of the divine. A glimpse that connects you to the millions watching it along with you, in the instant forging an intense memory. As Owen charged away with hands outstretched, the bar became a mosh pit in which we all lost ourselves. The English fans, me, my prospective donor pogo-ing around in abandon like giddy childhood friends.

Yet, in English football, elation must always be negated by self-destructive agony, and so it was no surprise when the Argentinians struck back. Their players had demonstrated fierce intelligence to adapt in-game and began to stifle Owen and cut off his supply from midfield. On the stroke of halftime, they found a leveler via Javier Zanetti, who archly finished off a cunning, synchronized free kick, an agony that paled in comparison to the disaster that followed seventy-four seconds into the second half.

David Beckham was fouled by Diego Simeone, a canny veteran who was a self-styled villain. First, Simeone flattened England's young prince, then he antagonized his opponent by pushing himself up from the turf, using the back of his victim as a springboard. A masterful moment of dark arts gamesmanship, designed to goad his prey. Beckham, then as young and inexperienced as he was handsome, could not help but be provoked. Lying face down, he kicked out ever so slightly. The tiniest of flicks, but enough for Diego Simeone to fall backward in utter agony, triggering an uproar from his teammates. The dour Danish referee Kim Milton Nielsen took a theatrical moment of reflection before waving a red card in David Beckham's face. The ultimate punishment. England's great young hope had been duped into an act of petulance and could do nothing but walk off the field, knowing that his team would now be down a man, and if defeated, it would be him who the English tabloids would bury without mercy. It felt harsh, but also right by the letter of the law. Watching in that bar, this occurrence felt tumultuous and definitive. English history has so many dark benchmark moments. Norman Conquest. The Great Plague of London. Dunkirk. Watching it live, Beckham's dismissal was just as epic.

The mood in the bar collapsed like a lung. Even as the ten men of England proceeded to fight heroically with discipline and Churchillian-finest-hour tenacity. At the very last, they even put the ball in the back of the net. The normally stoic Sol Campbell rose up to head home a corner and charge away in ecstatic delirium, cruelly unaware the goal had been ruled off for a foul in the buildup. Also unaware: my donor, who was not only still present, but was so emotionally invested in the match, he threw his pint of Guinness in the air in celebration and then had to sit there having to act chill, like he knew the goal did not count, even as drops of the black stuff now dripped off his hair, shirt, and pants.

The moment the game went to penalties, it was clear to everyone how it would end. This was the psychological crucible at which the English nation had so often failed. Every time an England player took that long, trudging walk to the penalty spot, they were not only trying to score goals but also to exorcise ghosts. The last English shooter was bulldog midfielder David Batty, who had bravely volunteered for the task despite never taking a kick before in competitive play. He predictably crumbled, firing his kick straight into the Argentinian keeper's palms.

As the Argentine players began to celebrate, removing their jerseys and waving them as they raced downfield, the Irish bar fell silent. Each of us, even my donor, was left to contemplate their own personal feeling of failure and wasted talent. Once again England had come so close, but now we all had four more years to ruminate on the peculiarly cruel nature of their defeat. Beckham would of course go on to be savaged by the English media, but, in the moment, we were left numbed by the weight of a new agony to add to the nation's pantheon of English footballing loss.

I would like to tell you this afternoon concluded with the donor writing a large check, handing it over, and disappearing into the Chicago night. But there is no such romance in football. As we stumbled out into the awkwardness of the early Chicago evening, he shook my hand, leaned in, and said, "If you don't tell, I won't tell." Like England at the 1998 World Cup, I never saw him again.

There is a finality to loss at the World Cup. Yet, the tournament moves on at a rollicking pace, never waiting for any nation to wallow in their misery. The global audience was soon captivated by the collision of two journeys of destiny. The year

1998 was supposed to be Ronaldo's Cup. The original Ronaldo. The Brazilian, with the gap-tooth smile who was known as "O Fenômeno" (The Phenomenon). He was then just twenty-one years old and widely agreed to be the best player in the world. His breathtaking pace, cartoonish acceleration, and clinical finishing made him more video game than human, blowing past defenders in a blur of motion and deft touch. A one-man herd propelling Brazil toward their fifth World Cup, which felt close enough to touch.

The team that stood between them and glory was the home nation France, which had shed the traumas of countless noble semifinal failures past by clipping the pluck-filled Croatians. Their talisman was a balding hero, Zinedine Zidane. The son of poor Algerian immigrants, who was part of a scintillating, multiracial team known as the "Black, Blanc, Beur" (Black, White, Arab), dominated by stars from former colonies such as Lilian Thuram, born in Guadeloupe; Marcel Desailly, who hailed from Ghana; and Patrick Vieira, who was born in Senegal.

The French were a defensively robust team, who took a collective delight in smothering opponents, but France was also a country riven by deep ethnic tensions around the issue of immigration, and it was with horror that the global football fanbase had to watch on as the tournament became infected with crude, craven political hate. Jean-Marie Le Pen, the leader of France's far-right-wing National Front, seized on the opportunity to inflame division by alleging that the team "did not look French," speaking with a venomous relish about the mélange's ability to represent "the true spirit of France."

As an English-born fan, despising the French was threaded into my DNA. But even I could not help admiring these men winning game after game under the pressure of unbearable national scrutiny. It was clear these footballers were playing for something more than just sporting glory. The deeper into the tournament they battled, the more the French nation rallied round and embraced these men as their own. It was joyful to watch nightly news reports broadcast from a celebratory Paris overrun by flotillas of tiny Citroëns and Renaults after every knockout victory, taking to the streets with large tricolores in tow. It felt as if they were drowning out Le Pen's vile hatred, one celebratory car horn blast after another.

The World Cup final was broadcast on a Sunday afternoon in DC. For the first time ever, the final featured the host nation and the defending champions. Overwhelmed with childish excitement, I was moved to invite the members of my five-a-side indoor league team to my home to experience it with me. Week in, week out, we let off steam together on Tuesday and Thursday nights, and the group had become an anchor of my social life, and while I had never had them over to my apartment before, I felt like the World Cup final was as good a time as any for firsts.

The five-a-side league was a decent standard, populated with people like me: recent college graduates, high on ambition, low on the professional ladder, operating in the administration or random nonprofits scattered all over the city. They were all American, and most had played soccer through college.

I was slow of speed, but quick of mind and a decent finisher, but above all, competing alongside these guys was an eye-opening cultural exchange. I quickly learned how vastly different American soccer players were to the English kids I came of age with. In Liverpool, the game was physical, and we all mastered the art of throwing a crafty elbow into an opponent's ribs when the opportunity presented itself. American soccer players were horrified by these random acts of violence. They were such naive, decent human beings. They also followed up any mistake—and football is a game that consists of constant decision making and decision making gone awry—by stopping and raising a hand to apologize to their teammates with the self-evident acknowledgment of "My Bad." A righteous gesture that I never truly understood, as the quickest way to redeem yourself after losing the ball was to win it right back. In short, English football felt like a knife fight. American soccer felt like a game of checkers.

It was while sitting there in my apartment, poised to watch the World Cup final with all seven of my teammates crushed onto my couch, that a far more profound difference between American and English soccer players revealed itself. As my guests crushed beers and destroyed an extra-large pepperoni pizza, it became clear that even though soccer was an important athletic pursuit in their own lives, none of them had ever watched a live game. Indeed, most appeared to have little interest. An astounding phenomenon I had never considered before, never mind encountered. Akin to an accomplished writer with no interest in reading. As the minutes to kickoff counted down, my teammates showed little to no curiosity for the images broadcast on the screen, idly swapping on-the-job war stories and observations on the Orioles' pitching rotation.

I sat and seethed in my rocking chair that did not rock properly, a heavy wooden piece of furniture, one of many I had found discarded in a Chicago alleyway and brought with me to DC. Even though it was impossible to drown out the blasphemy of side conversations, I attempted to lock into the game. In truth, the drama trumped the action. In the buildup to kickoff, Ronaldo's name had mysteriously been left off the Brazilian lineup. It seemed like a glitch. By kickoff, he was back in the starting eleven. But when he stepped onto the pitch that evening, it was clear that something was wrong. Ronaldo was the last one out of the tunnel. As the camera followed him onto the field, he was subdued and glassy-eyed. The rumor mill went into overdrive: He was suffering from an ankle injury, or some kind of stomach complaint. There was a suggestion, later confirmed, that he had experienced a fit before the game and was in no state to play, only for Nike, Brazil's sponsors, to insist upon his reinstatement.

The only thing for certain was that Brazil capitulated, with their phenomenon barely able to touch the ball. When he did, he was lethargic, slow to react, almost dazed, missing all the pop and power of the usual Ronaldo. With their star player sleepwalking around the field, Brazil went down 2–0 by halftime, Zidane leaping around like a man possessed, delivering a pair of first-half headers that propelled his team to an improbably easy victory. The French scored again in the final moments of the second half, causing the Brazilians to slink off the field as the French players erupted around them in jubilation. Only two of my guests were still around to watch with me as the Brazilian team trudged up the steps through the euphoric crowd to accept their runner-up medals, and the camera trained itself on the face of Ronaldo. He was not angry, not in tears like some of his teammates. He looked bewildered and slightly bemused. The look of an extraordinarily gifted athlete who woke up in someone else's body.

The impact of the World Cup was transformative for the French, shattering their old sense of self as noble failures. The victorious multiracial Black, Blanc, Beur team enabled the nation to reimagine itself as the "La France qui gagne," a

France who won things. A new myth was forged overnight—one that aligned seamlessly with the political and economic self-confidence that abounded throughout French society at that time. Zidane's two headers obliterated the mystique of Brazilian invincibility and silenced the French right wing. The victorious squad was proclaimed the face of a new France—a proudly multicultural nation that could be the best in the world. The streets of Paris had not seen such celebration since Liberation. The slogan "Zidane président!" (Zidane for president!) was graffitied all over the city, and Zizou's face was beamed over one hundred feet wide against the side of the Arc de Triomphe.

All of these images were dizzying. A reminder of the power of football and the enormous societal changes it could catalyze. While all of that could not have been more inspiring, that night, as I collected all the crushed cans of beer into a black trash bag, I could not have felt more dead inside. On the evidence of the damp squib of a World Cup final party I had just hosted, America's interest in the game I loved was even colder than the tangle of pizza crusts that lined the oily boxes scattered across my floor. I was angry at myself for expecting more and wished I had done the easy thing and gone and watched the game down in Planet Fred with my fellow expats. The hallowed few who truly loved the sport and knew that the only way to treat American wannabe "fans" was to slap them on the cheek and advise them to stroll on.

Chapter 7

2002 World Cup, Korea/Japan

THE 2002 WORLD Cup is the one I watched live the least. I was living in New York City, newly married to a New York woman, Vanessa, whom I had first met playing coed soccer in Washington, DC. I would be lying if I did not confess that it was her composure on the ball, and the way she saw time and space with her passing, that first made my heart cleave.

We had gotten engaged quickly, admittedly by accident, an event which also happened thanks to football. We had dated for about two months when I made the ill-advised decision to engage in a mid-game fistfight with two hulking center backs, who happened to be identical twin brothers. The referee eventually sent all three of us off, but that dismissal only meant I was suddenly left alone on the sideline with the same two giants with whom I had just exchanged punches. Cue more pushing and shoving and being such a general distraction that the exasperated referee finally ran up to us and brandished his red card in our direction for a second time, to which I said, "You already sent us off, mate." Fair play to the ref, as he quickly improvised the power of sending us out of the park and ordering me and the twins to sit in our respective cars. Which I did for an hour, waiting for the game to end, so that Nessa, who was the only one of us who could drive at that time, could get us both out of there in one piece.

Cue the end of the game, when Vanessa stormed toward our vehicle. I had plenty of time to stew on the skirmish, and the aftermath. Thinking I was hard done, I honestly thought I would receive some sympathy for my bravery under fire. After all, I had heroically fought not one, but two enormous opponents, and they were identical bloody twins to boot. But from the distance of about twelve steps away, I could see Nessa was not of the same mindset. There was almost-cartoonesque steam coming out of her ears, and I slumped in the passenger seat and braced myself for the squall to come.

"I am so ashamed of the way you behaved, Roger. It was embarrassing to watch," Nessa screamed as her opening gambit, using my full name, which, to this day, she only does when she is *really* angry. "When we have kids, you will never, *ever* coach their football team." Those last twelve words changed my life. "What?" I stammered. "Does that mean we are getting married?" There was a silence. "I guess," she said with a shrug. "So..." I asked. "Does that mean that technically, we are engaged?" And that was that. We agreed we were, quickly left DC and the looming threat of Giant Twin Revenge that I could never shake, got married, and moved to New York City. We arrived with dreams of living in the kind of bright, airy SoHo loft we had seen on *Friends* and ended up only having enough money for a soulless one bedroom on the Upper West Side.

I kept working in nonprofits, all the time refining my writing and dabbling, in its early days, with the sense of connectivity the internet provided. I was fascinated to glimpse how niche audiences could be built into true communities. As an early experiment, I started a website putting out an APB for 1980s bar mitzvah photographs, which fascinated me as the perfect mirror reflecting the kitsch music, style, and culture of that time. I then stood back as thousands proceeded to wing my way from points all over the country. *Gawker* covered this project. *The New York Times* Style section followed suit. A book deal ensued, and I spent months organizing and scanning my way into becoming a first-time author.

Those same powers of internet connectivity made English club football feel ever more important in my life. It fundamentally changed the way we Americans could access and experience Premier League football. In the past, I had to wait for the monthly stuffed envelope of press clippings my mother would faithfully cull from the local newspaper to follow along the intricate details. Now, the proliferation of rudimentary fan message boards made her mailings redundant, forging an instant link to the telenovela levels of news, gossip, and rumors surrounding the club I loved. I lived for the Everton message boards Blue Kipper and ToffeeWeb, dialing up AOL and logging on several times a day to feast on every morsel of news about tactical possibilities, injuries, and transfers as if they were Holy Gospels.

My ritual of weekends at the sports bar continued, but now they proved more heavily populated. I was not alone. Early Saturday morning, I hopped crosstown to the East Side to raise a breakfast beer at the Kinsale Tavern, an Irish bar on Third Avenue. In stark contrast to the English-only underground Fight Club vibe at Planet Fred in DC, the Kinsale was thronging, packed full of American early adopters, who had started to commune at the crack of dawn and formed an ardent, accepting, joyous culture. The vibe was less bar, more a portal to another land filled with passion, pints, and pie. Albeit one now rife with American accents, eager to connect and talk the language of football. Now, the only interlopers were the occasional random creepy taxi driver stopping in before an early morning pickup at JFK to neck down two scotches before heading off to the airport, which was always disconcerting to witness.

Despite the swelling community forming around football, there were two powerful reasons that made this "the World Cup which almost entirely passed me by." The first was personal. My wife was three months pregnant with the baby who would turn out to be our eldest kid, Samson. His impending arrival filled me with an acute sense of existential angst. To that point, I had lived like a kid, free to chase impulses with little thought of risk. If I wanted to try and fight a pair of twins on the football field, *Let's go!* My move to Chicago from Liverpool had been a leap into the unknown with no consideration of the downside. The imminent arrival of a family—a human being dependent on my creative output—meant that I felt, for the first time, not exactly maturity, more a sense of weighted responsibility that was rushing toward me. That summer I was gripped by a self-involved fog of preoccupation as I attempted to work out exactly what it all meant.

The other reason was practical. Yes, football had never meant more to me, but the World Cup had never put itself in a place to mean less. This was the year FIFA elected for the first time to hold the tournament outside of Europe and the Americas, heading to Japan and South Korea. Two regional rivals hastily conjuring a marriage of convenience, born of a fractious and deeply competitive joint bid. The two countries were soccer crazy, thanks in no small part to the fetishization of fashion-forward Manchester United midfielder David Beckham, who was beloved throughout Asia, but they were thirteen hours ahead of New York City, which meant most of the tournament was played in the middle of the night. So, the first week of the World Cup forced me to unbox a TiVo, which someone had given me for our wedding. You may know this device as a primitive DVR, but I had never had the time, nor the inclination to unpack it. The World Cup provided the impetus as the games kicked off in the wee morning hours. For the first two weeks of the tournament I would wake up in the morning and summon up the games that had occurred overnight, watching them all at triple speed as I dressed for work, winding and rewinding the action with the TiVo's signature doorbell ringing noise popping in my ears as an accompanying soundtrack.

South Korea and Japan had originally competed for sole hosting duties, and their rivalry continued long after they had banded together, in the form of a frenzied stadium construction competition. Both countries tossed state-of-the-art facilities around like giant roulette chips, some of them even landing on cities that were not actually home to soccer teams. South Korea built the World Cup Fountain in the Hangang River, at 633 feet high the world's second tallest, and the Japanese countered by constructing a stadium that used a computer system to control the growth rate of the grass, which felt like a Isaac Asimov novel come alive.

The coverage surrounding the buildup to the tournament veered between the saccharine sap of "soccer amidst the cherry blossoms" sentimentality and vaguely terrifying articles about how fans traveling to Korea would be served free samples of cooked dog in an attempt to defuse any preexisting cultural prejudice they may harbor around snacking on man's best friend. I read about how free samples of dog meat stew and soup would be made available in paper cups outside the ten Korean stadiums, accompanied by brochures in multiple European languages detailing the nutritional advantages of canine cuisine. These articles made me nostalgic for the simpler days when World Cups past had merely been used by dictators for propaganda purposes.

The competitive geopolitical battle between the two host nations gave this tournament a surreal edge. Things turned nasty during the opening ceremony, held in Seoul, when the South Koreans forgot to mention their Japanese partners—payback perhaps, as the Japanese had erased the word "Korea" from the World Cup logo on the tickets for the matches held in their country. The result was a strangely bipolar competition, in which Korea used the tournament to demystify itself to the world while Japan was relaxed, seemingly content to enjoy the spectacle and poke at their cohosts.

The football also had a dreamlike tinge. This was the first World Cup in which the traditional power base of Europe and South America was challenged by the underdog new world of Africa, Asia, and, yes, the US. Senegal kicked things off by beating their former colonizer, the defending champions France, who, with Zidane hobbled and barely able to play, exited without scoring a single goal. I watched the game on replay in another Irish bar on lower Third Avenue, Molly's, whose signature feature was the old-school sawdust that persevered on its floor. Like approximately 79 percent of the rest of New York City at that time, I was attempting to break into documentary filmmaking and was pitching a footballing concept to a film producer, who had just won an award at Sundance. He mostly talked about himself and how great the burger was at this place. The burger was indeed excellent, but the football was better, and as his mouth opened and closed in perpetual self-adulation, I watched the action unfurl on a small television set over his shoulder. As the Senegalese joyously rendered the twin stereotypes of French invincibility and African naivete obsolete, it became a supreme effort to prevent my jaw from dropping.

In previous World Cups, emerging nations with no tournament pedigree and few recognized stars expected to be slaughtered. However, in this new global era, their individual players knew that a standout performance or single dazzling goal could trigger a big money move to an Italian, English, or Spanish league club. In this tournament, the smaller nations were often more motivated, cohesive, and fearless than the superpowers, whose fat cat players were preoccupied with sponsor obligations, book deals, and image rights. This was an incredible time for my love of all things American—the Chicago Bears, Tracy Chapman, and Public Enemy—to continue to transfer itself from supporting England to the US Men's National Team. Watching those Senegalese "Lions of Teranga" run rampant filled my heart with wonder. If they could do it, why couldn't the American boys also shock the world?

The US team indeed arrived with a swaggering sense of optimism, determined to erase the embarrassment of 1998's arrogant implosion. I followed along with my naive hope swelling as the squad's chemistry developed through qualifying. I had joined a crowd of forty thousand fans traveling to Foxboro to watch them beat Jamaica on the day the US invaded Afghanistan, a cacophonous event that suggested interest was growing behind their progress. Yes, the NFL hashmarks on the field may still have been visible, the optics of which gave the game a slight

JV feel, but the fans wore red and American flags and chanted "F bin Laden" throughout. The team's manager, Bruce Arena, was a strange mix of arrogance and insecurity, which perhaps should have been expected of a man who began his career as a lacrosse coach at the University of Virginia and was now about to lead his team into a World Cup. An "only in America" self-made footballing story.

With his thick New York accent, Arena tried to present himself as a mafia family boss, if a mafia family boss exclusively wore blue USA soccer polos and khakis. Bruce was a dour, sphincter-lipped personality. *The New York Times* called him "often as pleasant as an ingrown toenail." He presided over an American squad evenly split between European and domestic-based players. About half were holdovers from the 1998 disaster. Twenty-year-old Landon Donovan was the fresh-faced young stud of the team and was one of seven players somehow lulled into an immensely homoerotic photo shoot by *The New York Times Magazine*, overseen by an ex-Armani creative director Matthias Vriens-McGrath, who once boasted, "I can make anything look sexy. If you ask me to take a photograph of a tomato, it's going to end up looking like a hot tomato." Thus, we were treated to the sight of striker Brian McBride in head-to-toe Prada, pants tight, but not as tight as his grip on a fence post, which he looked like he was poised to jerk off. Goalkeeper Kasey Keller with his shorts hiked way north, while flashing his wedding ring as if teasing, "You can look, but don't touch." Landon's photo became the most famous. He was in a silky purple Jacquard button-down, mouth open, about to do borderline nonconsensual things with a water fountain. The whole thing felt like the "least sexy, sexy photo spread" I had ever seen, and as I flicked through the pages aghast, struck by the desperate extent the players would go through to advance the profile of their game in their country, I calculated they had just inadvertently set it back by at least ten years or so.

If that photo shoot was the marker of form, I braced myself for the United States to repeat their last-place finish in 1998. Arena, though, kept hawking his belief that his team could win it all. I did not share his confidence. Indeed, I am embarrassed to say, I did not watch their first game against Portugal live. It kicked off at 5 a.m. ET, and I did not expect much from it. This was against the so-called golden generation of Portuguese talent led by global superstar Figo, recently the most expensive player in the world and reigning world player of the year. The team were ranked number 5 in the world. I woke up to watch the game fast-forward on my trusty TiVo. The US had a World Cup record of eight losses, one draw, and just one win since 1990. I expected them to be utterly outclassed and hoped, at best, for a valiant low-scoring defeat.

Instead, I witnessed otherwise as the game kicked off at Suwon Stadium, with its roof shaped like a bird's wings. A fitting place for the USA's World Cup journey to take flight. The Portugal team wore gold chains and had olive skin and a healthy level of Mediterranean body hair. They looked, collectively, like the guy your girlfriend told you not to worry about. They were definitely suave, savvy, and exuded the confidence of men who wore Speedos when not being paid to play soccer at an elite level. All their best players had developed at the same time, winning consecutive Under-20 World Cups in 1989 and 1991. This same collective had just come off a semifinal appearance in Euro 2000. The 2002 World Cup was meant to be the moment all their promise became real when it mattered. Instead, they were cold-cocked by a storming opener from the Yanks.

Four minutes into the game, the artful midfielder John O'Brien tapped in from close range and I could not believe my bleary eyes. Bruce Arena merely celebrated by hiking up his khakis. Twenty-six minutes later, a Landon Donovan cross was haplessly deflected by Jorge Costa into his own net. You saw Landon's orthodontist's work up close as the cameras zoomed into his celebration and he shrugged his hands in an ecstatic apology. Just after the half-hour mark, the brawny target man Brian McBride, whose nickname was the distinctly unclever "McHead," delivered a thunderous diving headbutt of a strike to put the United States up 3–0, a scoreline that felt like it had been ripped from the most imaginative fan fiction.

Portugal mounted a ferocious comeback, scoring before halftime, and then ratcheting up the pressure. The stress on the American backline was sufficient to compel defender Jeff Agoos to synapse, volleying the ball spectacularly into the net, which made it 3–2 with nineteen minutes left to play. But the United States held on for the win, and as I clicked my TiVo remote control to savor every American goal for a second time to make sure that actually all had happened, I don't know who looked more stunned. The Portuguese golden generation, the American players, or me watching seven thousand miles away. Quivering. Fingers shaking so hard I could not properly do up my tie. I had to run to work through Manhattan streets that were entirely unaware their best male footballers had pulled off one of the greatest shocks in our nation's history.

The United States proceeded to tie hosts South Korea in another game I watched "as live" alone at breakfast time via TiVo. Clint Mathis, the team's young hotshot, opened the scoring with a delicious trap and volley out of nowhere. Clint was the self-styled bad boy of the American squad. A rebellious free spirit who had reacted to being benched for the Portugal game by having his roommate shave his hair into a clownish mohawk. The rest of the squad gave Mathis the nickname "Cletus" after the redneck *Simpsons* character. A nickname he not only owned but ended up getting tattooed on his back. Coach Arena used to publicly complain about Mathis's fitness, cryptically demeaning his "refueling" habits. The man was the self-dubbed Dennis Rodman of the squad, but here it felt like he had justified his presence by giving the United States one foot in the knockout round promised land.

Yet, our dreams were shattered late on when Ahn Jung-hwan headed home a free kick, triggering ecstatic scenes for the hosts, as he celebrated with a poorly synchronized speed skate mime in a crafty allusion to the recent Winter Olympics in Salt Lake City in which a Korean short track speed skating star Kim Dong-sung had been controversially disqualified for blocking after an official protest, which enabled an American Apolo Ohno to win gold instead. I rewound the celebration twice to make sure mine eyes had processed it correctly. The ignominy of being trolled in the World Cup for speed skating misdemeanors.

The final group stage game was a reality check as we were handed a bare-bottom spanking by Poland, a result that ultimately did not matter as the Koreans, perhaps out of embarrassment for their speed skating banter, did the United States an enormous favor, shocking a bedraggled Portugal 1–0. As the score filtered through to Taejon, the substitutes on the American bench leapt up and suddenly started cheering and clapping even though their team were down 3–0. The US were through to the knockout rounds, and even better, they would face regional archrivals Mexico. An achievement that earned the squad a televised pregame phone call from no less a figure than President George W. Bush himself, who phoned and offered a backhanded compliment: "A lot of people that don't know anything about soccer, like me, are all excited and pulling for you." The US team were sitting around awkwardly in training gear in a sparse locker room in Jeonju, listening on a plain white speakerphone. Arena was the only one to speak. He didn't full-on predict victory but declared his team would submit a performance worthy of the greatest country in the world. After hanging up, the players giggled nervously among themselves. "That was pretty good." "That was great!"

The game kicked off at 2:30 a.m. ET and I did get up to watch this one live. With a place in the quarterfinals on the line, I sat alone, groggily, on our tiny couch in my boxer shorts to witness a bloodbath as the US and Mexican players descended upon one another like Cain and Abel. Which is what they were in a way, Cain and Abel in cleats. The two countries share a border that spans nearly 2,000 miles and *a lot* of history. Over the nineteenth century, the US had annexed more territory from its southern neighbor than did any of the marauding European powers—think of every Spanish town in California or that one state unimaginatively named *New* Mexico. Not to mention the constant militarized monitoring of the border by US officials. Against that backdrop, and the long and painful immigration conflict, football had remained the one arena in which Mexico didn't have to genuflect to their affluent, self-satisfied, gringo-neighbor up north. However, as the United States started to take football more seriously, that dominance was eroding, which only made the Mexican players more venomous. Now this cocky US team feared no one.

Over the course of ninety fiercely fought minutes, ten yellow cards were handed out. The apex of the violence saw Mexico's pantomime villain defender, Rafa Márquez, sent off for attempting to kung-fu kick Cobi Jones's backside while simultaneously trying to decapitate him with a headbutt. This was an act of violence so furiously creative, I felt guilty clicking my TiVo replay button three or four times to attempt to understand his thinking. In between the crafty elbows and late tackles, there was a smattering of football. Mexico dominated the time of possession by a 2–1 margin, outshot the US, and enjoyed eight corners to the US's three. But when the final whistle blew, Brian McBride and Donovan had both scored—and the Mexicans hadn't. Dos a Cero. The United States had not just won a massive World Cup game convincingly, they placed an albatross around the neck of their archrival in the process. When Landon Donovan sealed the win, he stripped topless to show off his barely postpubescent bod, proudly presenting what looks like six or seven newly sprouted tufts of chest hair. Each one a symbol of America's sudden nascent footballing virility. As the victorious American players hugged each other at the final whistle, in a Manhattan yet to wake up, anything felt possible. After the game, as the US players were cracking beers on the team bus, they realized they had pulled up next to the Mexicans. The entire team went over to the windows to raise their beers and taunt them. What could be more American than that?

As a reward for their valor, the United States was given the quarterfinal gift of meeting powerhouse Germany. In the days before the game, I had flown home to England for a vacation with my entire family. From the moment Vanessa and I landed at Heathrow airport and made our way to Paddington Station to catch the train to Cornwall, it was thrilling to be reacquainted with a nation that lived for the World Cup. Every few feet of our journey, from the moment we arrived at passport control, all the way to the arrivals' platform at Truro station, some screen somewhere was guaranteed to be broadcasting the game, always with a crowd surrounding it, fixated on the football. Traveling across the south of England, it was stunning to see English jerseys being worn on bodies both athletic and ill-advised, scarves flying out of every car window, and flags draped off building balconies. It was the World Cup as it was meant to be. An event that stopped the nation, bonded strangers together, and encouraged irresponsible daytime drinking.

Another silver-lining of being in England? More reasonable kickoff times. At 7:30 a.m. ET, I tuned in to watch our American boys face Destiny (aka, the Germans), from the couch in our Cornwall rental holiday home, with only Vanessa for company alongside me. The US Men's Soccer team were not yet enough of a draw to tempt the rest of the family out of bed that early, and no English person truly enjoyed watching Germany. Even a Germany that were weaker than the one which had run over the US 2-0 in the opening game of the previous World Cup. This squad was older, and slower, but still German and so to be intrinsically feared.

From the off, the US played audaciously, relying on their defensive organization and willingness to snipe forward bravely in moments on the counterattack. When the Germans took the lead in the 39th minute, it felt doubly deflating precisely because the Americans had their chances but missed them. The German goal came off a set piece, a Teutonic forte as they require practice, precision, and planning. Their star, Michael Ballack, a footballing tank, split his defenders and headed home. Still, I admired the resiliency with which the Americans responded, creating opportunities with forceful football.

Landon Donovan relished the stage and the moment. Faking out defenders, testing the goalkeeper, with the fearlessness of a kid living purely in the moment.

Four minutes into the second half, I was three breakfast beers in and feeling as dangerous as the US, who were experiencing a spell of dominance. A floated corner kick was flicked toward defender Gregg Berhalter, who volleyed a shot toward the goal. Monstrous German goalkeeper Oliver Kahn spread his wings to smother, but the ball bounced under him and spun toward the goal line where defender Torsten Frings was stationed. Frings was able to scoop the ball away to safety but replays showed he did so illegally with a stealthy use of a hand. Watching live, it was clear Frings knew what had just happened by the extent to which he attempted to summon the most innocent of looks. The Americans surrounded the referee begging for as clear and obvious a handball penalty as you will see in the light of day. Even my pregnant wife had bolted off the couch and screamed at the television for a red card. However, the only man whose opinion counted was Scottish referee Hugh Dallas. He claimed he saw nothing and let play continue. We slumped back down into the scratchy embrace of the rental couch. The frustration and disbelief you experience in those cruel moments of injustice as a fan is worse than conceding a goal. The sense of being impotent as you are wronged is double agony.

Instead of having a player sent off and conceding a penalty kick, Frings had taken a calculated gamble and been rewarded for it. A moment that would have broken lesser teams but, to their credit, the US continued to probe. The closest they came was a Tony Sanneh header, which went into the side netting. And so, the USA was eliminated, but with mixed emotions. As an Englishman, I knew there was no disgrace to losing to a German team, yet a semifinal against South Korea had been within touching distance. Instead, the US were on their way home, but they departed having earned the world's respect as footballers for the first time in the modern period. The respect of everyone other than my older brother, Nigel, who walked in five minutes before the final whistle, in his dressing gown and underpants, just in time to mock my anguish at the Americans' elimination. "You are like Benedict Arnold in reverse," he quipped, before stumbling off into the kitchen to make a cup of tea.

Knee-deep into my fifth beer, I sat on the floor alongside my wife who, by now, had taken up the whole couch, and we both wallowed in a proud disappointment. In the days to come, Bruce Arena, in his typically modest way, called the run "close to, if not equal to or better than" the Miracle on Ice at the 1980 Olympics. Landon Donovan ultimately won the tournament's best young player award. He went on a talk show tour and became the most well-known American soccer player of his generation. Upon returning to New York, I watched him guest on *Last Call with Carson Daly* alongside musical guest N.E.R.D. and felt that it just did not get any bigger than that. Just as important, it seemed that American football now had a booming future. It had truly, belatedly, arrived.

All of that was still to pass. Back in the Cornish coast, we had the small matter of three hours to kill until England took the field for their quarterfinal against Brazil. Their run thus far had been propelled by traditionally, irrationally high hopes and scant evidence to back them up. David Beckham had experienced a resurrection of quasi-biblical proportions since becoming the national scapegoat four years earlier, flicking out that regretfully angry cleat at the wily Argentine Diego Simeone in Saint-Étienne, and shattering his team's hearts in the process. That incident marred his life for the subsequent eighteen months, as he and his wife were mercilessly abused by football fans all over the country, on a weekly basis. He was jeered at and spat upon, his name cursed, and his effigy hung in pubs. Some even had the temerity to doubt his fashion choices. But then, three years later, Goldenballs unleashed one of his signature long-range free kick poems against Greece to assure England's automatic qualification for this World Cup, trotting away with arms outstretched, an image instantly cementing itself into every schoolkid's top ten list of great moments of postwar English history. The nation hastily dug out the Beckham posters that had been banished to closet, proving there is little more futile in this world than trying to hold on to old grudges in the face of really, really, really, ridiculously good-looking football played by a really, really, really, ridiculously good-looking man.

However, football is a constant reminder of how cruel and unromantic it can be. Seven weeks before the World Cup, Beckham crumpled under a tackle in a Champions League game and broke the second metatarsal in his left foot. That bone instantly became known as the "Beckham bone" as the English media and public followed the medical reports of its rehabilitation, as the safeguarding of the nation's democratic future hinged upon its healing. England's desperate desire to experience glory, and their realization that the standard of English coaching was suboptimal, meant the English Football Association took the extraordinary and previously unthinkable step of hiring a foreign manager they prayed could bring the state-of-the-art tactical savvy to make their dreams come true. Sven-Göran Eriksson was that man. An innovative, icy Swede with a sly sense of humor, who had won titles in Italy and was expected to deliver

English World Cup glory the second he accepted the job. In a bold decision, Eriksson elected to select Beckham for Japan, knowing his inclusion was a gamble, all the while willing him back to full health with an element of magical thinking.

I watched the first game in New York on my TiVo. A nervy 1–1 stalemate against Sven-Göran's home nation of Sweden, for which Beckham was selected, playing for an hour, there in body, not in spirit. One English newspaper compared his performance to "the last scene of El Cid, when the crusader army lash the dead Charlton Heston to his saddle and send him out at the head of his troops, knowing that merely the sight of him will strike fear into the enemy's hearts." The Beckham we saw was shattered and tentative, neither of which was surprising as this was his first competitive match in over seven weeks and that the metatarsal bone in his left foot had barely healed.

The good news: Beckham was not a corpse on a horse. He lived and walked amongst us, and next up for the English was their grand nemesis, Argentina. Sometimes football feels like it has been written by some secret cabal of scriptwriters. This was one of those times. An epic opportunity for Beckham to exact revenge on the Argentines, who had previously tormented him and, for a time, shattered his world.

I had watched that game in an Upper West Side Irish bar, which had opened it doors at 7 a.m., marketing the occasion as a "British Beers for Breakfast extravaganza." Despite it being a workday morning, the pub was surprisingly busy, filled mostly with expats and a smattering of American Anglophiles wearing football gear or Oasis tour shirts. We were all there to witness a game akin to a national exorcism and a personal atonement for Beckham. England repelled the Argentinians, becoming stronger with every Michael Owen–inspired foray. The England speedster burst into the box just before halftime. Mauricio Pochettino, the Argentine defender, stuck out a trembling leg, which Owen obliged by falling over. The conned referee gave a penalty and Owen had, quite deliciously, handed the Argentinians a taste of their own gamesmanship medicine. Beckham stepped up to the spot to deliver his penalty of justice. English history remembers it as a heroic act of wonder. In truth it was a nervous blast of energy straight down the middle. Somehow the immobile keeper let it fly past him and the entire country of England went into rapture. Watching on in the Upper West Side bar, I felt a happiness for all those around me, but I also realized that the emotional heft of a US win now moved me far more than any English victory. I was clearly traveling in the opposite direction to the gaggle of American Anglophiles who were in attendance, many of whom were hugging each other as if they were more English that Dame Maggie Smith.

Bookmakers instantly halved the odds of England winning the World Cup from 16/1 to 7/1 as punters all over the nation acted on their renewed belief. Ninety minutes earlier, England had appeared tepid. Suddenly they were perceived as world beaters. The Argentines, for their part, had been robbed by a dubious penalty, but their nation was so enchanted by the dark art side of football that the Buenos Aires newspapers were not outraged. Instead, their headlines nodded their approval. "They've learnt," wrote one.

England proceeded to the knockout rounds where they made short work of Denmark in a one-sided game and now faced the vaunted Brazil of mono-named legends Ronaldo, Rivaldo, and Cafu with confidence surging. My family faithfully poured into the lounge in our rental home. It was large but oddly underfurnished. My wife and my father were given pride of place on the couch. The rest of us, including my mother and sister, sat on the floor around the boxy, old-school television. Everyone was heightened by a sense of expectation, apart from my poor wife, who was merely overwhelmed by early pregnancy morning sickness. This had been exacerbated by my father's unquenchable desire to make each family car journey an off-roading experience, clattering down tiny Cornish farm roads in the shadow of the area's thick hedges at dangerously high speeds.

The game kicked off in the afternoon. My parents had driven out to buy some special local pasties and clotted cream scones. This was a game so filled with occasion that even my mum came in to watch with us, making random observations about the hair of the different players as she munched on a pastie. We all felt sure we were poised to witness English glory on the ultimate journey to tournament victory. If this team could beat Argentina, then thirty-six years of hurt since we last won the World Cup could finally end.

By the time the English took to the field on a boiling hot day in Shizuoka Stadium, I was most aware of the difference between watching England and the United States play. Witnessing David Beckham stretch through his warmups, I knew that every English pub and television set in the land was tuned in to this moment. That this was very much the collective national experience that I sincerely hoped for future American games. The game began so well from an English perspective. In the 23rd minute, Michael Owen opened the scoring, taking advantage of a Brazilian error. Sometimes the ball rolls in and you feel only exaltation. Sometimes it goes in and you fear your team has scored too early. "Now we have something precious to lose," my father, ever the pessimist, quipped, while attempting to butter a scone on his lap. For him, taking the lead only catalyzed a strange feeling of watching a game in which the outcome was never a doubt, and not in a good way.

My dad had watched too much English fecklessness in his lifetime to be wrong. The Brazilians were indeed undeterred, summoning an equalizer just before halftime. Then. The Moment. Brazil won a free kick in a seemingly innocuous position out on the right. Their goofy-jester-prince Ronaldinho stood over the ball. Every other football player on the planet would have knocked it into the box and hoped one of his teammates could head it goalbound. Ronaldinho, an effervescent talent, ultimately done in by a combination of his love of nightlife, late night bongo playing, and women, was not every other player. He stepped up and floated a 35-yard moonshot over the flailing English goalkeeper, David Seaman. A gent who, with his bold choice of mustache and greased-back ponytail, looked like a cross between a porn star and a founding father of the United States—think Alexander Hamilton if he were a stripper. After the ball spun into the top corner, the air in our rental house lounge felt like it had been sucked out. The camera cut to close-ups of Seaman, who looked like a man who had seen his haircut in the mirror for the first time and desperately regretted his style choice. "Silly man," muttered my mother as Seaman broke down in tears. The British commentators prattled about how lucky Ronaldinho's goal had been because he could not have meant it. Just because no Englishman had the touch or skill or verve to pull off that shot did not mean Ronaldinho had not intended it. This was the single most Brazilian moment of flair I had ever seen live with my own eyes, and it hurt as much as I admired it. A strike that did not just beat an opponent but humiliated them to the withering point of destruction.

England's tournament had ended with a whimper. Even after Ronaldinho managed to get himself sent off, England never really responded. It was as if the manner of the second Brazil goal had broken them. My dad, who had told me he did not really care about the English team anymore, sat there on the couch, covered in scone crumbs, and ashen-faced in a way I had only seen on him before at funerals. I realized this was a man who cared so much, he did not want to reveal the depths of his desire for them to succeed, for fear of being embarrassed by it. Like millions of English people, he had allowed himself to be fooled by the win against a generationally poor Argentine team fifteen days earlier. That win had been mere cruel misdirection.

To cheer us up, my mum pulled out a cheap plastic football she had purchased at the village store earlier that morning and gave it to my brother's young kids. Within minutes, my whole family found ourselves outside in the front yard for a multigenerational kick around. My wife, though pregnant, could not help herself as she flung herself into the game. My father was astonished by the spectacle. He had never seen a woman play soccer before. Women's football back then was a peripheral pursuit in England. "What are you doing?" he asked out loud, as shocked as if she had just announced she was a lesbian. My wife quickly nutmegged my brother. "She's actually quite good," my father was forced to admit, still stupefied by the spectacle.

We were in transit home to the United States during the World Cup semifinals. They featured two unexpected underdogs—Turkey and host South Korea. Turkey was a true under-the-radar phenomenon, having shrugged off an opening game loss to drop China and tie with Costa Rica, then defeat hosts Japan and France's conquerors Senegal, employing a robust physicality to batter all-comers.

South Korea's journey was altogether more controversial. After experiencing its nation's first World Cup victory in fifteen attempts, the Koreans prospered thanks to their organization, pluck, and the fanatical support of their cultic followers who, in their red T-shirts branded with the ubiquitous phrase "Be the reds!" unleashed some of the most passionate fan choreography the tournament had ever seen. One misguided fan doused himself in paint thinner and set himself on fire, leaving a suicide note that explained his intention to "be a ghost, the twelfth player on the pitch, and do my best for the team." When the fans could not pull the Korean team through, the referees occasionally stepped in suspiciously, most controversially in victories against Italy and Spain in the knockout stages. The heavily favored Italians had a goal wrongly disallowed after their star striker Francesco Totti was unfairly sent off, then the Koreans tied the game late just as regulation was about to expire. In overtime, Ahn Jung-hwan scored the sudden-death golden goal to seal the victory and instantly become a national hero, a position that entitled him to free life insurance, exemption from military service, and free flights on the Korean national airline for life.

Yet, in a World Cup studded with shocking results and the sense of a new world order forming, the final saw order restored. And me flying back from the West Coast for work in a day before internet on planes. The TiVo once again saving the day to assert its dominance as my own personal tournament MVP. Serial winners Brazil and Germany had emerged to face each other. Two superpowers who, despite their peerless successes, were quite incredibly facing each other for the first time at the World Cup in the 2002 final. The game in Yokohama was billed as the battle between two footballing stereotypes: Brazilian flair and German pragmatism. In truth, Brazil had been vulnerable in the path to the final, losing an unprecedented six games, emerging from the experience as a much more physically robust team fusing defensive steel onto their traditional attacking flamboyance, a delicate and often unachievable tactical balance. Germany had limped through to the playoffs themselves, having relied upon the intimidating play of goalkeeper captain Oliver Kahn and potency of midfielder Michael Ballack, which had propelled them to a string of 1–0 victories. It was Ballack who scored the only goal of the game against South Korea in the semis, a match in which he picked up his second yellow card of the knockout phase, sidelining him for the final and rendering him powerless to prevent Ronaldo from experiencing a glory he had to wait years to experience.

Four years earlier, buck-toothed and bug-eyed, Ronaldo had toiled in the 1998 final, sleepwalking through the biggest game of his life with the look of an extraordinarily gifted athlete who had woken up in a mere mortal's body. His Brazilian team proceeded to implode against France, 3–0. A loss that led to prolonged and extensive investigations by the Brazilian Parliament into why Ronaldo had originally been left out of the starting lineup, then reinserted just before kickoff. Those investigations proved inconclusive. The only certainty was that Ronaldo's reputation had been tarnished, his durability suspect.

After two operations on his damaged right knee and almost two unhappy years of rehabilitation, the breathtaking turbocharged life-force returned just in time for the 2002 World Cup, clad in a chrome pair of cleats, and proceeded to heal the mental and physical wounds of the past with a resplendent performance that was akin to a human stampede. The only thing more staggering than his eight goals scored was his haircut. A now-iconic monk tonsure, which became one of the few elite footballer hairstyles to never catch on.

The Brazilian saved the most quintessentially Ronaldo for his first goal of the final. After losing a tackle on the edge of the box, he bounced back onto his feet, stealing the ball with the speed of a cut purse. One spin collapsed the German midfield, and he flicked the ball to his teammate Rivaldo, who shot from 24 yards. The drive went straight to the keeper, but the deflection rolled back out. Even though Ronaldo was barely in the camera's frame when Rivaldo shot, it is he who swooped in to blast the ball into the open net. Watching it back in replay, it looked like there were four Brazilians involved in that play. And there are. It's just that three of them were Ronaldo.

After scoring both goals in the final, Ronaldo led Brazil to World Cup glory for that elusive fifth time. As Brazil claimed the cup, thousands of origami cranes, symbols of luck and long life, fell to the field, a stunning spectacle that surpassed almost everything that had taken place in the previous ninety minutes. It was a fitting end to a joyous, passionate tournament whose most moving aspect was fan fever in general, and in particular the 12,000 Koreans who registered to become "volunteer supporters" of *other* nations. When Ronaldo was asked in the press conference what felt better, winning the World Cup or sex, he thought for a moment. "This," he replied. You could see it in the smile as Ronaldo scored his second goal in the final. The emotion he had just experienced was not just the giddiness of victory or the orgasmic satisfaction of scoring on the biggest stage in the world. It is also the sheer relief of the world's best striker in finding himself, finally, back in his body. With the whole world paying witness.

Brazil's performance was so epic that on December 25, when our son Samson was born, we received not one, but two baby Ronaldo kits as baby naming gifts. My mother added to our collection of tiny polyester replicas by proudly dispatching a full-England onesie with Beckham's name on the back, replete with baby football booties. I made sure that cursed outfit went nowhere near my newborn's body. That was pretty much the sum amount of the important decisions I made in the first week of his existence. I would like to write profound thoughts about how looking down at the face of my firstborn changed my life and propelled me into a new phase as a hunter-gatherer. The truth was, the first time I looked down at Samson and saw his snubbed nose and soft fluffy peach-fuzz baby hair crewcut, he looked just like Liverpool's iconic midfielder Steven Gerrard, the star player of my team's archrivals, and the resemblance made me feel physically sick. For the first two weeks of my son's life, I could barely look at him nor change his diaper. Thankfully, like many babies, his features changed rapidly in the first few weeks, and the likeness faded. Once it had, I delighted in dressing Samson in the US jersey my friend Jamie had thoughtfully sent over, holding him in my arms, late at night, and rocking him to sleep, dreaming only of his representing the United States in World Cups to come.

Chapter 8

2006 World Cup, Germany

THE 2006 WORLD Cup changed my life. In the same way as the birth of Jesus separates world history into BC and AD, my existence can be split into "Before World Cup 2006" and "After World Cup 2006." The tournament gave me the idea that changed the entire trajectory of my being. The remarkable thing is that there was little drama from a football perspective about the moment. It was not prompted by an underdog victory or wonder goal. Instead, it was a split second during a pregame show that triggered an idea, which plunged my life into a sudden, new, mission-driven direction.

That is a pretty amazing achievement for a football tournament taking place nearly four thousand miles away in Germany that I mostly watched while perched on my couch in New York City. Indeed, I had zero idea about any of this when the World Cup approached. Storytelling was the one thing I cared about most in my life at that point. Maybe first equal, alongside my family. By that time, we had two kids, both boys. Mentally, I was still very much in a frenzied state of searching, desperate to identify a path to a future I could feel passionate about, one that also offered even a faint sense of financial security. That duality mostly translated into me firing book after book out into the world. Colorful cultural histories about things I was personally fascinated by: Ping-Pong, lost vinyl, and that beloved Jewish American institution of summer camp. Each somehow proved to be evermore niche than the last.

I told myself I was still finding my voice, so, in the run-up to the 2006 World Cup, I was surprised, and slightly giddy, when that once-vaunted outlet *The New Republic* reached out through a friend of a friend to invite me to contribute to their World Cup blog. It was a lo-fi affair, but I jumped at the opportunity to bang out a few paragraphs and see my thoughts, and my byline, alongside those of real writers like the novelist Aleksandar Hemon, and journalists Daniel Alarcón and León Krauze, all whom I admired, all from different nations, supporting different teams, but bonding over an ecstatic worship of the tournament that had shaped our lives.

And this tournament was some powerful muse. Ebullient enough to achieve something most of the planet never thought was possible—worldwide admiration of all things German. That host nation whose history is rife with attempts to grab the world's attention—most often by force—achieved that goal this time around, not by might, but with politeness, a barrage of würst, and revealing a hithertofore well-concealed inimitable sense of self-awareness, and even humor. Thanks to its remarkable organization, hospitality, and the plucky play of its national team on the field, Germany used this one month to rebrand itself as a cuddly underdog, triggering a wave of self-love within the country, which had not been experienced since World War II.

The great game-changing invention was the official "Fan

Fest." These were epically large public viewing spaces in which ticketless fans could gather around gigantic jumbotrons to watch the games, drink the town dry, and become part of the spectacle themselves. The Berlin fan zone alone could bring nearly one million fans together in the shadow of the Brandenburg Gate. It felt as if the whole of Europe had emptied itself into each German host city, and the sheer size, scale, and energy was utterly intoxicating to witness. I can assume being a part of it was even more so.

I watched the opening day unfurl from the Upper West Side and was mesmerized by the football yet intimidated by the gnawing responsibility I now felt to identify storylines sufficiently highfalutin to serve up to *The New Republic*'s audience. The other writers appeared to have no such problems. Each appeared more adept than the last at diving deep into the geopolitical ramifications of the event and find no shortage of narrative. Eight teams had qualified for the first time that year, and the effervescence and pride felt by the likes of Angola, the Czech Republic, Ukraine, Ghana, the Ivory Coast, Trinidad and Tobago, and Togo gave the tournament a new energy. My fellow writers, most of whom appeared to have black belts in political theory and cultural anthropology, found plenty to write about. One contributor after another effortlessly dropped their theses on Serbia and Montenegro, two nations officially separated into two countries a week prior, after Montenegro voted for independence as the final step in the breakup of the former Socialist Federal Republic of Yugoslavia. FIFA forced them to play as one since that's how they had qualified, and that is how FIFA rolls.

There was a piece that Hemon wrote about the debut on the world stage of Argentine wunderkind Lionel Messi, who at that time was just eighteen years old. Though injured in the run-up to the tournament, Messi had to carry the crushing weight of Argentinian expectations that he could be the next Maradona and deliver a third world title on his slender shoulders, despite his injured thigh and early Beatles shaggy bowl cut. A year earlier the Barcelona prodigy had taken Argentina to victory in the FIFA World Youth Championship and was fast-tracked into his country's squad for Germany 2006. Argentina would ultimately be clipped by host Germany in the quarterfinal, and Messi was mystifyingly never even brought off the substitutes bench. Hemon effortlessly wove a profound Greek mythological comparison into his writing. The exact contours of the allusion were lost on me, but I remember reading it and marveling at the construct and quality of the knowledge and storytelling, doubting that I could ever think of anything so compelling or engaging.

Yet, on the second day of the tournament, I experienced *Revelation*. June 10, 2006, was the moment my life changed. First some context: ESPN had made laudable attempts to step up the breadth of their coverage, but the actual quality of it—the investment they had made in the detail of their production—was visible. Their lead commentator was Dave O'Brien, a baseball guy jammed into covering football. O'Brien admitted to anyone listening that he had only called eight soccer games before the tournament, and the way he sounded—it felt like that was also the sum total of games he had watched in his lifetime. Anyone who understood the rudimentary basics knew just how foreign they were to O'Brien. Alongside him sat Marcelo Balboa, a mustache- and mullet-sporting defender from the US 1994 World Cup team, bringing to the broadcast booth the same "tenacious effort over natural skill" ethic he had unfurled on the field.

Even before the tournament started, an online petition had been circulated by an English professor from Fort Wayne, Indiana, demanding they both be replaced. It racked up thousands of signatures, and O'Brien didn't help his cause amongst the soccer cognoscenti by saying in response, "There's kind of a petulant little clique of soccer fans. There's not many of them, but they're mean-spirited . . . and they're not really the audience we want to reach anyway." In fact, that was exactly the audience ESPN needed to capture, at least first and foremost.

So, forty-eight hours into the World Cup, I tuned in to watch England begin their assault on the title against Paraguay. The two teams emerged from the tunnel, and the cameras zoomed in and lingered upon England captain-turned-human-global-billboard vaguely visible from outer space David Beckham. Balboa chose that moment to drop this pearl of broadcasting wisdom: "The world's most famous footballer, Charlie Beckham takes the field." I then reflexively screamed at my television, "Good God, if only they had someone who knew what they were talking about covering this sport, football would grow in a heartbeat." My wife, who was reading some kind of romance novel on the couch alongside me, did not even look up, but instead muttered, "Why don't you do it, love." And it hit me in that moment, like Archimedes screaming "Eureka" in the bath, Sir Isaac Newton staring at a falling apple to discover universal gravitation, or Marty McFly figuring out how he could harness enough electricity to power a DeLorean time machine, that my god, she was right. Football should be my calling.

I had already noticed that the seeds of America's fascination with football had truly started to take root. This was the first foreign-held tournament where the energy it made—the dent it created—in the American sporting consciousness was palpable. Five billion viewers were projected to watch the tournament worldwide, and my fellow fans and I at the Kinsale Tavern were no longer a fringe minority. *Time Out* wrote a feature about how the cognoscenti had become clued up. Hipsters were spreading word about exactly which Brazilian barbecue spots in Brooklyn or Ghanaian stew joints in Queens were the prime places to experience the opening round. Finance bros in cubicle after cubicle across the city were getting hooked on the daily action, keeping up with the narrative on their Bloomberg monitors. *SportsCenter* wove the highlights into its crucial ecosystem, speaking about soccer not as some freak sideshow curiosity, but as if it truly believed its audience was following along.

That noise surrounding the tournament was amplified by the fact that this was the time when social media was in its infancy. Though still primitive, these platforms enabled a crackling sense of connectivity and conversation to bubble up around the game, one that transcended geographical borders and felt, for the moment, truly democratized. No one dismissed your opinion just because of where you were from, because they could no longer hear an American accent. If you tweeted an intelligently framed idea about a match, it could catch fire and go global. Audiences, truly niche audiences about just about anything, could be built around passions and storytelling.

Tapping into that passion, the first *New Republic* piece I elected to write was a short screed describing how Dave O'Brien's ignorance was not just an ear bleed in its own right, it was a threat to the very growth of soccer in the United States. I fired up my state-of-the-art Dell laptop, which weighed half a ton but never felt lighter than in that moment, as I swung it onto my knee and banged out my column, which culminated in a call to action—that my fellow-football loving readers call ESPN's customer service line and demand they do better with their soccer-commentating hires. The words flowed in a way they never had before. Within half an hour of my hitting send, the *New Republic* editor emailed back, telling me I had written a piece worthy of the home page. Upon seeing my byline for the first time, I could only have felt prouder if I had actually taken the field to play in the World Cup.

The piece hit a nerve. Funneled in by social media, it spawned a real debate about O'Brien's half-assed efforts and the extent to which they damaged the game. One reader wrote underneath that generations of terrible baseball commentators had never hurt the popularity of that sport. I wrote a second piece in response, attempting to explain that baseball was endemic to America's DNA, but soccer was a novel unknown to vast segments of the potential audience, begging for more nuanced and contextualized storytelling.

The notion of internet virality was still a new one, and to be clear the foment surrounding my writing was a mere blip by modern-Kardashian or Jake Paul–sized standards. But to be heard in this call-and-response fashion was to feel the kindling of a real footballing audience in my chosen homeland. One reader designed a graphic with O'Brien's face slashed by the diagonal of a red no-entry road sign, with the ESPN customer service number around the outside. That image was a tangible symbol of my sudden new readership. I wasted no time before mocking it up as a T-shirt, which I modeled, posting a slightly blurry photograph of myself, alongside a third story. After a mere ninety minutes, I received an email from someone at ESPN asking me in pleading fashion to stop giving out their phone number. Emboldened by the realization I must have encouraged enough people to ring to have become annoying, I sensed a modicum of leverage and asked for a meeting with whomever was responsible for their soccer coverage. Within twenty-four hours, I was patched in to a personality-less Canadian who opened by confiding that he knew nothing about soccer, covered the NHL and NASCAR beats but had been forced to take over World Cup coverage because no one else was available or willing. I asked him why they did not have smarter, more knowledgeable people providing accurate and compelling soccer content. In an exasperated tone he screamed down the phone, "There is NO ONE," before asking, "Can you do it?" He offered me the princely sum of $100 per article, to which I quickly agreed, and told me we would start after the World Cup. I put the phone down as exhilarated as if he had just offered to sell me untouched beachfront land to develop.

The rest of the World Cup was a total buzz. This was the tournament in which soccer's "New World Order" was expected to upset the traditional powers, and although Australia, Ghana, and even Switzerland had their moments, they fell away, leaving the usual heavyweights—France, Italy, Germany, and Brazil—to pound their way into the later rounds.

The United States had arrived, once again, with bravado and longed to be seen as one of those heavyweights. Coach Bruce Arena was still at the helm, appearing in Germany with his khakis overconfidently hiked up after the delirium of 2002's quarterfinal wind in his sails as the only American manager to lead the nation in two World Cups. The US swaggered into Germany having finished at the top of regional qualifying for the first time in seventy-two years, a feat capped by a stirring Dos a Cero victory over dread rivals Mexico. This was a battle-hardened squad with many of the players experiencing their third tournament, and Captain America, Claudio Reyna, his fourth.

The US had reached as high as 4th in the FIFA world rankings a few months before the World Cup. FIFA's rankings always demand cognitive dissonance. Every fan knows to take them with a pinch of salt. While they are not exactly totally made up, they did seem to be pulled out of a very corrupt organization's collective anus. However . . . *fourth place. Holy Crap.* It felt like we were about to make some noise for sure. US Soccer fans traditionally had two gears—the sky is falling, or "why even hold the tournament, just give us the trophy now," and the mood very much tilted toward the latter this round. Deep inside the US football fan bubble, the sense of surging confidence was off the charts as the team careened toward its first game moment of truth. Our squad had come so far from the days of stonewashed denim jerseys.

This US team had a small gaggle of accomplished players who were surging in the best leagues in the world. Clint Dempsey was the one I loved to watch the most. A gunslinging American original, he had learned the intricacies of the game as a kid on dirt fields in the Latino men's leagues of Nacogdoches, Texas, in which elbows to the face were as common as inch-perfect passes. He oozed the tenacity required to emerge from that crucible intact. He was a player who seemed fueled by fury, pounding his chest and letting his eyes bulge wildly every time he scored. Clint once broke his own club captain's tooth in a fistfight. He broke his own jaw and played with it wired shut. He broke the scoring record for Americans in the Premier League playing for Fulham. He even found a moment to drop a rap video, "Don't Tread," ahead of the World Cup, featuring a pair of Texan rappers—the late great Big Hawk and

XO. I watched the video on repeat in the run-up to kickoff, I loved it so much. The opening lines, "In the beginning, we were those kids, That played on the dirt fields, But with determination, We came from the bottom, And rose to the top," appeared to capture the ferocious spirit of the entire American team.

Unfortunately, the draw was unkind. The United States found themselves thrust into the dreaded Group of Death alongside number 2-ranked Czech Republic, number 12 Italy, and Ghana, one of the most potent teams in Africa. The American media roared with unified faith ahead of the first game against the Czechs in Gelsenkirchen. I happened to be in Lake Placid for a wedding, and in a gracious move the bride and groom changed the time of the ceremony to ensure they were married by kickoff—a healthy sign for the rise of football in America if you were looking for one, and I was drawing strength from every little detail. The game ran on a screen during the reception. The wedding planner was so proud of the perfection she had choreographed events to the kickoff timing. The smug smile on her face was gone just five minutes into the game. That is as long as it took for colossal Czech striker Jan Koller to rise like a giant sequoia towering over shrubs and head the ball violently into the American goal. A bewildered United States instantly folded, managing just three shots on goal and falling to a 3–0 defeat. The wedding DJ was told to "get this party started" before the first half had even ended. I sat dumbstruck at my table alone, stunned that this US team looked like a World Cup newcomer all over again.

Bruce Arena proceeded to blame everyone apart from himself for the rout, calling out his best player, Landon Donovan, for his lack of fight. The truth was the team still had everything to play for as they faced Italy in the second game. A clash that coincided with my wife Vanessa's thirtieth birthday, which we had elected to celebrate by returning to Washington, DC, for a romantic revisiting of many of our original haunts. She spent the month before the trip building a list of the top ten places she considered "must-visit," including the bar where we first met and the bridge where we first kissed. Planet Fred, the dingy football bar where I had watched countless Premier League games with that grimy crew of English expats, did not make the list. But God bless her generosity. Come gameday, she agreed to accompany me and watch by my side.

We rolled up to the bar half an hour before kickoff and, to my astonishment, found a line snaking around the block and back down N Street. It was a blazingly hot DC summer day, and Vanessa was not best pleased at the idea of lining up in the full glare of the white-hot sun. But as we lathered ourselves in sunscreen while taking our place in the queue, I was absolutely ecstatic. This thronging crowd would not have been bigger nor more electric if the Beatles had reformed and announced they were playing a secret gig in the bar. I was utterly gobsmacked at the sight and sweaty smell: Americans, lining up to watch a soccer match in my lifetime. These were my people. This was the living, breathing football audience to which I had committed my life.

The United States faced an Italy team who were almost Italian to an offensively cliched degree. A blur of slicked back long hair and thin black headbands. Legends abounded: Gianluigi Buffon in goal; Fabio Cannavaro and Alessandro Nesta in defense; Andrea Pirlo and Francesco Totti pulling the strings. They opened the scoring in the 22nd minute. Andrea Pirlo was the Donatello of free kicks and Alberto Gilardino dove to head the ball in, then celebrated by kneeling and playing an imaginary violin. The moment was crushingly deflating but that also posed the question in my mind—how would *you* celebrate if you had the eyes of the world on you after scoring in the World Cup, knowing children would instantly be copycatting your theatrics in schoolyards all over the planet?

I pondered potential poses for just five minutes, until the United States fought their way back into the game via a Cristian Zaccardo own goal. This is always an odd feeling to witness. The opposing players, all too familiar with the agony of that sporting act of self-immolation themselves, never know quite how to celebrate. As American fans there was also the frustration that our boys could not even score goals that counted for them.

The game deteriorated into a bare-knuckle battle. The Italian slab of midfield marble, Daniele De Rossi, elbowed Brian McBride in the head, leaving the Midwesterner with blood pouring down his nose and face. This gave the United States a fleeting man advantage but if Italy had a red, our impulse to show we are number one demonstrated itself in the worst possible way, as we then earned two and had to kill off much of the second half with nine men, which they just about did to earn their first-ever point in a European World Cup after eight straight losses. But a victory in the next game was needed to hold on.

The bar area inside Planet Fred was a dispirited place at the final whistle. There was a sense of an opportunity frittered away because of our own ill-discipline. "This team is alive," Kasey Keller said unconvincingly in his postgame interview, sounding less like a footballer and more like Dr. Frankenstein talking about his monster. Despite the disappointment, I felt strangely ebullient. My focus was on the big picture. The crowd. The number of jerseys being worn. The sense of commitment—

and the extent of the disappointment—were all the positive indicators in my mind.

In a must-win game, the US faced the Black Stars of Ghana, who were an unknown quantity to most American fans before the match. Ghana had brought the youngest roster to this, their first World Cup appearance. And they utterly battered us. Ghana opened the scoring early, the legendary Claudio Reyna dallied on the ball, was dispossessed, and Haminu Draman celebrated his resulting goal by kneeling and putting his forehead to the turf. Reyna was substituted out and retired the next day. Clint Dempsey made his World Cup debut and did what he always did, took his shot, equalizing with a delicious volley with the outside of his boot. God bless Clint, who always lived out Bruce Arena's famous quote, "He tries shit." Yet Ghana was unfazed, responding almost immediately via a penalty. The United States had run out of energy and hope.

It would have all felt so immensely deflating if it was not for two things. The first was that it felt like this World Cup was a breakthrough moment, culturally. Although the United States campaign had been a brutal reality check, television ratings continued to rise as the competition progressed, an impressive sign that the game was at last finding a strong audience in the States. The ratings news reinforced my anecdotal bar-based evidence that the audience for the game was surging. The ratings for the final far outstripped the audience for the NBA Finals. A number that was seen by brands as a tipping point to begin investing in the sport and make this the moment soccer flipped over to being economically viable in the United States. Much of it thanks to Dave O'Brien. Connected to all of that was my own sense of personal breakthrough. ESPN followed up on their word and gave me a book deal to write about the history of football. I immediately immersed myself in the project by hitting eBay hard to reclaim the footballing ephemera that defined my childhood: the 1978 Top Trumps cards, the 1982 Panini World Cup sticker book, and the England World Cup vinyl that had acted like fairytale breadcrumbs marking the path through the magical forest of my own sporting fandom. As I held these items in my hands again, I imagined writing a book that could enable American readers to develop the same emotional connection to the game that I had developed in my life.

With the United States out, the one personal connection left for me was to watch England disappoint an overexpectant fanbase, and destroy the sanity of their manager, in that now all-too-familiar tournament trope. The entire nation was on broken metatarsal watch once again, this time for twenty-year-old marvel Wayne Rooney, who had announced himself as a world-class prodigy, instantly establishing himself as the team's focal point. His arrival had been explosive, bursting onto the global scene as a snarling ball of aggression, impossible to ignore. The media quizzed the Liverpudlian on where he watched the previous World Cup as a sixteen-year-old unknown. "Just at me mate's," he said, clearly not able to remember, "or 'round my gran's or in the pub."

Despite question marks around Rooney's fitness, the English players arrived with a tabloid-headline-fueled bluster. Star striker Michael Owen unwisely promised England was the "best team in the tournament, player for player." Defender Rio Ferdinand talked in confident cliches about how it was "time England delivered the goods to lift the cup." I was now wise to the vicious British cycle of overconfidence, underperforming, and self-loathing. Indeed, by this point, the thrill of watching England was similar to rubbernecking. As far as I was concerned, they could not have been more doomed if the squad contained reckless Icarus himself and headed straight toward the sun.

The team had been sequestered in an isolated castle-turned-hotel in the spa town of Baden-Baden in the Black Forest. The remote sequestered setting had an unforeseen knock-on effect. Nature abhors a vacuum, as do the tabloid paparazzi. As the players were shielded from the media, the journalists turned their attention to a juicier subject. Their wives and girlfriends, or WAGs, who reveled in the attention, proceeding to shop, champagne-swill, and table dance their way onto the front pages in their Prada heels, skin-tight jeans, and fake tans. The competition between the girls led to fissures within the England camp itself, proving to be fuel for the fire burning alongside their inevitable march to failure.

Baden-Baden became a circus in which the actual football was secondary to the main event: WAG Carnage. Inspired by their spiritual leader, Victoria Beckham, these designer proto-influencers drank, shopped, and partied with a ferocity far more aggressive than their men on the field. Laying siege to the town's boutiques, the media breathlessly covered every detail as five of the WAGs dropped $75,000 in less than an hour. They then celebrated their spree by knocking back $6,000 worth of champagne and engaging in a drunken sing-along till 4 a.m. at one of Baden-Baden's toniest nightclubs. When a group of German men began chanting that Germany would win the World Cup, Elen Rives, the model girlfriend of Chelsea star Frank Lampard, wittily retorted, "F*** off and leave us alone."

I flew back to England in time for the quarterfinal clash with Portugal, which we watched at my aunt's home in Manchester. The drive to Manchester was memorable for the sheer number of English flags being flown behind every vehicle. The cross of

St. George appeared on bedsheets draped from windows and over front doors of homes. The level of national pride and flag waving was still an uncharacteristic and new tradition. When I was a kid, it was rare to see such an expression, particularly in Liverpool, which always felt more like an independent republic rather than part of the bigger whole. The flags in Manchester, and alas all over, were a sign of just how central football's grip had become on the culture of my birth nation as opposed to its former status as a working-class pursuit and the purview of hooligans.

The day was also marked by the fact it took place on a rare hot summer afternoon. The kind British homes are not built for because air-conditioning is not a thing. The English just open all their windows in the summer, which is utterly ineffective. A dead wind meant a thick hot blanket of air just hung heavy in the living room as we gathered round the television, both excited for the football but irritated by the heat in equal measure. My dad, brother, and uncle sat jammed on my aunt's finest couch, trying desperately not to brush against each other accidentally with their sweaty limbs. Perspiring, and beer groggy, we watched England self-destruct. In the 62nd minute, Wayne Rooney, who had been goaded by wily veteran Portuguese Ricardo Carvalho throughout the game, lost his cool and stamped on the prone defender's family jewels. We knew the second he did it that a red card was incoming and all was lost. "For forty years I have watched this shite," my father, who so rarely swore, screamed in exasperation. While Rooney was being sent off, his Manchester United teammate Cristiano Ronaldo was caught on camera winking at the Portuguese bench, suggesting to the world that baiting Rooney had been an official part of the country's game plan.

England held on gamely with ten men, but their perseverance only prolonged the pain. They lost a penalty shoot-out when Portuguese goalkeeper Ricardo became the first man to save three penalty kicks. As England's Jamie Carragher blew the final shot, my attention moved from the loss, for which I, as an American fan, felt so little, and more to my family, who sat in sweaty sadness bordering on mourning. I looked at their naivete with a sense of astonishment. In contrast to the American fan base, who practiced self-deception based on innocence and an inflated sense of self-belief, the English had a multi-generational experience of collective trauma to draw upon, which should have acted as a guide. The only thing shocking about the team's exit was the extent to which any of this English self-destruction still took them by surprise. It was as if I were witnessing a form of national mass delusion. The English Brits truly believed that because the Premier League was the richest and most glamorous in the world, victory should result as some kind of transitive property. In truth, there was not a single moment on the field that suggested England were true challengers in the World Cup, and they had not been for decades. Each of their performances were overshadowed by the WAGs soap opera that surrounded them. As a capper, no fewer than three members of the 2006 squad quickly pumped out tell-all books about their tournament as soon as the team were eliminated. Controversial midfielder Joey Barton went so far as to lampoon the culture of English football at the time as "I played like shit, here's my book."

In contrast to Beckham's 1998 Red Card, the English media did not vilify Wayne Rooney. Instead, they focused their anger on Ronaldo for his treachery against a clubmate. Portugal proceeded to become the tournament heels and were booed by fans from that point on. They faced France in the semifinal, a team who had been a delightful surprise that year. They were much maligned at the outset for their advanced average age, and their own fans were slow to warm to them as they progressed. But the country became believers once Zidane slotted home the only goal of the semifinal against the Portuguese from the penalty spot, triggering a frenzied night of national celebration in which five people were reportedly killed. A defeated Ronaldo returned to Manchester United with Rooney. Former English legend Alan Shearer told a live British viewing public with absolute gravitas that "Wayne Rooney should go back to the United training ground and 'stick one' on Ronaldo." Yes, he was suggesting that Rooney knock his teammate out.

All four semifinalists were European. The Germans faced that Italian team who had struggled to cope with the United States earlier in the tournament. In reality, the team had arrived in Germany beleaguered after a match-fixing scandal had rocked their domestic league and proceeded to demonstrate that they are never more dangerous than when they are playing to save face. The Germans had become the darlings of their own party, led by their coach and Motivations-Meister Jürgen Klinsmann, their former striking hero who now patrolled the sidelines clad head-to-toe in Hugo Boss. Having lived largely in self-imposed exile in California since 1998, Klinsmann had been a controversial selection, but the physical and mental training techniques he brought with him from American sports scientists were perceived to equip the squad with the positivity and pluck that he now—more management guru than soccer manager—demanded.

As an Englishman, it was remarkable to witness the impact

of this team in this moment. Football was all about patriotic fandom. But despite their past successes, German fans had avoided ostentatious signs of support for two quite massive and obvious historical reasons—the first and second World Wars. Their team's 2006 journey transformed all that. A million German fans filled Berlin's fan park talking about "ultimate victory" and chanting "Berlin, Berlin, wir fahren nach Berlin." (We're going to Berlin.) Even though the plucky Germans lost 2-0 when Italy scored late goals in the 119th and 120th minutes the national mood did not change. The players were doubled over in agony and tears, but Germany underwent a national catharsis, ignited by, but far transcending, football. It was permissible to be a fan again.

I watched the final between Italy and France alone. We were due to go to *another* wedding, friends of my wife's family who had elected to be married on a boat departing Manhattan's South Street Seaport in the late afternoon. I remember trying to explain to my wife how selfish it was to choose to be married on World Cup final day, but my arguments were drowned out by her hairdryer as she prepped and primped in our bedroom. I forgot about the injustice of it all as the game kicked off, revealing itself to become the stuff of legend. Soccer as reimagined by Vince McMahon.

Zinedine Zidane dominated the game as both hero and villain. The French icon had been plagued by injuries and announced that he would retire from the sport at the tournament's end. He then proceeded, at age thirty-four, to prove that time had eroded few of his skills by dragging his team on an unlikely and spectacular run into the final. His performances were imperious as the aging team eliminated first Spain and then Brazil, a game in which Zizou played with such guile and mastery that it was as if he were the only real Brazilian on the field.

In the final, Zidane opened the scoring in the 7th minute, with a cheeky chip of a penalty kick. That penalty had been conceded by Italian defender Marco Materazzi, who immediately redeemed himself by heading home a corner kick twelve minutes later. This game was so open, it was riveting to witness, yet somehow it stayed 1–1. During the break, my wife screamed at me from the bedroom, reminding me to get dressed for the wedding. Forgoing a shower, I changed into a dinner jacket while standing inches away from the action pulsating on the television screen in front of me. I proceeded to watch, numb with shock, as a moment of madness occurred. Zidane and Materazzi clashed off the ball. Zidane initially walked away, then took one step forward, lowered his handsome, bald head, and drove it with full force into the Italian's midriff, knocking him over. The referee brandished a red card. The violence of this attack was especially shocking in a sport that is renowned for simulated injuries and melodramatic overreactions.

Zidane trooped off the field in disgrace, head down, a defeated gladiator, past the World Cup trophy pitch side without so much as a sideways glance. I watched on in agony. In 1998, we saw Zizou use a World Cup final to unify a fractured nation. Now, just eight years later, he had used one to shatter its collective heart, whilst simultaneously delivering ESPN's *SportsCenter* with its all-time favorite soccer clip. This was his last action as a professional footballer before he slunk off into retirement with ignominy, leaving the world to decipher the complicated legacy of a man who had roamed the field and dominated play with such furious intensity that, at times, he appeared to be a demigod. Now, he had never seemed more mortal. A man like the rest of us, living while a cartoon angel and devil argued on his shoulders.

The aftershocks of Zidane's dismissal meant I must have buttoned up the front of my shirt with muscle memory. As the game was about to go to penalties, my wife said sharply, "Roger, we have to go." Remember, she rarely calls me by my full name. It is reserved for our rare arguments and moments of extreme stress, and its utilization is akin to an emotional alarm bell. "Babe," I said. "It is the World Cup final . . . the wedding will have to wait." "Roger," she said, "the wedding is on a *boat*. If we don't leave now, it will have left the dock without us on board."

Retrospectively, I realize this moment must rank as the greatest testament of my love for my wife. Dumbstruck, I let her click off the television broadcast of the 2006 World Cup final and followed her, with seething obedience, out of the apartment and into the street. Being yanked away from the World Cup in a pre-smart phone era was emotionally devastating. Akin to a spaceman being cut off from the air supply mid-moon walk. I followed my wife in body, yet not in mind. By the time we had reached South Ferry and boarded the wedding boat, I was in a very, very dark place. A mood worsened when I heard the Italians ultimately won on penalties. Surrounded by Americans who were giddily celebrating the impending nuptials and seemingly unbothered we had all missed one of the most psychologically fascinating culminations the World Cup had ever seen sent me into a spiral of doom. I attacked the bar with the same fury Zidane had propelled his cranium into Materazzi's chest and vented by skulking around the periphery of the celebration, scowling and avoiding human contact.

It was at the bar that I encountered a man whose countenance was different to all the others. Indeed, his curt dismissiveness and body language seemed to indicate he had no interest in being on a wedding boat on the Hudson River, which had the effect of making me feel like I was looking in the mirror. As he ordered a glass of Malbec, I heard his English accent. Though it was the plummy tone of a Southerner, I still warmed to his general disregard for all those who surrounded him.

"Are you furious not to be watching the World Cup final?" I ventured.

"Furious enough to have contemplated sinking this boat," he replied.

"I'm Rog," I said, extending my hand.

"Michael Davies," he replied.

And this is how I met Davo. The man with whom I would begin my podcasting career. We sat there all night, talking about the tournament, England's self-immolation, my dreams of American glory, and the German moral victory as if we had known each other our whole lives. Football can do that. Make instant connections that feel profound. When the boat docked back on dry land around midnight, we shook hands and vowed to cover the next World Cup together. We had no idea in the moment how much that promise would transform our futures, just as the happy couple had no idea their marriage was doomed and would end in divorce. Yet, the moral of the story is pretty obvious: If you are ever forced to leave a World Cup final to witness a wedding you could not give two craps about but which happens to be taking place on a boat, make every opportunity to drag yourself up that gangplank before the vessel departs. It might just change your life.

Chapter 9

2010 World Cup, South Africa

I WAS SEATED behind a microphone in a recording studio facing a man I had met at a bar on a boat at a wedding almost four years earlier, to the day. The 2010 World Cup was just two days old. A producer pushed a button to patch a phone call straight into our headphones. Liam Neeson's singular Irish brogue boomed into our ears. This was only my second interview of any kind. I clumsily attempted to make small talk about the actor's football fandom. I then nervously asked him what compelled him to play Hannibal in the new movie reboot of *The A-Team*. "Was it the script that just spoke to you?" I ventured gamely, attempting to summon the cliched rhythms of celebrity interviews I had seen in such respected outlets as *Entertainment Tonight*. "It was money, you idiot," the actor boomed dismissively in reply.

How did this surreal reality become my life? That is the story of the 2010 World Cup.

Every journey begins with a first step. My plunge into football cognoscenti started with a plan to establish myself as a writer for ESPN's website. The sad Canadian hockey editor glumly gave me a year-round offer to join their team, which, in my excitement, I misread. I believed the contract offered me $250 an hour, to which my wife shrugged when I broke the news to her. "That's not terrible," she said. "It's what entry level lawyers are paid in New York City." I proudly called ESPN to accept the offer of the aforementioned "two hundred and fifty dollars an hour" only for the editor to crush my soul by responding, "Sorry guy, I don't know where you got that from. We don't pay two hundred and fifty dollars an hour. We pay two fifty for *every finished article*." For context, a finished article took me roughly four days to write. My hasty attempts to negotiate were instantly and curtly rebuffed. There would be no negotiation. "You either accept the offer, or we will just move on to someone else," I was told with menace. "We actually don't care about the words," the editor admitted. "We just care about the advertisements we sell and jam around your writing." So humbled, I signed on.

By that point, I had become all too familiar with this style of humiliating outcome as I hurtled breathlessly along in my one-man crusade to expand the vacuum that was American football coverage after the 2006 World Cup. It felt like everyone in the media had moved to the point where they knew they wanted, and needed, football coverage, but no outlet had anything resembling the budget to pay for it. I was left with no choice but to leap in and hustle, praying I could patch together a gaggle of projects that would enable me to eke out a living.

I produced a documentary film about an Arab football team that became cup champions of Israel, winning the right to represent the nation on the European stage. That doc won a prize at the Tribeca Film Festival but made exactly zero dollars. I began to craft a book on the history of football for the ESPN publishing imprint. It was rough going. I had been paired with an old magazine crony who had seemingly leveraged both the fact he watched Arsenal on a weekly basis and his connections in the publishing industry to position himself as a football savant. I quickly learned there were two challenges with this partnership. My cowriter knew little about international football and struggled with writer's block. Our initial collaboration revolved around me doing the writing and him adding his name, which felt like playing football with a teammate who kept tapping in goals that were already going into the net. Our relationship was friction-filled.

None of these ventures were close to earners. As giddy as I was for the opportunity to master new skills by attaching myself to projects in a multitude of media, I always dreaded the moment I had to come back home and break the news to my wife, then pregnant with our fourth child, of exactly how little income they would bring. These conversations developed their own rhythm. I would open by breathlessly telling her about some new documentary I had been asked to be interviewed for, or a new book for which I had been invited to write an introduction, and she would excitedly and logically inquire as to how much it paid. That practical question always felt like a punch straight to the solar plexus. Instead of telling her, "Nothing," I would use the phrase, "It's a loss leader." And God bless Vanessa, she would do her best to feign enthusiasm as she hugged me, whispering, "Great. Another loss leader."

Attempting to find a way to make a living in football felt akin to being forced to sprint breathlessly through a maze wearing a blindfold. Feeling the financial pressure of three kids, with one on the way, and little sense of how I was going to support them in the long term was quite the motivator. I worked so hard, maniacally trying to meet anyone and everyone with even a loose connection to the sport. Most were not fertile encounters. The most debilitating was a night spent with an Oscar-winning documentary producer from England, who had made a pair of critically acclaimed football movies. He asked me to meet for dinner at Raoul's, the iconic bistro in SoHo. On my way downtown, I had visions of a meeting of minds with a pathfinding kindred spirit who had also glimpsed the possibility of the future of the game in the United States and would undoubtedly want to leap into business with me. When I set out my thesis over an enormous steak that his partner had ordered, he stopped me quickly to laugh at the idea football would ever be a sustainable business in the United States. "There will never be a way to make a living just covering football over here," he managed to spit out between steak-filled mouth guffaws. "Americans will never care about the sport *that* much." I then got stuck with the bill and rode the late-night subway back uptown in a stupor. This was a man who had covered football here to great acclaim. If he was dismissing the future of the sport, what chance was there for me to find a path to follow? I felt like a climber reaching for a handhold drilled into a mountainside, only for it to come loose in my grip, sending me into freefall.

I checked in with Michael Davies sporadically, dropping into his offices over in the no-man's-land west of SoHo. Michael had built his business on the back of a life-changing decision to import the British quiz sensation *Who Wants to Be a Millionaire?* to the United States. His studio was a small setup that was a buzz of energy when his anchor show, *Watch What Happens Live*, was filming, but strangely silent on down days. Michael had a charming habit of telling me how busy he was when I arrived and then proceeding to talk for hours. We chatted about the same things with a hearty passion: football, England, and English culture, flipping among the three in profoundly personal ways. Michael loved to swap stories about the sacred fragments of the English experience baked into our youths—the books we read, the '80s music that shaped us (mostly Wham! and the Human League), and the television shows.

These conversations were exhilarating, and we both pursued them with the thrill of characters in a fairytale finding breadcrumbs leading them along a trail through an enchanted forest. By the time I would leave Michael's office, it was inevitably dark outside, and I would stagger into the near empty streets around his office in an almost trance state. Michael and I were so different as human beings. He was from the toney South of England; I was from the hardened postindustrial North. He supported Chelsea, a super team owned by an oligarch; I supported humble Everton, owned by a local supporter who struggled to find enough money to keep the lights on. And let's face it, Michael had the trappings of success, and I was still jumping over the turnstile to ride the subway downtown to meet him. Yet, the cultural touchpoints of our lives made it feel like we had grown up the best of friends, willing to share the most profound stories about the trauma and pressure of seventh grade school discos, early, innocent dreams of America forged by watching *Hart to Hart* and *Diff'rent Strokes*, and above all, football heroes like Brian Robson, Gary Lineker, and Paul Gascoigne that had lain dormant inside both of us during our lives in the United States because no one else shared the same memories.

The 2010 World Cup now charged toward us. The ESPN book I had spent three years writing was slated to come out on the eve of the tournament. Darkness struck shortly after I finished the first draft. My publisher broke the news via a short, cruel email informing me that I would be taking a backseat in promoting the book. A brutal and blindsiding act, quickly followed up with a phone call, in which I was told, "I will make it my job to ensure no one hires you in any media job for any outlet in any capacity. That will be my occupation from this day on. It will also be my hobby." I was a grown man, but once we hung up, I was left quivering, and cold with shock. I had worked so bloody hard and had hustled so much to research and write that book, but in a single phone call, I felt I had been TKO'd by a bully who had effectively ended my career.

I could not sleep that night. I also could not find the right words to break this ruinous development to my wife, fearing for the baby when she learned her husband was now effectively unemployed and unemployable. Life is not like a Hollywood movie, apart from on those rare occasions when it very much is. Suddenly, mine became akin to the finale to one of the *Godfather* trilogy. You are probably familiar with the highly choreographed scenes in which every life-threatening enemy is murdered in a coordinated coda, played out against pulsating opera music; one foe is garroted, another stabbed in the heart, and yet another shot from close range in a drive-by. That is almost exactly what happened to me next but without the actual assassinations.

The very next day, ESPN announced an enormous company-wide downsizing, beginning with the firing of a multitude of heavily salaried, deadwood senior staff. Chief amongst them—all of my coauthor's allies whose involvement had tormented me sadistically for months. The leverage they had savored in putting a foot on my throat was removed in an instant. I felt an overwhelming sense of reprieve, like a prisoner released from death row or Jeff Bridges in *Fearless*. The plane had crashed, but somehow, I was free to walk away from the wreckage with all my limbs intact.

As Churchill once said, "There is nothing more exhilarating than to be shot at with no result." So liberated, I drove straight up to Bristol, Connecticut, with Michael Davies to meet with John Skipper, the tall, gaunt, charming North Carolinian who was then head of content for ESPN. Skipper welcomed us into his large, nearly barren office. On the wall was one tiny, framed memento. I walked up to stare at it before sitting down and was delighted to discover it was a 2006 World Cup final ticket. "I'm a soccer guy," Skipper said as he caught me gawking. I was honestly trying to work out if this was some slick scheme, and his assistant spent the entire day constantly replacing the frame to match it with the exact interests of guest after guest—a World Series ticket when Peter Gammons dropped by, or a rare Super Bowl one for Al Michaels. Whatever the case, I was thrilled. My blood was pumping. "I believe soccer is going to be the sport of the future," Skipper said, pointing at his ticket. "Sport of the future . . . as it has been since 1972," I joked in return. The rest of the meeting was a blur of football enthusiasm and a meeting of the minds. Skipper excitedly described a new technology that I was vaguely familiar with. "There's this new thing called podcasts," he said. "Let's try this thing out. We will give you and Michael one for the World Cup. Podcast and write for us every single day. Knock yourselves out."

I honestly had no real idea of what we had just signed up for but my excitement levels were "just won the Mega Millions" high. This had been some reversal of fortune. One minute, I felt that the powers that be at ESPN were about to treat me like Joe Pesci at the end of *Goodfellas*. The next I had my own podcast, even though I had no real understanding of what that word actually meant. I soon learned that at ESPN, when Skipper wanted something done, it happened. Yet I also quickly discovered that the underlings who the president passed you down to, did not always share his enthusiasm. We were introduced to the network's new podcasting head, and he asked us what we wanted to call our show. Feeling empowered and a little ditzy I sent back the suggestion "The Martin Tyler Experience," choosing a title that paid homage to Tyler, England's most famous football commentator whom ESPN had just signed at some cost to be the face of their World Cup broadcast. We promptly received a short email back informing us our show would be called *Off the Ball*. Confused, I fired back that there were already roughly 500+ soccer blogs, websites, and at least two dozen podcasts by that name, only to receive a one-line email back saying, "I don't give a f**k. that is what you are called." Decision made then.

The next day we were sent an opening sting, which would act as the show's theme song. It sounded like it had been ripped from Akron's number 3-rated morning drive local radio show in the 1980s. A deep thirty cigarettes a day and two brandies a night voice bellowed "Off the Ball. . . . With Michael Davies and Roger Bennett," as crazy sound effects blipped and exploded aggressively in the background. Even though the man mispronounced Michael's last name, I loved it. Yes, it was cheesy, but it was all ours. I sat up all night, on the eve of the tournament, playing the sting over and over, until it had etched its soundwaves onto the surface of my inner ear.

The sense of adventure that gripped my World Cup experience that year was a tiny echo of the tournament itself, which in a bold gamble had been given to South Africa, a first for the continent. Africa was seen as a brave new world for football to celebrate. Just sixteen years after apartheid, this was perceived as an audacious and profoundly symbolic move by FIFA, who turned their brightest spotlight on Nelson Mandela's newly democratic nation with its tortured history and global sports boycotts of the recent past. There was proud talk of nation building, a $75 billion investment in highway and airport infrastructure, and the creation of 415,000 jobs. Football was positioned as the ultimate healer for a nation in which rich white Afrikaners traditionally played rugby, with FIFA president Sepp Blatter making the intrepid proclamation, "We are giving hope to the world that perhaps through football we can become better human beings."

Below the talk and gestures, there was an agonizing fear. The mindboggling statistics of annual murders, car jackings, and sexual assaults in South Africa were bandied round by the media more than the qualifying teams' football results. There were repeated concerns that the organizers (who were later alleged to have won the World Cup bid corruptly) were incapable of organizing the basics of security and transport. Stories broke alleging there would not be enough electricity on the country's grid to support basic tournament broadcasting. Rumors flew that, in the year running up to kickoff, FIFA had bailed on their plans and was poised to take its crown jewel elsewhere.

And yet, on June 11, the tournament began. Host South Africa welcomed Mexico in Soccer City stadium in their largest city, Johannesburg. Michael and I went with a film crew dispatched by ESPN to watch the opening ceremony at a South African restaurant in deepest Brooklyn. It was absolutely jampacked. It felt like every South African in New York State had come together to witness this moment and were now surrounded by everyone else, crushed onto the street outside, who wanted to watch South Africans watch history being made. The South Africans themselves were in full force, dressed in the yellow of their national team jersey; some proudly wore traditional Zulu dress. I am a cynical human being. FIFA's long-running reputation for greed, self-interest, and corruption made it easy to feel suspicious of every one of their motives, but when FIFA president Sepp Blatter opened the tournament, after a deft performance by the iconic jazz trumpeter Hugh Masekela, even I was overwhelmed by the power of the moment. Standing at the back of the restaurant, surrounded by South African diaspora in Brooklyn, it was impossible not to feel the welling of pride. Some of my fellow viewers started sobbing; others just hugged silently. Then a giant man at the back near the door put what looked like a novelty plastic kid's trumpet to his mouth and let out a single-note screech that sounded like a hive of tormented bees had just been let loose in the restaurant, and the place exploded in a wall of noise.

The game was ecstasy. In truth, every South African was afraid their team would humiliate themselves on the world stage. After the pulsating thrill of the opening ceremony, once the match kicked off, a sense of fretfulness and anxiety kicked in, sitting heavily in the room, but all of that was lanced in the 55th minute. A tiny attacker, Siphiwe Tshabalala, stepped up and thrashed the ball with the perfect combination of masterful technique and ebullient mischief, turning it into a flaming comet that left his boot and hurtled, roaring, into the back of the Mexican net.

"Goal for all of Africa," screamed the commentator with a truly poetic flair.

Tshabalala and his teammates assembled in the corner and executed the kind of spontaneous line dance I had previously only seen amidst the dry ice of a bar mitzvah disco. Everyone in the crowded bar instantly mimicked it, as if it were some kind of traditional set of moves with which they were intimately familiar, rather than a moment of World Cup–inspired improvisation. The mood in the room was near religious. The only time I had experienced anything like it was a night spent in London when the Berlin Wall came down, during which I watched Germans dance together in front of their embassy. It was magical, a fusing of national pride and history. The fact that Rafa Márquez equalized for the Mexicans with only eleven minutes remaining was almost beside the point. Tshabalala had scored. Soccer City had danced. And South Africa had given the world a thunderbolt, exclamation-point moment of national pride.

Michael and I charged back to SoHo to broadcast with a sense of national mission. As we plugged in our microphones, excitement levels remained Brooklyn-bar high. I did not know exactly what I was going to say. I had a few notes scribbled in the bar on a beer- and sweat-soaked piece of paper. We also had no idea who would listen to any of it anyway. Podcasting sounded as flimsy a communication device as the empty cans we tied together with string as kids. None of that mattered. As the *Off the Ball* sting fired up in live-recording reality for the first time, I was buzzing at levels known only to Siphiwe Tshabalala.

Michael opened the show, and we riffed backward and forward on our Brooklyn experience. We cut to a guest. Somehow, we had managed to book Wolfgang Puck as our guinea pig. It did not matter what we asked him; he did not listen. Chef Puck was energized, just like we were, and he kept talking about sharing this memory with his kids, and their excitement, in between persistent plugs for a new concept restaurant I did not quite understand that he was opening somewhere in California. It was a terrible interview, but for vibes, it could not be beat. And about forty minutes later, we were finished. Show Number One was in the books. We sat back in our seats for a moment and stared at each other in silence, in a semi-state of shock over what we had just accomplished. Then, once our producers departed to send it off into the world via the podosphere, I was hit by a wave of exhaustion that was so overpowering, I lay down on the floor under the recording table and went right to sleep.

I did not know it then, but that was the moment football truly became my life. That first podcast sent out over ESPN's platform only had about twenty thousand listeners. But it was who they were that changed everything. They were an audience of Americans for whom we had just raised a footballing freak flag, and they flocked to us, sending in ideas and insights, coming together and communing with us and each other. The conversation we had, where we talked about the football, the tactics, the players, but also reveled in sidelines, like the market cap of oversized comedy sunglasses in South Africa, which seemed to be enormous, the players who were attempting to cover impending baldness in different head sectors, or wondering why the Danes had such a banging official World Cup song. Somehow, that conversation, about this Danish song recorded by a band named Nephew, made its way to Aarhus, because the very next morning, I woke up to an email from Nephew's lead singer volunteering to come on and explain to America what was distinctly Danish about the slapping tune, "The Danish Way to Rock."

Nephew's lead singer did indeed join us in a cameo on episode 2, alongside that truly terrible interview with Liam Neeson, the low of which occurred when I attempted to rib him for switching allegiances in the club he supported from Manchester United to archrivals Liverpool. "How on earth did that happen?" I said with a derisory laugh, "You can't change teams." Liam Neeson then proceeded to tell a long and emotionally detailed story involving his wife's recent traumatic death from a skiing accident, attending a Liverpool game, and having the crowd serenade his wife's memory, which made him switch allegiance on the spot. A story so painful and harrowing, I did not know how to follow it up, and so just let an eternity of radio silence fill the air before thanking him for coming on and letting him exit. I was racked with guilt that I had just thrown my second-ever guest into a doom spiral of agonizing memory.

It did not matter. We had no idea how to edit our shows back then, so we put everything out, blemishes and all, and our audience seemed to love it. The smart cohesive parts *and* the behind-the-scenes cockups. I laughingly called the show "Suboptimal Radio" and that tagline stuck. The rough edges infused the podcast with a maker-feel, which only encouraged listener engagement via email and via social media. This was the World Cup in which Twitter truly exploded, the players were all experimenting with the platform in real time, and we thrived because of the sheer amount of ridiculous content we were suddenly privy to. There were others who were smarter at breaking down the tactical approach of the Argentinian side, but few who could beat our analysis of Brazilian legend Kaká tweeting: "@Realkaka: nothing to do? Pray. Something to do? Pray . . . Pray all the time!!" Almost simultaneously, third-string US striker Edson Buddle barked, "@edsonbuddle: The shop on my website is opening soon! Create a design for a shirt that I like and win a prize. Send designs to Shirt@EdsonBuddle.com."

These Twitter conversations added to the fantastical nature of our episodes from the very beginning. A surrealness reinforced by the fact that pretty much every famous person in the entertainment or sporting realms in America who loved soccer, but had never had an outlet in the United States, suddenly lined up to come onto our higgledy-piggledy show. It was an eclectic bunch. We welcomed Spanish NBA star Marc Gasol one day, Booker Prize–winning novelist Howard Jacobson the next. Seth Meyers wandered on to talk about his love of Dutch football, followed by the lead singer of Weezer, who was obsessed with all facets of the game. It did not seem to matter who came on. Our listeners loved hearing famous people talk about football with passion that matched their own, and listening to their takes on the daily drama of the World Cup.

My life was now utterly ruled by the rhythm of the tournament. The podcast. The writing. And then—a daily television hit. After being belatedly reinstated onto the book's promotion cycle, I appeared on *Morning Joe* and met Joe Scarborough, the host, who I knew only as a former Republican politician, but soon learned was soccer mad. Joe loved the opportunity to talk about his passions and, without consulting with his producers, promptly invited me to appear every morning in the 6 a.m. block.

The experience was slightly bizarre. My wife immediately brought me a shirt, tie, and jacket. I wore the same one every single day on the show, which was shot in a signature style by roving camera crews who circled a central desk at which the likes of Tom Brokaw and Al Sharpton were perched—neither of whom had an inkling, nor cared a jot, about football. I found it easy to deal with their interrupting and shouting. It honestly reminded me of nights in my childhood spent arguing around my family dinner table in Liverpool. The real trick was to make football relevant to this audience. I would appear in between segments with New York City mayor Michael Bloomberg, or a Nobel Prize–winning economist who had arrived to talk about the threat of stagflation. I was treading water and loving every second.

I quickly learned how to frame the World Cup through the widest possible lens for an American audience who had little knowledge—or, in most cases, any prior interest—in the game. The equation I employed was to keep my segment moving and to focus on the culture, geopolitics, and circus of the World Cup, knowing that if the football action would not engage the American sports fan, videos of South American fans firing bottle rockets out of their butt cheeks, enormous fan zones in which thousands of beers would be flung skyward in moments of ecstasy, or stories of an octopus in a German aquarium who predicted results with an unerring accuracy certainly would.

My days took on a familiar rhythm. At 5 a.m., I would be picked up by a town car to appear on *Morning Joe*. After taping the hit, I hurtled over to Michael's office, enormous coffee liberated from the MSNBC green room in hand, to bang out a preview of the games for ESPN's home page. If the timing was right, I would have ten minutes to research a script for whatever guest was coming on, or at least to Google whether they had lost their partner to any kind of tragedy so I could avoid awkwardness and dead air. Then the games kicked off, and I would keep one eye on the action, the other on the burbling conversation on Twitter. It felt so good to have fans—or as we called them from the beginning, GFOPs, or "Great Friends of the Pod." This joke began organically when we talked about real people we loved, pretending they were listening to the show—like England's temperamental genius, Wayne Rooney. "Shout-out to Big Wayne," I would say, "we know you are an avid listener, Wazza, a Great Friend of the Pod." This moniker became one that our listeners self-adopted when they would email in, signing off their letters with "Josh Kail in Philadelphia, Great Friend of the Pod." I was so validated by this reciprocal connection, and by the mountain of emails pouring in from our listeners, I attempted to treat them all with the care and respect I used to write to my own mother.

The show quickly developed its own insider language, forming a semifictional ecosystem that folded in on itself by the end of the first week. The day before the World Cup kicked off, I had taken a moment to try and imagine my dream audience members, writing their names on a Post-it, which I stuck on my bathroom mirror. I had this idea that our ideal listener would be an intelligent American who was just beginning to wrap their mind around the game of football. One person came to mind. *Moneyball* MLB stats king Billy Beane, who was rumored to have fallen in love with European club football.

In the first week of the tournament, I referred to this "audience of one" during a broadcast, hailing Billy Beane, in my customary, self-deluded way, as a "Great Friend of the Pod." By the end of the week, my phone pinged with an unrecognized message. The text was brief. It was from Billy Beane. He proclaimed himself to be an avid listener and explained that he had asked an ESPN NBA correspondent we both knew to connect us so he could come on. I honestly believed this was my wife taking the piss and phoned her up to call her on her bullshit, only to find out that the text was legit. Billy Beane had actually been listening to our crap from the beginning, which meant he had heard my debacle with poor Liam Neeson. God bless Billy. He still wanted to come on and talk to us.

Our vibes were high, but in truth, the football at this World Cup was terrible. The reasons for that were self-inflicted. Football is a very simple game that does not require much equipment. In a way, FIFA only had one job: to make sure the ball that will be kicked in the games actually worked. In 2010, they failed in the most calamitous way, unveiling an Adidas ball, the Jabulani—its name deriving from the Zulu word "to celebrate." The Jabulani had been hailed as a scientific miracle, the product of laboratory testing to produce aerodynamic grooves and ridges capable of delivering perfect flight. Yet there had been one crucial oversight in the creative process. The ball had been laboratory-tested in the middle of England, far from South Africa's high altitudes. The change of continent and thinning of the air saw the Jabulani begin to knuckle-ball, and accelerate unpredictably, as if it had a mind of its own. With the eyes of the world watching in horror, the world's best footballers were rendered impotent by the tournament ball, suddenly unable to pass accurately, shoot with precision, or make saves with any degree of confidence. It was slapstick as coaches, players, and poor goalkeepers—the ones most exposed by its irregular flight—condemned it as the worst they had ever seen. The football was blunted by the fact that free expression and creativity had been rendered an impossibility because the ball simply could not be controlled.

That the ball's comic flight path made the action hard to watch was only half the problem. It was also excruciating to listen to. I discovered that the cheap plastic trumpet I had first encountered at the South African bar in Brooklyn was known as the "vuvuzela," and there turned out to be millions of the damn things across South Africa. The local custom was for fans to blow them in an incessant drone throughout the game. Their agonized screech became the soundtrack of the 2010 tournament, as omnipresent as the World Cup's official anthem, Shakira's "Waka Waka." Lionel Messi alleged that playing in a vuvuzela-filled stadium was "like being deaf" and every game felt like it was experiencing a drive-by from a local herd of anxious elephants. Commentators fretted aloud as if 2010 might be the first tournament the world elected to watch with the volume turned down.

Despite all of this, I remained enthralled, utterly lost in the subplots and the surging opportunity to engage with an American audience who were experiencing a similar overwhelming connection to football, and to each other. This was happening because the US Men's National Team were an enormous driver from the outset. A fearless underdog collective yet again, they were led by a taciturn manager, Bob Bradley, a bald-headed, lips-pursed stoic who employed a pragmatic style of missionary-position football born of double trainings and suicide runs. Along with Bob came his son, Michael, a similarly bald Mini-Me, who was seen as the beneficiary of nepotism early in his career but persevered to reveal himself to be a single-minded midfield monster, grinding his way to success in Europe, where he picked up nicknames like "Il Marine," "Lex Luthor," and "Alien" along the way. A year before the World Cup, our boys had beaten Euro champions Spain, ending the Spaniards' fantastical 35-game unbeaten run. A defeat so unexpected and humiliating that nearly all the Spanish players refused to exchange shirts and stormed off the field, like the Detroit Pistons when they were finally done in by Michael Jordan's Bulls. I had watched the game at home alone with my jaw dropped as the

US went eye-to-eye with a giant and competently felled them. It felt like a slither of every US fan's dream coming true. It was with this sentiment that we entered the 2010 stage.

We had good reason to harbor that Spain-conquering confidence. Even though there was still the death rattle coming from soccer haters like Glenn Beck, who declared that "we (Americans) don't like soccer," and no less an expert G. Gordon Liddy with "this game originated with the South American Indians and instead of a ball, they used to use the head, the decapitated head, of an enemy warrior," the cultural wave was tilting irrevocably toward soccer. Kobe Bryant, who had spent part of his formative years falling in love with football when his father hooped in Italy, charged over to South Africa to cheer the US on, admitting he had really wanted to be a soccer player as a kid. Kobe was not alone. Only host South Africa bought more World Cup tickets than American fans, who came loaded down with an arsenal of US flag bandanas, scarves, and capes. Television personality John Oliver seized the moment, inviting the US players onto *The Daily Show* and asking them how they "came out" to their parents as soccer players.

The US was a respectable 14th in the FIFA rankings that year. The roster was packed with classic names. Tim Howard, the latest in a line of bald goalkeeping giants, stood tall. Clint Dempsey simmered out wide, and Landon Donovan ran the tempo. His hairline was receding, but his skills were still verdant. The draw had pitted us against England, Slovenia, and Algeria. When the draw had been made, skeezy English tabloid *The Sun* printed a front page "England Algeria Slovenia Yanks. EASY." Subhead: "Best English group since the Beatles." I stayed at home to watch the opening game between the United States and England with my two older children: Samson, then aged seven, and Ber, who was four. It felt like such a big moment, my father flew out to savor it with us. This was an England team stuffed to the gills with Premier League superstars like Wayne Rooney, Frank Lampard, and Steven Gerrard, for whom the media doubled the traditionally crushing pressure by hailing them as a "Golden Generation." Their salaries and media clout dwarfed those of the American team. I looked at my young kids with sympathy as they sat there in their new US jerseys ahead of kickoff. Football was everything to them, yet they were too young to know they should be afraid.

It did not start well. Inside four minutes, the US defense was carved apart and England captain Steven Gerrard calmly rolled one home. My father could not help himself and laughed directly in Ber's face, reducing him to tears. Football has rarely felt more "Hello Darkness My Old Friend" for me in that moment. I put my sobbing son on my knee and held him with one arm, while tweeting with my phone in the other: "Shoot on sight. The English keeper is dodgy." I had approximately 124 Twitter followers back then. I think the tweet received one like, but it remains an insight of which I am proud, because my prediction about English goalkeeper Robert Green could not have become more prescient if I were a prognosticating octopus from Germany. Five minutes before halftime, Clint Dempsey turned inside and out to carve out a few feet of space from his marker, Gerrard, and let fly a tame zero-percentage left-footed shot which was so weak, he had already turned away, certain that Green would save it. Instead, the ball bobbled right through the keeper, as if he were Patrick Swayze in *Ghost*. There was delirium in my house, as my American children danced around their distressed English grandfather to celebrate an impressive result that earned a *New York Post* headline: "USA Wins 1–1."

Subhead: "Greatest tie against the British since Bunker Hill." I remember Joe Scarborough's ecstasy on *Morning Joe* the next day as he talked about how in Alabama they call a draw "kissing your cousin," but this was one incredible kiss. I was not exactly sure what to say in response and elected to let the Reverend Al Sharpton field that one.

Next up, the United States would face Slovenia, a tiny nation around the size of New Jersey newly splintered off from Yugoslavia. Prime Minister Borut Pahor had promised to clean the players' boots if they qualified, a promise he carried through after a fairy-tale playoff win against Russia earned them a place in their second World Cup. The Slovenians were fearless and forced the US to fight back from a 2–0 hole at halftime, for an anticlimactic tie. If the England game was a draw that felt like a win, this one felt like a loss, and it meant we now needed to beat Algeria in the final group game to qualify for the knockout rounds. We were at all or nothing.

To mark the occasion, *Morning Joe* rented a bar in Tribeca to watch the match. The game was an early-morning kickoff. The entire production staff was there, and the Bloody Marys flowed freely. I was seated in pride of place, between Joe and cohost Mika Brzezinski. The three of us being filmed by a phalanx of cameras. The game entered stoppage time with neither team able to score a goal. In the bar, the buzz of breakfast beers had worn off and it felt as if a funeral was about to break out. Joe loved football. He wanted to grow it by highlighting it on his show. American failure was not the story he wanted to tell.

Into the 91st minute, the ball was in goalkeeper Tim Howard's hands. He bounced the Jabulani, then hurtled it up field to a speeding Landon Donovan, whom he found like Joe Montana going long to Jerry Rice. Donovan streaked forward, starting a chain reaction that led to Clint Dempsey stabbing the ball off the Algerian keeper. It rolled back into the penalty area, and a still-searing Donovan swooped in to stroke it home, an astonishing moment in context and in and of itself. Twelve seconds from front to back, from one goal to another, leaving the US players in a dogpile by the corner flag and ESPN's British commentator Ian Darke meeting the moment by improvisationally proclaiming: "Go, go USA! It's incredible! You could not write a script like this."

In the bar, Mika grabbed the table we were sitting at and flipped it over. Beers spilled everywhere in a scene of ecstatic carnage. Donovan had not just delivered the United States into the knockout round, he had given American soccer an out-of-body, *SportsCenter*-worthy moment, one that would be played on repeat throughout the summer, along with YouTube videos of scenes like ours unfolding in bars across the nation. The US men had finally delivered a moment in which the refusal to quit refracted the best qualities we like to see in ourselves. The next day on the show, we debated where the moment ranked in American history, up there with the Boston Tea Party, D-Day, and the week we kicked Piers Morgan out of the country.

That single moment made our podcast more than any other. A torrent of young Americans was won over to the sport with that goal, all of them seemingly hungry to learn more and connect to others of similar frame of mind. There were thousands of football podcasts for them to choose from, but most were from England, where the reference points and cultural norms were unfamiliar. One of the first letters we received was from a listener asking, "What part of London is Newcastle in?" It was a funny question, but it did not make me laugh. That letter taught me our mission: to speak to American fans, and American fans alone, with a sense of passion, detail, and backstory tailor-made of the moment. This approach was clearly resonating. My evening regimen suddenly included nightly stops on NPR and PBS NewsHour. Charlie Rose had seen me on *Morning Joe* and invited me to come on, screaming at his assistants in between takes. At the end of the interview, he shook my hand while shouting, "Can someone get me my running shoes so I can have lunch with Nancy Pelosi, I'm LATE!"

My life became so mono-focused that at 3 a.m. one morning, when my wife went into labor with our fourth child, she calmly woke me and told me that if I needed to write my daily match preview, I should do it immediately as she was about to give birth. I walked to my desk in my boxer shorts, banged out one thousand words on Spain's exquisite midfield, then drove her to the hospital and kept one eye on the game while she gave birth. My suggestion that we call our son Clint fell on deaf ears. He was named Oz.

The United States surged into the knockout rounds, first in their group, with second-placed England having to play, and lose, once again, to Germany. The US would face a nemesis of its own in the Round of 16: the Black Stars of Ghana. I had a premonition their pulsating journey would come to an end the moment US Soccer arranged a celebration with Bill Clinton. The ex-president arrived to smash Budweisers with the players. President Obama called in to their party and told the players how proud he was, and I watched in horror. I realized these footballers had left the US with no one really caring about them. As they listened to Clinton's jokes, they now knew the whole nation was watching, which felt like tightrope walkers looking down.

To make matters worse, the US was on the wide-open side

of the knockout bracket. The winner would play the victor in the South Korea–Uruguay clash, either of which seemed beatable. Judging by their tweets and letters, many of our listeners were dreaming of just strolling to the semifinal by right. Coach Bob Bradley did not help by declaring, "We can go to the end." I screamed when I saw Mick Jagger in attendance to cheer on the United States. He had already developed a long and deserved reputation for bringing the mark of death to every England World Cup campaign. Every game he attended in person, the Three Lions lost. Watching Jagger sit by Bill Clinton told me the game was over before a ball had been kicked. That turned out to be agonizingly true. Again, the US leaked early. Kevin-Prince Boateng ran straight through the middle, finishing with aplomb inside five minutes. Bob Bradley took the unorthodox step of making substitutions inside half an hour, something coaches never do but it worked. Landon Donovan leveled the score with a penalty. That man was all sideburns and composure. The game went into extra time. The United States seemed shattered and emotionally spent. The ecstasy of the Algerian win coupled with the shock of Reggie Bush's sprinkled stardust will do that to you. We were so shorn of energy and ideas that the winning Ghanaian goal felt like a guillotine blade falling. A long ball up the middle, striker Asamoah Gyan raced onto it, burst between the central defenders, and volleyed over an exposed Howard. All of that positivity. All of that promise. All of the energy of the nation finally riding the football wave, and we were out in an instant.

Three days later, Bob Bradley came onto *Morning Joe*. He arrived in the studio in his full US Soccer tracksuit garb, like one of those NHL players in a Wendy's commercial where Wendy's knows that most viewers have no idea who the hell they are, so they make them wear a jersey with their name on it so there can be no doubt. I introduced Bradley on live television by saying "Good to see you, Bob," and he snapped back, "It would be better if you could not see me and I was still there with my team in South Africa," and I realized in that moment the size of the wound and the trauma the defeat had inflicted on this man. I was sitting with someone who had given this journey his all. He had believed in it totally and utterly, and despite the agony of failure, knew just how close he had come to making real American sports history.

Even with the United States out, the real winner of the tournament was the ratings, which kept increasing even once the US boys had caught their flight home. America was really hooked on World Cup magic. Lionel Messi once again arrived with much fanfare, having blasted a startling 47 goals for Barcelona in the 2009–10 season, yet wilted once more, failing to find the back of the net in five games. As rumors of fatigue and burnout swirled, Argentina was not helped by the erratic leadership of icon Diego Maradona, who now brought his manic aura to the sideline as manager. Maradona had beaten cocaine addiction and obesity by finding God, to whom he gave the affectionate nickname "The Beard." When his team barely scraped through qualification, Diego suggested their best help was "The Beard who saved me many times—I hope he saves me this time, too."

The Argentinians were blessed with almost too much striking firepower. Their six strikers had smashed 133 league goals for their clubs between them. Maradona decided to ostentatiously shoehorn as many of them as he could into his lineup and let them loose, a tactic-less strategy that came a cropper the first moment they faced a savvy opponent, Germany, who destroyed them 4–0 in the quarterfinal. Messi limped away from South Africa as if he had barely been there.

The United States–slayers Ghana met an agonizing fate of their own in the quarterfinals against Uruguay. By becoming only the third African team ever to reach that stage, they represented the hope of an entire continent. The game was tied at 1–1 going into dying seconds of extra time. Ghana's Dominic Adiyiah stabbed a follow-up goalward past the goalkeeper, only for Luis Suárez, the Uruguayan striker, to use both hands to palm the shot away on the goal line. The referee gave Suárez an immediate red card and awarded a penalty. Ghanaian goal-scoring hero Asamoah Gyan stepped up to the spot. He had already scored two penalties in the tournament, yet with all of Africa behind him, skimmed the crossbar and sent the ball into an agonized crowd. Suárez, who was still in the act of leaving the field as the penalty thundered over the bar, was caught by cameras, turning round, pumping his fists, and laughing hysterically. His instinctive gamble had paid off. Uruguay won the ensuing shoot-out and the world was left to debate whether Suárez's actions were those of a despicable cheat or a true rational professional. Ghana exited after coming within a fingertip of taking African football to new heights of respect—only to be thwarted by one of the most controversial moments of gamesmanship a World Cup has ever seen. For his part, a gloating Suárez reveled in his heel role, telling reporters after the game that "the hand of God now belongs to me," referencing Diego Maradona's famous handball goal against England in the quarterfinals of the 1986 World Cup. "I made the save of the tournament."

The Cup ultimately belonged to Spain. Their slick passing had papercut all opponents to death at Euro 2008, enabling the nation to cast aside their reputation as prime-time chokers in the process. They entered the tournament with the pressure of being the bookies' favorites and wobbled in their first game, a defeat against Switzerland that made many wonder if they were ready to withstand the pressure of expectation. But in a tournament undermined by the Jabulani, the Spanish midfield—rife with tiny, possession-hungry, technically superlative, Smurf-ish stars like Xavi and Andrés Iniesta—were able to skip through crevices of space left vulnerable by even the most organized defenses. Their lightning-quick passes and movement meant adversaries could only chase shadows. So proficient was their whirling, one-touch game, which denied opponents basic possession of the ball, that many called watching them play boring. Their obsession with possession served both an offensive and defensive purpose. If their opponents cannot touch the ball, they cannot score. I found it mesmerizing watching these wizards toss the ball around, back and forth with casual velocity, as if they were tossing a hacky sack around some high school quad.

They faced the physically challenging Dutch in the final. An occasion Michael Davies proudly marked by procuring a state-of-the-art 3-D television from his bosses at Sony. The tournament had made history by becoming the first sporting event to broadcast a number of games in multiple dimensions. We sat there with this newfangled technology in front of our podcasting desk, both of us trying to look cool in the heavy 3-D glasses the screen required. I looked over at Michael, who sat behind his desk in the goggles, resembling a blind jazz musician in the 1950s, as he assured me, "This technology is going to change the industry." I found that hard to believe. Not only was the game a bloodbath requiring fourteen yellow cards and one red, but the much-hyped 3-D broadcast just reduced the game to a blurry-looking wash, the players resembling avatars from a 1990s arcade game.

A game of strangled intent was settled in extra time by a moment of human poetry. In the 116th minute of extra time, 5'7" Iniesta, who had been subjected to a terrible physical beatdown throughout the game, gained his revenge, summoning the courage to use his bruised and battered legs to dispatch a vicious volley into the far corner of the net. His Spain became the eighth nation to win the title. The cynical Dutch cemented their place as the tournament's nearly team, deservedly on this day becoming losing finalists for the third time. More than anything, the goal was a relief. The game had been such an eyesore, few neutrals would have wanted it to drag on a moment more. Yet the final of a World Cup is always bittersweet. In contrast to the breathless excitement of the group stage, when the football is fast and furious, I always feel a sense of mourning at the end of a tournament that has filled my life and given millions of fans a sense of connection to the global game. I remember walking down to the studio ahead of the final, feeling a heaviness, an impending sense of the unknown in terms of what would happen to our podcast once the final whistle blew.

After we taped our last podcast of the tournament, Michael poured a pair of brandies and toasted the future. We were both exhausted. We both also felt like we had, through our work and the community we had built, just won the World Cup. The very next day, we had a conference call to debrief with our ESPN handlers. Michael was always an optimist. He had a single motto in life, "Stay in Charge," which, when he explained it to me, essentially boiled down to always pretending you were in control, even when you were not. This was most certainly one of the latter occasions. Michael pitched our podcast to the ESPN honchos as if we were one of the television shows he ran. He calmly asked them for a cool twenty-five thousand dollars an episode. I didn't even have time to gulp as they threw their heads back and guffawed, then countered with: "We have two hundred and fifty dollars an episode budgeted. No one cares about soccer outside of a World Cup. That's what we pay for podcasts. Take it or leave it." I wilted at those words, and girded my loins for the long, familiar—yet suddenly sad—subway ride home to tell my wife.

Chapter 10

2014 World Cup, Brazil

BY THE TIME the 2014 World Cup rolled around, I had attempted to transform myself into American football's version of Cher's "Believe" to pop music. A voice that is always faintly audible across the nation. The first step was ensuring our podcast surged to become America's "most listened to" football show. A humblebrag that sounds far more impressive and arduous an achievement than it actually was. Sports podcast pathfinder Bill Simmons had been given a new signature platform by ESPN, Grantland, and he needed a fresh supply of shows to distribute. All we had to do was accept his offer to partner. The financial arrangement was as follows: zero dollars in exchange for Grantland's enormous promotional muscle. To everyone but my wife (sigh: "another loss leader") this felt like a fair deal. Bill's own show had become a pioneering juggernaut in sports podcasting. His halo, coupled with his generous support, instantly exposed us to a weekly audience in the hundreds of thousands.

We changed the name of the show to *Men in Blazers* the second we were liberated from ESPN. As a kid in England, I had been mesmerized by any glimpse ever snatched of American sports broadcasting on British television. Back in the day, every American broadcaster wore matching brightly colored blazers when on air. Each network had a different hue. It did not seem to matter if the words they spoke made sense. It was as if the power of their blazer conferred meaning. As a kid, I had always loved Harris Tweed, and the fact that this name gave me the chance to wear it again sealed the deal. And that's how we called our show *Men in Blazers*. I was honestly shocked how quickly our audience grew, and how connected and deeply devoted that audience was. The 2010 World Cup had made an enormous number of Americans fall in love with football, leaving an avid, curious, hungry new fanbase in its wake, like a rogue wave depositing a mound of flotsam and jetsam on an Atlantic beach. We made it our mission to wire them together into a joyous community. The act of podcasting about the English Premier League on a weekly basis was central to that. The power lay in the intimacy of the medium. Broadcasting directly into people's ears and speaking so personally allowed us to develop an insider language for, and with, the listeners. A language that was rooted in the act of watching English football together across the United States with a spirit of exhilarated discovery.

The beloved young adult author John Green was an early listener and guest, and when he came on the show, he took the time after taping to warn me that the secret of building a niche community was to always tend to it personally, even as it grew. His actual advice was to obsess about the depth of connection, as much as the breadth of it. I asked him what that meant in practice, and he told me to continue handwriting messages back to fans who sent in deeply personal letters, despite the size of the task. John was a man who signed hundreds of thousands of his new books upon publication. They all became instant bestsellers, and so that advice became my guiding light, to treat each listener as if we were in a one-on-one relationship.

The moment everything crystallized was the night of our first-ever live show. I had become friendly with Bob Ley, the ESPN broadcasting legend, who had long been the sole voice brave enough to talk with knowledge and love for the sport of soccer on the network. A doppelgänger for a middle-aged Kenny Loggins, Bob had been at ESPN for what felt like forever. If someone told me he had been present at the 1930 World Cup semifinal in which the US were cruelly pipped 6–1 by a speedy Argentinian side on a rain-soaked field in Montevideo, I would have believed them.

Bob was in the midst of a contract renegotiation with ESPN. It was evidently not progressing well. In one of many budget-driven belt-tightening moves by "The Worldwide Leader in Sports," the broadcaster had made a series of demeaning, paltry offers to him. We had been toying with the idea of executing a live taping for a while—encouraged by another remarkable fan of the show, John Johnson, who happened to be both a football fan and a multi-Tony Award winning Broadway theater producer. John had reached out and urged us to consider taping our show with a live audience. I called Bob up and asked him if we could celebrate his career live onstage in New York City, making up the idea of a "Men in Blazers Golden Blazer" mid-conversation, in a desperate effort to make the occasion sound loftier and more thought out than it actually was. While I was on the phone, I clicked through Amazon to find a golden blazer we could afford, and found one at the discount price of $29.99. Mostly because it was garish, sequined, and on sale. It was with that garb that we would spend a night honoring a man who had dedicated his life to growing the game in the United States.

The show was booked for Joe's Pub in NoHo New York. The day the box office opened, I was driving up to ESPN to appear on their evening football show. To this day, I remain an ardent pessimist whenever we launch something. My modus is to brace for disaster until proven otherwise. The box office opened at midday, and at 12:03, I was thundering up to Bristol, Connecticut, in my reliable Toyota Sienna with its glamorous multiple infant car seats, when my phone blew up. I pulled over onto the hard shoulder and looked at the device, which was smothered with desperate texted ticket requests from people from all parts of my life. The gig itself had sold out inside ninety seconds.

Come showtime, we unfurled an act that was essentially a ninety-minute Bob Ley tribute/infomercial, reliving the lonely and thankless path our guest had plowed, as the standard bearer for soccer, through the '80s and '90s wilderness when his attempts to talk with passion about the sport was to open himself to brazen mockery from his fellow cohosts. We published the finished product on our Grantland site, and within twenty-four hours, Bob Ley received the kind of respectful offer from ESPN that he should have been handed in the first place. Bob signed on for one more World Cup, safe in the knowledge he could retire in the wake with his dignity intact and on his own terms. It was all so surreal to experience. I was still shocked that the powers that be listened to our show and took our opinions seriously, and so attributed the new contract to the mystical power of a $29.99 sequined blazer.

The other colossal outcome of the night was far more personal: the impact of meeting our audience face-to-face for the first time. That happened once the show had finished, and we charged to a nearby bar to raise a pint with our listeners and hear their stories. It was shocking how many had flown in from all points. There were: a large group of college kids who had paratrooped in from Los Angeles; a gaggle of marketers from Denver who had conspired to bill the show as some form of business trip; a hulking Chicagoan, Jason Kennedy, who bounded round the bar in a Liverpool tracksuit top, buying beers for his fellow football fans as if he had not just met them but known them his whole life—an act he repeated dozens of times as he made it his business to turn up at every show we put on for the next six years, traveling with us across the nation like some kind of Deadhead.

I stood in the center of that bar, shattered by our onstage exertions, but also utterly enthralled by the scene going on all around me. Here was this very American audience, all clad in English football jerseys. They had been strangers when the night began but were now all drinking, talking, and forming friendships, bonded not only by the love of our show but also a shared hunger to commune with fellow travelers, fellow Americans who had been bitten by the soccer bug and fallen in love with the Premier League three thousand plus miles away. A passion they had thus far largely experienced solo, watching early-morning kickoffs at ungodly hours in their pajamas, had now been ignited and given a place to grow through our giddy little podcast. This scene showed me that what *Men in Blazers* was about was less broadcasting, and more community building.

The pod was the heartbeat of everything we created, but I scrambled to be everywhere, maintaining my ESPN byline and making any documentary film I could. This was partly by design—I had seen a gap in the market and did my part to fill it. It was also by financial necessity. Football still paid terribly. To give yourself to it, you had no choice but to be a hustler. I kept appearing on *Morning Joe* long after the World Cup finished. The show's producers invited me to return on a weekly basis to do a quick hit review of the weekend's action on Monday mornings. Football did not really belong on a show covering global and domestic politics in such serious form, yet Joe Scarborough had fallen hard for the game and insisted on being given the opportunity to talk about his growing love of Liverpool Football Club.

The segment was typically a rapid-fire four-minute crash through the weekend soccer headlines—a conversation between me and Joe—with the rest of the regular political pundits looking on in a bemused silence. This confusion revealed itself the third time I appeared. Former ad man Donny Deutsch interrupted my flow by cutting me off with a rant about how this American show should have no place for European soccer.

Live broadcasts are an eerie experience. The need to keep talking means the mouth often engages without passing the words through the required mental filters. Instinct just takes over. Without missing a beat, I cut Deutsch off by asking him if he had any grandchildren. "I do but what has that got to do with it?" he responded, sounding suddenly age-conscious. "You are an old man, Donny Deutsch," I heard myself saying. "Soccer is the fastest growing sport for Americans under the age of thirty in America. You might have grown up playing stickball on the street in Queens, but today the young audience is following Premier League football. This is not for you, old man." Suitably chastised, Deutsch was silenced as if his battery pack had been ripped out.

Two weeks later I was on again. I charged into my opening with enthusiasm only to be interrupted again. This time by Tom Brokaw. "Wait a minute, wait a minute," the veteran broadcasting legend interjected. "We are in America!" he exclaimed. "Where we care about ball sports like baseball and NFL football. Talking about *soccer* is simply anti-American." Brokaw's rant went on and on, as he pronounced the word *soccer* with such scorn that I quickly became lost inside my own head. I thought about unleashing the ageist attack I had used to ensnare Deutsch, but this was *Tom Brokaw* who was steamrolling me. Television royalty. Humiliating him would be like ridiculing the queen to her face. So I sat there silently for four minutes, dying inside as the man who wrote *The Greatest Generation* mocked me and the sport I loved on live television.

Utterly humiliated, and believing my television broadcast career had just been well and truly ended, I somehow crawled out of the studio. To my surprise the show producer said, "Same time next week, Roger?" as I headed for the door. I just about managed to stammer, "I will never, EVER go on live television when Brokaw is sitting at the desk."

I did the show every week for two years without incident. Brokaw was politely ushered off anytime he was on set before my arrival. Then in early January, I took to the set and, to my horror, Brokaw was still in place opposite Joe Scarborough as the clock ticked down before live broadcast resumed. "I am not going on with bloody Brokaw," I hissed. "Don't worry, he is a changed man," said the producer, shoving me into my seat just in time as the last commercial ended.

The introductory music kicked in, my segment began, and I leaped into my opening. I had gotten roughly five words out and blow me down, if Brokaw did not lean forward and interrupt me once more. "Wait a minute . . . wait a minute," he said, using words that had populated my recurring nightmares ever since I had last heard him utter them. "I once said soccer is un-American," he began, as I sat chilled, finding myself gasping for air. "Yet, since then, I have had the opportunity to travel to England with my sons-in-law to watch Premier League games, and I have to admit, I have developed a new appreciation for the game," he said with a quiet pride while across the desk, the blood drained back into my face. "We even fly coach," he concluded, handing the conversation back to me so I could charge through the Manchester United–Sunderland highlights package.

The second the segment was over, I was overwhelmed by a greater sense of shock than after Brokaw's first attack. If even Tom Brokaw had fallen in love with Premier League soccer, the game had well and truly arrived in the United States. Soccer was America's Sport of the Future no more.

The *Morning Joe* gig gave me a distinctive platform and voice. It may not have been the most watched breakfast show in the world, but pound for pound, none had a more influential viewership. Producers from NPR and PBS started to flock my way whenever they needed an expert, not because I was necessarily good. More because I was the only one they knew. My cell phone voice mail became cluttered with requests for "the *Morning Joe* soccer guy." The show also gave me a unique place apart from the rest of the press pack. A status that became cemented in 2011 when the United States Men's National Team announced a German, Jürgen Klinsmann, would be their next manager.

Jürgen was an enigmatic life-force. A legend as a footballer. He had been a feared striker with a dyed blond mop top, who won both the World Cup and the Euros as a player. Tenacious enough to win over the suspicious jingoistic English media when he arrived at Tottenham in 1994, late in his career as a thirty-year-old. A *Guardian* writer welcomed him with a feature entitled "Why I Hate Jürgen Klinsmann," describing his cunning, flopping gamesmanship as everything the British game stood against. Within a couple of months, Jürgen had lashed home 29 goals and won everyone over with his ethereal talent, forcing the English scribe to recant with a second feature, "Why I Love Jürgen Klinsmann."

Klinsmann had become the German national team's coach in 2004 and oversaw the Nationalmannschaft's transition from a cold-blooded, robotic winner into something the world never thought was possible: a German team the rest of the world could admire and root for. His career in the wake had been admittedly erratic. Klinsmann had relocated to live in California and fused a helicopter-flying, management-consultant-speak LA vibe to his natural Teutonic meticulousness. He lasted less than a season as manager of Bayern Munich, a disastrous spell that undermined his status as an elite coach. Yet a combination of his availability and proximity on the West Coast meant he became coveted by the powers that be at US Soccer, and when he agreed to lead us into the 2014 World Cup as the first globally renowned footballing personality to coach the US boys, it was hailed as a real coup.

I ran down to witness Klinsmann's opening press conference in person. It was held at Niketown in New York, and I arrived with a genuine sense of excitement and watched him enthusiastically hold court on his footballing theories, which were a strange mix of fearless optimism and psychobabble. "I think, yes, the youth teams should reflect the mixture of your culture, it should reflect what's going on in this country," Klinsmann began, proceeding to hypothesize that the way a football team plays should reflect the nation's mentality. It was bold and compelling, but the idea that the United States men should play in a certain "American style" sounded all the crazier because he punctuated every sentence with his signature laugh. A half cackle, half shriek that the transcription service who typed up my recording, perhaps heavily influenced by Christoph Waltz's work, would later describe as "Loud German Laughter." Jürgen capped the press conference off by quipping, "I hope we find a way to discover a Lionel Messi in the United States. That would be awesome." I wrote the following in my notes: "You can't fault him for optimism." Jürgen's appeared as wildly deluded as my own.

Not everyone was as welcoming as I was, though. Watching Klinsmann's first year with the US team was akin to witnessing a donor organ rejected by the host body, as he attempted to foster a style of perpetual experimentation, tweaking personnel, positions, formations, and even nationalities. These demands, methodology, and tactics did not jive with the culture of the players he inherited, causing a swarming sense of uncertainty. A nucleus of the American players still played in the domestic American MLS, a league he constantly belittled and disparaged, urging his team to strive to play in Europe, as if that leap was something they could just make happen of their own free will. When Clint Dempsey, then by far the most talented maverick in the US player pool, secured a move from a mid-level team, Fulham, to Tottenham Hotspur, an aspiring power, Klinsmann made the ill-advised decision to tweak his star player in the media. He told *The Wall Street Journal*, "Dempsey has not accomplished shit yet," making sure the Yank understood there is always *another* level.

I felt sad watching all of this unspool. So much seemed to be getting lost in translation. The bulk of the American press pack had never seen Klinsmann play and so did not truly appreciate the heights of his accomplishments, instead laughing at his flashy habit of helicoptering to work to skip the SoCal traffic, his Porsche SUV license plate that read FLYHELI, and the $2.5 million he made per year, which was an enormous number for a soccer coach at the time in this nation. Jürgen also seemed to have elected not to care about the lack of experience of most of the players who were now his charges. I hoped I could act as a sort of translator here and flew out to California to spend an afternoon with Jürgen. My goal was to write a feature for ESPN that showed the arc of the coach's journey via the management lessons he had learned from each of the legendary coaches he had played for, including Arsène Wenger and Giovanni Trapattoni. My goal was to give Jürgen's eccentricity a backstory and some context.

I met Jürgen in a hotel coffee shop in Torrance. He was buzzing. The multiple double espressos he pounded through the course of our conversation may have had something to do with that. He had the unsettling habit of shrieking midsentence "Espresso!" in a slightly menacing Teutonic accent. A PR assistant would quickly and nervously appear to deposit a double shot in front of him, which he would then theatrically down. In the hour and a half we spent together, it was never entirely clear to me whether the trim coach was suffering a perpetual caffeine rush or thriving off the challenge of infusing US Soccer with his philosophy and experience.

In truth, I found engaging with the man to be fascinating. He was the rare former footballing superstar eager to exchange freewheeling ideas about current events in the present rather than rely on personal achievements in the past as a crutch. He began our meeting by expounding on the challenges facing

Boeing after a malfunction with their Dreamliner aircraft. As he did so, I watched his mouth open and close without really listening to the words, just marveling at how easy it could be to forget that he was once one of the most feared forwards in football. Before I left, I asked him what fears kept him awake at night. "I sleep well," he snapped. "I stop drinking my espressos at 4 p.m." With that, he looked at his watch, discovered it was exactly 3:50 p.m., and, giggling with delight, ordered one more.

The piece I wrote did huge numbers for ESPN. I never asked Jürgen what he thought about it, but from that point on he came to me whenever he wanted his viewpoint to be given a fair articulation. We were not exactly friends. Jürgen is a prickly, sensitive human being. A strange mix of arrogance and insecurity. But it quickly became clear within ESPN that if they wanted to do something that involved Klinsmann, I was as close to a Jürgen whisperer as there could be. There were times when he was exasperating. Once he decided he was going to have the US team play in the tactically complex style of Pep Guardiola. "I want them to attack with ten players and defend with ten players," he proclaimed, "like Lionel Messi's Barcelona." A fantastical idea to which I could only retort, "Jürgen, just because I want to quarterback the Chicago Bears or date supermodels does not mean I can." We just sat there in an awkward silence for a moment, which he shattered by turning in the general direction of his assistant and screaming "Espresso!"

A year before the World Cup kicked off, ESPN dispatched me to Brazil to cover the Confederations Cup. An eight-team dry run for the World Cup designed to offer the host nation a chance to work out kinks regarding travel, hotels, and stadium infrastructure. The World Cup that year had been hailed as a profound moment for football to return to its spiritual home.

There was one challenge, though: Football's spiritual home was going through a period of chaotic political turmoil. When I landed in São Paulo—as impressed as I was that the urinal cakes in the airport bathrooms were in the shape of goals (a proper football country)—I quickly realized that I had arrived in a nation in tumult.

In Brazilian history, through military dictatorships, false new dawns, and startling social inequality, football had always served as a consistently all-powerful distraction. On the eve of the 2014 World Cup, it had become a fire starter; the estimated $1 trillion in public works spending, political wrangling, and corruption surrounding the build-out for the tournament had become an all-too-tangible symbol of decades of government self-interest run amok. As I traveled between the eastern towns of Salvador, Fortaleza, and Recife, the daily scenes of demonstrations and street violence represented a deeply buried resentment shaken free as young Brazilians rose up to protest transport costs and social inequality, or as one protestor explained to me, "a Scandinavian level of taxation with an Albanian level of services."

There was one opening-round game I had to cover between Nigeria and Uruguay that was played in a half-empty stadium in Salvador with a large cloud of tear gas hanging over the field. The whole match was accompanied by the sound of riots taking place in the streets outside the stadium. Explosions crackled throughout. I was both grateful and unnerved by the one Brazilian journalist who sat next to me and provided a constant commentary after each loud bang. "Tear gas," he would mutter while typing his match report. "Oh, that one was a gunshot." His efforts to be helpful actually had the complete opposite effect.

I inevitably got caught up in a police riot while attempting to cover a game in Fortaleza's Arena Castelão, trapped between an advancing mob of protestors and a ring of security. Another Brazilian journalist pulled me out of a police scrum and wondered out loud if his nation could be trusted to host the tournament in a year's time. However, amid the violence and chaos, or maybe fueled by it, the Brazilian national team proceeded to play delirious football. Each game prefaced by the bellowing of the national anthem by the thousands of fans in attendance, which, after the turmoil in the streets, felt akin to a psychic release for an entire nation. When FIFA started to cut the anthem short, the players and the massive crowds in the stadium would finish it off a cappella style, like Springsteen fans screaming along with "Born to Run."

The spirit created in those moments felt almost mystical. The team, propelled by a young, undeniable Neymar, was unstoppable, overwhelming the vaunted Spanish in the final 3–0. A game that made the entire country experience a football-propelled self-love as antidote to the trauma of the protests. On my final night in Brazil, I drove back to my hotel postgame to find the quiet streets littered with debris, smashed glass, and smoldering trash cans. I went out for a beer with my driver, who attempted to put the events of the week into perspective. I showed him a line from an essay I had just read by Brazilian novelist Tatiana Salem Levy, who wrote, "The requirement that one be cheerful in Rio can be as oppressive as the grey sky in Paris, London, or Berlin," and he laughed out loud admitting, "The bad thing about the Brazilian personality is we don't take anything seriously, but when this tournament kicked off, a match was lit in this country."

We headed back to the hotel, driving past a colorful street

performer cruising alongside our car on a tricked-out push bike he had fashioned in national colors, with flashing lights, blaring funk music, and towing a giant Brazilian flag. "We may have no money and no hope, but I wanted everyone to know 'I am a Brazilian with plenty of pride and plenty of love,'" he shouted, quoting a popular football chant. "This man is the true Brazilian spirit," the driver said to me. "It's people like him that make me believe this country is going to be okay, unless, that is, Argentina wins the World Cup."

As the World Cup neared, the time and energy I had devoted to my strange relationship with Jürgen Klinsmann began to pay off. SXSW launched their first sports conference and asked me if I could tempt Jürgen to appear with me on the main stage. To my delight, Klinsmann agreed, and we spent a kinetic hour and a half thrashing out his leadership philosophy before a standing-room-only ballroom, with the young audience hooked on his every word, as the two of us argued about the sources of his eternal optimism. "The glass is always half full," he said. "No, it is not. It is completely empty and cracked," I replied. Jürgen snorted and said, "You just see the world like that because you are English," to which I responded, "It is worse than that, Jürgen. I'm not just English, I am Jewish, too. I have a double dose of pessimism." Jürgen stared at me, not quite sure what to say next. I expected him to shriek "Espresso!" but instead he elected to throw his head back and let out a very loud cackle like a German red-tailed hawk.

After the show, I was taken aside by John Skipper, who had spent most of the conference proudly parading data boy wonder Nate Silver around as ESPN's splashy new acquisition. With taut jaw, he told me the network had a problem for which I was the solution. As World Cup broadcasters, ESPN longed to film a *Hard Knocks* style behind-the-scenes documentary of the US team's preparation for the tournament. They had approached Jürgen with the idea. I was not surprised to hear that the manager had agreed, because he clearly adored the spotlight. However, Skipper proceeded to tell me Jürgen had one condition. "He is demanding that the network allow you to direct it, Roger."

I suddenly felt like the kid from *The Last Starfighter*, plucked from anonymity to save the world. The truth was evident to all parties. I had never directed a massive multipart fly-on-the-wall documentary. However, unless I stepped into the breach, ESPN had no course of action. Luckily, I had a good friend, Jonathan Hock, who was a pioneering Emmy Award–winning sports documentarian. A gent who had made some of the most emotionally nuanced *30 for 30* ESPN had ever broadcast. ESPN trusted him, and so we partnered together as rookie director and battle-hardened producer, like some kind of buddy-cop-movie caper.

Within two weeks, I found myself embedded with a four-camera team, living, eating, and traveling alongside the US World Cup hopefuls as they prepared for Brazil. It was a unique perspective from which to thunder toward the tournament. I saw everything up close. The drama was real. Upon qualifying, the US had been drawn into the Group of Death once again: Germany, Portugal, Ghana. All old foes. Germany and Portugal were second and fourth in the FIFA rankings. The logistics of the tournament were just as daunting. The size of Brazil meant the team would have to travel about nine thousand miles between the three cities in the opening round, experiencing three intensely different ecosystems in the process. There was muggy heat in Natal, the smothering

Amazonian rainforest humidity of Manaus, and the threat of monsoons in Recife. The enormity of the challenge that lay ahead, coupled with a persistent low-grade friction between Klinsmann's always unconventional, often erratic ideas and his confused players, meant the mood in camp was perpetually tense.

We flew across Europe as the team prepared for all that was to come, capturing the way the most successful players on the team—maverick captain Clint Dempsey, long-standing goalkeeper Tim Howard, and trusted goalscorer Jozy Altidore—respected each other but were all so different, they did not really interact off the field, keeping to themselves. Hypercompetitive midfielder Michael Bradley had an incredible simmering intensity that never relented. Landon Donovan, the long-time star, cut a jumpy, nervous figure, uncertain in his own skin. Desperate for new talent, which he believed could upgrade the tactical IQ of his team, Klinsmann constantly auditioned any German player who had American roots. A strange legacy of the Cold War was the number of players in the German league, the Bundesliga, who had American serviceman fathers. One was a hulking midfielder, Jermaine Jones, who joked at the procession of fellow Germans who arrived for their first US camp with a newly inked Stars and Stripes tattoo on their person to demonstrate their commitment. Jones subsequently strolled into the very next camp with an enormous American flag tattooed into a star shape near his knee.

The film shoot was like a crash course in this mode of storytelling for me, a formative experience in which I learned how to put largely inarticulate human beings at ease, establish an emotional trust, and act as a conduit to help them speak their feelings. In the run-up to the World Cup, the squad was based in a hotel near an industrial park in Stanford. We were given an unprecedented amount of access, filming in and around camp and capturing every training session, then setting up a small studio by the gym in which we captured daily conversations with key players so they could articulate their emotions and experiences in the first person. I watched the dynamic of the squad form in real time. The loneliness, the grinding repetitive ritual of travel, the loose connections between the players. There were real highs—witnessing meaningful relationships forged, even as they were competing against each other for limited slots on the final World Cup roster. There were also true lows, like the afternoon the team scrimmaged with Stanford University men's soccer team and were strangely, and surreally, outclassed.

The sterility of the camp's location gave the atmosphere an airless quality. The truth about international football is that the players experience a lot of dead downtime. The boredom of the breaks exists in stark contrast to the high stress of training sessions in which one missed shot or one blown covering tackle can lead to a player being cut. High drama ensued when Klinsmann elected to cut Landon Donovan, the team's legendary star. Albeit a thirty-two-year-old one who had taken a four-month sabbatical from playing to backpack in Cambodia and returned not match ready. Still, Donovan was then the US all-time leader with 57 goals and 58 assists.

When Jürgen announced his decision, it felt like the unimaginable had happened. The sense of loss that rippled through camp honestly felt like news of a death. A silence gripped the locker room. Donovan walked to a shower stall, sat down, and sobbed. Michael Bradley, DaMarcus Beasley, and Kyle Beckerman hugged and consoled him. There was a certain rationality to the decision. Jürgen was fighting for control of his team. This move was

Coaching 101 to eliminate a fading locker room king to gain the attention of the rest of the squad. Landon's form was not that of a starter, and Klinsmann was experienced enough to know he should not bring along an enemy to sit on the substitutes' bench. Landon would be a distractive threat who would instantly have all the leverage. If the US performed poorly in the first game, the media would demand that Landon get off the bench. So Jürgen whacked him like Leonardo DiCaprio at the end of *The Departed*. Like DiCaprio, Landon had thought he was on safe ground, only to be ambushed and shocked. His false hope blindsided by an attack he never saw coming.

In between shoots, Bill Simmons invited us to film a World Cup preview series, and I flew back from another shoot in Europe to tape them in Los Angeles. Grantland had rented out a downtown Irish bar, transforming it into a no-expenses-spared set. These were the last embers of swollen television budgets as symbolized by the decision to go with a six-camera shoot, about three more than needed. I wrote the scripts previewing every team's backstory in a fever dream on an overnight flight back from the UK. They were equal parts football knowledge, history, and geopolitics with a sprinkle of Monty Python–esque humor. I landed, went to my hotel room, and gave the scripts a last run-through. Davo and I taped thirty-two short films in a day and a half, and before I knew it, I was going back to US camp, filming the final week of training, unaware that the slightly dippy content we had just banged out would change the arc of our careers forever.

I raced back to Stanford as the final US roster was announced; it was young. Seven players were twenty-four or younger. Only six squad members had actually experienced a World Cup game before. Fresh-faced fullback DeAndre Yedlin was one year into his pro career with the Akron Zips, straight out of college football. I asked him why he thought he had made the squad, and he looked at my camera, blinked, and said, "I have no idea." Jürgen screamed a life truth at me when I posed the same question to him: "Sometimes you do not know enough to know you are meant to be afraid."

The day after the announcement, I received a call from an 860 number. Thinking it was just some routine ESPN producer working on our film, I picked it up. John Skipper was on the line. I had barely spoken to him since he handed us our podcast ahead of the 2010 World Cup. "I have just watched the World Cup things you shot for Grantland," he said. "I thought I would just flick through an episode or two but ended up watching four hours of your stuff." I did not know what to say and was lost for small talk, but, luckily, Skipper was a master of getting to the point and rolling to his next call. "I like what you guys are doing. I think you speak to a different audience. I want you to come to Brazil and broadcast the World Cup every day. Can we make that happen?" I had only felt like this once before in my life. Twice—I will include the moment my wonderful wife asked me to marry her. The other was when climbing Ben Nevis, the highest mountain in the United Kingdom, with my dad, and with shattered limbs, we broke through the clouds and reached the peak. That is how I felt in that second. A long, exhausting, grinding climb had amounted to something soaringly beautiful. A surge of happiness and relief overwhelmed me, because I knew my life was going to change. I muttered some kind of half-assed joke about having to check my diary. "You do that," said Skipper. "We'll see you guys in Rio."

At this point, the pace of my life was such that the idea of broadcasting a World Cup for a month just felt like another adventure to attack with the same fearless energy of DeAndre Yedlin. I truly believed everything was possible with a mix of hard work and a tinge of imposter syndrome. A couple of nights before the team left for Brazil, I was part of ESPN's "Sendoff Broadcast" live from 42nd Street in Times Square. The place was mobbed by fans and cops, and the energy was intense. I looked around from the set at thousands of supporters who had gathered to watch this team. It was as if my hopes for football in America had finally come true. I interviewed Jürgen Klinsmann live on air, but he was in atypically dour form. A control freak who was clearly not enjoying the chaos of a circus he did not oversee. That interview flowed into one involving Alexi Lalas. The former player turned opinionated analyst was standing in front of the entire squad, assembled as a collective onstage right behind him. Lalas was asked live whether he thought the US would get out of the group stage and reach the knockout rounds. He paused dramatically for a moment, then leaned into his microphone and uttered one word. "No."

There was a beat of silence. The players looming over Alexi recoiled. His prediction had not been well received. Jermaine Jones looked like he wanted to reach down, grab Lalas, and tear him limb from limb. Alexi looked back at them with a self-satisfied smirk, his move from long-haired hippie-ish guitar-playing US player to agent provocateur just beginning, like that of a footballing Kanye West or Morrissey.

That night we also held a World Cup send-off live show for *Men in Blazers* fans at the Town Hall in New York City. The show relived every US World Cup campaign with veteran players who had experienced them. The finale was meant to be an appearance by Klinsmann and a number of the star players that US Soccer had agreed to send over. I received a call right before we went onstage saying that Jürgen was in such a foul mood after the Times Square debacle that he had banned all players from further media appearances. I was devastated, but relieved when Kyle Beckerman, the dreadlocked pitbull of a midfielder whose play we had long championed, sauntered onto the stage, having turned up of his own accord. "I sneaked out of the team hotel, bro," he whispered to me. "I was not gonna let you down." Kyle was a remarkable human being who played the game with the kind of fight and tenacity the US team embodied. He talked with passion and excitement about all that was to come in Brazil, and then gamely lived out the finale of the show in which we talked about our vision of him scoring a 40-yard wonder goal in the World Cup final, and then played along as we had him raise aloft a crudely crafted version of the World Cup trophy—a mannequin's hand grasping a grapefruit spray-painted gold—before a bellowing crowd.

The last time I saw Klinsmann was in Jacksonville the day before the US flew to Rio. The mood in camp was off. There had clearly been a number of arguments behind the scenes, and Jürgen was still necking down espressos like a madman. I asked him if he remained confident. "I don't know," he said with an uncharacteristic pang of reticence, "but this is a World Cup and anything can happen there." Then he jumped up in the air and clicked his heels together like some kind of German Fred Astaire, squealed his high-pitched laugh, and charged straight out of the set through a door marked "Fire Exit Do Not Enter!" Very, very Jürgen.

I landed in Rio the day the World Cup kicked off. I had no idea what to expect. Our mission was still very unclear. We had had one production call with the small gaggle of ESPN producers. I would not say they understood our assignment any better than we did. It was quickly evident that the company had not exactly assigned us their top-level creative talent. The lead producer was Chris Wondolowski, who oddly and coincidentally shared the very same name as a third string striker on the US squad. No matter what we asked, Wondo just kept repeating, "We just want to show Brazil as a place that is more than about samba and sun and carnival." I remembered those words when I arrived at Rio airport's baggage claim carousel above which loomed an enormous advertising board bellowing, "WELCOME TO THE LAND OF SAMBA, SUN, AND CARNIVAL."

We went right from the airport to the set ESPN had constructed on the beach in Rio, overlooking a stunning view of Sugarloaf Mountain. It was an impressive feat of engineering. Multiple levels of studios purpose-built out of scaffold solely for the month to broadcast in a Tower of Babel's worth of languages. Upon arrival, we were greeted by a head producer. A gruff veteran of the NFL, who had seen the rise of football and jumped on it as a political move to strengthen his power within the network. He walked us into the English-language floor, which was a hive of activity as tech guys and writers charged around setting up for the opening ceremony, but as Michael and I were paraded around, everyone stopped, smirked, and stared. You know that feeling of everyone in the room being in on the joke but you? That is what I experienced in that moment as Davo and I were perfunctorily introduced to key staff, one by one.

The producer marched us into the main studio. It was expansive, stunning, and a little daunting to be honest. A panel of American 1994 veteran Alexi Lalas, Dutch legend Ruud van

Nistelrooy, and Brazilian World Cup winner Gilberto Silva waved at us as they were prepped to go on air.

"This is our studio," the producer boomed with pride, "but you won't be in here."

I did not quite understand what was happening, but the sneer on his face suggested I would not have to wait long to find out. He marched us out of the studio at some pace, leading us through a gauntlet of grinning staff, all of whom knew exactly what was going on. We headed to a deserted area of desks at the back of the complex where there was a door marked "closet," which he theatrically yanked open. I peeked my head in to discover that this cramped storage area had been quickly and cheaply retrofitted with a single fixed camera overhead, pointing down at a tiny desk. An old air-conditioning unit groaned, with a bucket placed underneath to catch the dripping.

"This is your spot," he said with a broad grin, as the entire office broke out in unified rip of belly laughter. "Just because Skipper wanted you to work the World Cup does not mean we wanted you to be here. The big studio is for real footballers," he said with a stinging contempt. "You guys can knock yourself out in there."

It was immediately clear this closet studio was intended to be a symbol of exile and ridicule, but as I saw it, the exile only meant we were not going to be forced to operate in the starchy confines of that colossal main studio with its polished woods and enormous crews. Our improvised, rambling conversational style would have been lost in that vastness. I did not love being the butt of an elaborately choreographed office-wide joke, but I much preferred the intimacy of the closet with its tight-cropped single camera. The leaky air conditioner could be fixed. We could win the World Cup in there.

We had no time to dwell on this anyway. The opening game of the tournament, Brazil versus Croatia, kicked off within the hour, and Michael and I tried not to be noticed as we slid into the green room and began to watch with the legendary footballers who were now our fellow broadcasters. The ceremony largely consisted of the agony of Pitbull and Jennifer Lopez vampily dueting the official World Cup song, "We Are One (Ole Ola)," but it was followed by a poignant moment right before kickoff. The Brazilian players and fans bellowed out their national anthem while hosting the tournament for the first time since 1950. After all the social unrest of the past year, this felt truly cathartic. The green room makeup artist, a sweet Rio-born grandmother, stood up from her chair and sang softly to herself as a tear rolled down her cheek. She cried again as the Brazilian team proceeded to barnstorm to a 3–1 win against Croatia with two goals from Neymar, their twenty-two-year-old star who made light of the weight of his countrymen's expectations, playing like a manga comic book hero come to life. A turbocharged boy amongst leaden-footed men.

We streamed live that night for the first time, postgame, summing up the day as part of ESPN's wrap-up show. As we waited to make our debut, I listened to the segment preceding us. The Brazilian midfielder Gilberto Silva and Alexi Lalas prattled on about the tactical complexities of the game, most of which I knew were lost on the now vast American audience, the majority of whom were new to football. Then we came on, opening with a pretty terrible joke about how elated I was to discover that Barry Manilow was so venerated within Brazilian culture that they had named a beach, Copacabana, after one of his most famous songs.

I had experienced a crash course in live television from the surreal experiences on *Morning Joe*, so the adrenaline rush of our late-night hits and the long postgame hours that we hosted on ESPN.com after every big game felt almost normal. However, the entire experience of a big television tournament regimen broadcast live and onsite from the host-city studio was altogether another thing. In the last World Cup, we were responsible for a single daily half-hour podcast. Now we were broadcasting shows live from Rio at least four times a day. There were three games to keep up with daily, each of which was like a different language to be mastered. The spigot of news that bubbled alongside them demanded a third eye just to keep up. Fitting into the routine of production was also an adjustment. Beginning with living hotel life for a month, *Suite Life of Zack & Cody*–style, the endless cycle of bus rides to and from the broadcast complex, and learning how to fit in to a green room culture that included world-famous football figures was *a lot*. We watched alongside Michael Ballack, Ruud van Nistelrooy, and Roberto Martínez, and we tried to play it cool, making casual chatter to show we belonged, even as it was quite clear we did not belong, and the little fan voice inside us so wanted to scream out in exultation.

Every morning, I woke up early and walked along the boardwalk above Copacabana to marvel at the commitment of the thousands of Colombian and Argentinian fans who had arrived without tickets and were now sleeping at different ends of the beach. In between them were masses of Brazilians playing *Altinha*—a version of soccer where the players form a circle and use their feet, chest, and head to keep a ball airborne between them, performing dazzling keepie-uppies in large circles. Some even had their dogs joining in. By my rough accounting, there appeared to be hundreds of Brazilians and at least a handful of pets who were more technically gifted with a football than the US Men's National Team players.

After clearing my head, I proceeded to spend much of the next fourteen hours each day locked in and around our airless broadcast closet, which we had renamed Bob Ley's Panic Room. We did see the irony in coming all the way to Brazil, football's spiritual home, only to spend our days trapped in a windowless storage room. But the football was dizzying, and that was all that mattered. Defending champion Spain imploded, smashed 5–1 by the Netherlands, a rout that signaled the sudden end of an unprecedented era of dominance. England also crapped the bed, losing their first two games and exiting the tournament with one group game still to play, their worst showing since 1958.

These results, coupled with the rapturous experience of the world's fans savoring their nations' journeys around the stunningly diverse ecosystems of Brazil, gave our broadcasts a transcendent narrative. We soaked it up, attempting to capture the experience of watching the drama as part elite athletic event and part soap opera. We thrived on our ability to talk about what we were watching in a way that was authentic, human, and accessible for the flood of American fans experiencing a World Cup. The fact we were broadcast on ESPN's digital channels was also a gift. For the first time on record, the majority of young viewers followed the World Cup on their iPhones, as opposed to the traditional broadcast channels.

In the big studio, ESPN's heavyweight football analysts broke down tactics and statistics in a musty, traditional, missionary-position style. In our Panic Room, we spent more time marveling at how German manager Jogi Löw looked like the Bavarian love child of Dr. Oz and Dorothy Hamill and seemed utterly unashamed to plumb his nasal recesses brazenly for the world to see. Davo and I had a running joke about how jersey manufacturer Puma had elected to clad teams like Algeria, Uruguay, and Ivory Coast in such tight jerseys that every player's nipples were constantly revealed by the polyester sausage casing to such an extent we worried about collective chafing.

Above all, we celebrated the sideline antics of Mexico's passionate manager Miguel Herrera, who charged up and down the pitch rejoicing goals as if he was experiencing a hallucinatory fit or witnessing a barfight he was desperate to join. More than any, these kinds of conversations caught the imagination of our audience and helped turn Herrera into a meme. After his Mexico thrashed Croatia, we were invited onto *SportsCenter* to discuss our love for the man, where we affirmed that during the ninety minutes of that match, Herrera had singlehandedly expressed more joy than the entire English nation has experienced since Queen Victoria passed away in 1901.

The energy around our Panic Room was being felt across the ESPN compound. The big-named football talent started to request the opportunity to guest in our closet rather than to appear on the big set. There was no third seat, so viewers would be treated to the spectacle of Dutch legend Ruud van Nistelrooy or Premier League manager Roberto Martínez hovering awkwardly behind us as we peppered them with questions. The producer still iced us. He had a shtick in which he would hand out dozens of match tickets daily to reward staff of every level by giving them the once-in-a-life chance to watch a World Cup game at the legendary Maracanã Stadium. He delighted in the power of this ritual, like a crooked politician doling out patronage. Every day he would approach our Panic Room as if he were poised to give us a pair of tickets, then spin around dramatically at the last to psych us out.

We were honestly too busy to care. This US team had pluck and tenacity, and their World Cup journey gave us, and the watchers at home, something to focus on. The opening-round challenge could not have been tougher—Group of Death. Again. Germany, Portugal, Ghana. Again. Germany and Portugal were second and fourth in the FIFA rankings. Yet, our boys were supported by a vast army of fans. Just as it had in South Africa, the US led all other countries besides the host in ticket sales, buying over 200,000. The supporters' group, the American Outlaws, had 18,000 members nationwide fly in from over 140 chapters. This was the World Cup in which the American fan chant, "I believe that we will win," was omnipresent. We heard it crackle all over the streets of Rio as we moved around town, meeting the fans at night when we stumbled out to dinner.

In the opening game, Jürgen Klinsmann led his team against Ghana, the African regional power who had caused us borderline-national trauma twice before. This game felt almost biblical. It was played in remote Natal, a town that had experienced a Noah's Ark–worthy flood in the days up to kickoff. Upon arrival, American fans had to wade through knee-deep water to enter the stadium, but the trial proved worth it. Almost straight from the kickoff, the United States scored. Inside thirty seconds, captain Clint Dempsey charged down the flank like a cocksure sniper, cut inside, and unleashed a left-footed bolt into the net. I watched along with the broadcast talent in the ESPN green room in Rio. US women's legend Julie Foudy was sitting on the couch next to me. As Dempsey charged away to celebrate in bug-eyed ecstasy, she turned and silently hugged me. The goal felt like an elimination of doubt. This team I had lived with, whom I had watched face so much doubt and inner turmoil, were up 1–0.

Scoring early in a game is a rapturous experience, but it is also fear-tinged. The team you love now has something precious to lose and that can gnaw at their collective mentality. Having struck in an instant, the United States proceeded to drop back and attempt to hold on. A dangerous game. The action became a fearful exercise in holding on for dear life and the ensuing eighty-nine minutes feeling like an eternity. Ghana outshot us 21 to 8, so when the Black Stars equalized in the 82nd minute, the goal was accompanied by a sense of inevitability. Julie Foudy was known to eschew foul language, but even she greeted the strike with a short blast of profanities from our anxious perch on the couch.

Sometimes, in life and in football, there are teams that always seem to find a way to eclipse you. For the United States, Ghana had very much been that team. In this game, the US had been punished for striking early, then reverting into a defensive crouch. That sense of an opportunity wasted, which had been such a soundtrack to all of our World Cup dreams, threatened to unspool itself once again. But then, in the 86th minute, young German American defender John Brooks, who had ambled on as a substitute, managed to rise up to smash a thunderous downward header into the goal, charging away while touching his head in incredulous celebration, like he could not believe what his body had just done before collapsing to the turf in an exhausted fashion beautiful to witness.

I had spent time with Brooks—a sweet kid who had proudly tattooed a map of his hometown of Berlin on one elbow, Illinois with a star marking his family's original home of Chicago (or Chee-kah-gow as he pronounced it in his thickly accented

English) on the other. I knew he had quite literally dreamed of scoring a World Cup–winning goal for the United States, and the world had all just watched him make that real. The United States had been the better team for just the first thirty seconds and the last four minutes, but that was all that mattered.

The response on the homefront was instant and deafening. The internet was flooded with mesmerizing bar scenes, as Americans across the nation lost their minds, threw beers in the air, and connected to this team, to this sport, and to each other with a sense of national pride that is hard to match in other sporting pursuits. *The Guardian* wrote: "The most powerful nation on earth, awakening to the existence of soccer and the fact that its national team was still alive in the 'Group of Death,' went duly and very American-ly crazy."

All of this felt incredible. The United States was suddenly, madly, truly, deeply in love with football, and our little podcast was at the forefront. *SportsCenter*'s producers began to ask us to join them in prime time every night to sum up the daily action, preferring our slightly hyperbolic telling over the dry analysis of the footballing talent they had traditionally relied upon. Every time we went live and I saw our silly little *Men in Blazers* logo blown up to enormous size on the screens on the *SportsCenter* set, it was all I could do to stifle a laugh.

The United States then marched on to Manaus, a magical city deep in the Amazon rainforest, only accessible by plane or boat during the rainy season. The players had to have inoculations for typhoid, yellow fever, tetanus, hepatitis A, and influenza just to play the game. The Brazilian organizers had built a $290 million stadium smack dab in the middle of a hot zone, a stadium that would soon become a white elephant. But for now, it was built to look like a straw basket. That straw basket was muggy as hell. It was 84 degrees in Manaus with 70 percent humidity. Moths and mosquitoes circled the field. Worse still, we were facing Cristiano Ronaldo's Portugal. Ronaldo, that preening show-pony whose movement and Adonis musculature seemed otherworldly. The closest football has ever gotten to a mythic hero, capable of almost inhuman feats on the field. Our chances did not feel good. That feeling took just five minutes to harden and become truth. A scuffed clearance by defender Geoff Cameron gifted Portugal's mischievous Nani to scoop their opener. This US collective was resilient, though, and in the 64th minute, that dreadlocked German American Jermaine Jones, he of the stars and stripes kneecap tattoo, whipped an artfully curling drive through traffic and inside the far post from way downtown, or as he would say it, "Way Innenstadt."

Seventeen minutes later, we were back in dreamland. Clint Dempsey was again the hero, putting the USA ahead with his abs of steel, chesting the ball into the net, and letting a monstrous Texas roar careen out into the Amazonian air. Jürgen Klinsmann sprinted up and down the touchline like a toddler who had just been told he was going to Disneyland. I was watching, once again, in a packed ESPN green room. Foudy and I had both agreed to sit in our same lucky seats. As the room went berserk all around us, we just looked at each other in stunned silence. This was what we had dreamed about.

Yet, football allows for very few dreams to come true. Deep into stoppage time, Ronaldo enforced his will on proceedings, slinging a soaring cross across the face of the goal, to set up his stooping teammate Varela to head home. Less an equalizer, more a gut punch. At ninety-four minutes and thirty-three seconds we had just fallen victim to the latest goal ever scored in regulation time in World Cup history. We had been thirty seconds from knockout round qualification and could almost taste the sweaty, metallic champagne-y tang of Group of Death glory. Now we had to regroup and face Germany. I attempted to bring some perspective to our national pain by tweeting: "This may be as close as you will ever come to feeling English, America."

Clint Dempsey had a much more positive spin for the cameras before the game in Recife: "We're Americans. I think we like to do things the hard way." American fans once again had to wade through floodwaters and gridlock traffic just to make it to the stands. Still, they walked along the highway shoulder dressed as Uncle Sam, the Statue of Liberty, and Captain America. Will Ferrell had flown in specially for the match against Germany. US manager Jürgen Klinsmann was facing off against his old nose-picking sidekick, Jogi Löw. Low had succeeded him as manager of the German team and was so confident he probably would have stuck a finger down his shorts and sniffed it during matches without fear or shame.

Now we would finally see who the real master was. In truth, most of the German players hated Jürgen for his whacky, inconsistent, new-agey methods. They thought he was a fraud, a footballing medicine man, and were motivated to embarrass him. The other subplot was the host of German Americans who now rode with us. Jermaine Jones said that if he scored, he would not celebrate the goal. Luckily, for him, and sadly for the United States, he never had to make good on that. The US lost 1-0. The only goal came when Germany took a short corner and eventually crossed it. Tim Howard saved the ball, but Thomas Müller ruthlessly lashed the rebound home from the edge of the box. It turned out not to matter, though. On the sideline, US goalkeeper coach Chris Woods used his fingers to tell the score in the other game, raising two fingers with one hand, and one with the other, and then raising two thumbs up to signal, "We all good, baby." Portugal was beating Ghana, which meant the USA had done just enough to emerge from the Group of Death, advancing on goal difference over Portugal. Even though we were losing to Germany, as news of the Portuguese goals crackled around the stadium, a roar emerged and American fans started their "I Believe" chant.

Our broadcast postgame that evening played to record numbers. Michael and I wrapped scarves around our heads and blew into cheap plastic World Cup trophy replica noisemakers I had bought on the beach. Our audience on digital in that little Panic Room with its leaky air conditioner held its own in comparison to that of the gigantic, money-burning studio. As an Englishman who had dreamed of becoming an American since childhood, to celebrate this deeply patriotic moment felt euphoric in a way I had never previously experienced because my personal and professional journeys were colliding in a way that each reinforced the other. When the broadcast finished, I was so emotionally and mentally spent, I lay down on the floor of the Panic Room like John Brooks celebrating his winning goal against Ghana, only I did so to take a quick nap. ESPN's communications director woke me with the startling news that the *New York Times* arts section had called. They intended to write a feature with the working title: "The Men in Blazers Are Winning the World Cup."

I didn't sleep another minute that night. I did not want to miss watching a single live broadcast beamed in from home. The scenes were mesmerizing. President Obama celebrated on Air Force One; the Empire State Building was lit up red, white, and blue; and fans across the nation partied like it was 1999. Yes, the United States had been roundly outplayed but won our first game, conceded in the final minute of the next game to draw, then lost the third, but we were alive. And football is about emotions, not fact. Our audience was wildly jubilant, even though many were not sure what was going on. One tweet we received summed that up: "Don't really understand soccer. How many games do we have to tie or lose before we win the World Cup?"

In the first knockout "Round of 16," the United States faced Belgium in Salvador, a battle between the Statue of Liberty and Manneken Pis. It felt like the whole nation was riding with our team. Even that veritable institution Waffle House was tweeting about the game before kickoff, proclaiming: "We don't believe in Belgium waffles." Obama moved a cabinet meeting so he could watch. Fourteen million people stopped working, costing the US economy a reported $600 million.

On paper, this was an imbalanced contest. Belgium was a superpower. A talented squad stuffed to the max with globally renowned players in their prime, like the iconic visionary midfielder Kevin De Bruyne and big-buttocked wizard Eden Hazard. As I've repeatedly stated, we were not. And in the opening exchanges, the distance between the teams showed. This was a battle of fleet-footed technical skill against collective grit. And somehow, grit held out. Just. Belgium opened a can of whoop-ass, bludgeoning an enormous 38 shots on the US goal. American goalkeeper Tim Howard had the game of his life flinging every one of his limbs at the oncoming Flemish buzzsaw, swatting aside a record 16 saves. It was Marvel Comic Hero–levels of superpower. Tim blocked shots with his hands, his feet, his knees, and his heart. After the game, I spoke to Tim and he described his experience of the game as an infinite torment in which time dragged so slowly, he believed the stadium clocks had broken.

The United States were pummeled, but in football, every team has a puncher's chance, and the Americans fell to substitute Chris Wondolowski, the hippie-dippie striker who shared the name with our producer and talked and acted as if he could have been an extra in *Bill & Ted's Excellent Adventure*. In the last seconds of the game, the ball fell to him at close range. Wondo had been a goal machine in MLS, and with the net at his mercy, and just the goalkeeper to beat, he pulled his foot back and prepared to deliver a kill shot that would change his life forever. The shot was so easy, our producer Chris Wondolowski could have finished it. Instead, the moment was too much for Footballer Wondo and he whiffed the ball over the bar. A human agony that left him holding his hands together, as if praying for a time machine to let him take a redo.

The game went into extra time. I watched, back in my lucky seat on the couch, in a standing-room-only green room. There is a phrase in English football, "squeaky bum time," which connotes the anxiety experienced during the nerve-wracking final stages of a game. The ESPN green room fell silent, the only sound the tense clench of our collective bungholes.

That did not work. Belgium appeared to make light work of extra time, goals by the great ginger De Bruyne and a second by potent striker Romelu Lukaku made it feel like game over. But the US rallied at the death. Nineteen-year-old German American Julian Green, who many saw as a controversial selection in Landon Donovan's place, trotted onto the field as a substitute and pulled one back with a brilliantly struck volley with his first touch of the ball in the World Cup. Dempsey had a one-on-one chance at the death, but was denied, and that was that. I felt the finality of defeat and the agony of a journey that was suddenly over, but also a profound pride in our players, who had played their hearts out, gone toe to toe, and dragged mighty Belgium into a scrap. I know that is not an American outlook—appreciating a valiant defeat. Our nation is typically unforgiving around losers, but Howard's unearthly performance and a gratitude for the memories that had been made in this tournament made the players instant heroes. *Good Morning America* tweeted: "Tim Howard for President 2016." Tom Hanks tweeted: "Tim Howard remains a God."

The aftermath was incandescent. America felt alive to football. Every tournament feels like a national referendum on whether soccer belongs, and on this day, it truly felt like it had been welcomed in to stay. There had been viewing parties at Chicago's Soldier Field, at San Diego's Petco Park, at New York City's Bryant Park, at Pittsburgh's Market Square, at Washington DC's Freedom Plaza, and at Boston's City Hall. A record 24.7 million people watched the USA–Portugal match. More than any NBA Finals game *ever*. That blows any World Series away. But beyond the numbers, we finally had a men's team with players the masses knew and loved.

Our show that night was mournful yet proud. I was shocked by how emotionally devastated I was when we went on air and spent much of the conversation afraid I was going to break down and sob on a live broadcast. The back half of the show consisted of eulogizing the team's achievement by reading tweets from the world's journalists marveling at our boys. Even Henry Winter, one of the leaders of the traditionally dismissive English press pack, wrote approvingly: "The American choirs chanting 'I believe that we will win' simply reflect the inexorable rise of the sport in their country, and that they are now a respected force in the global game." I remember reading that and thinking, it does not matter who wins the tournament now, the US fans are the real darlings of the tournament—the size of the contingent, their noise, and their ebullient positivity. I had seen them all over Rio and can affirm, the United States did win the World Cup, but sadly only off the pitch.

The *New York Times* article came out on the front page of the arts section. It was headlined "At World Cup, Two Unknowns Are Surprise Stars." It was an incredibly generous piece, comparing our work to Dan Patrick and Keith Olbermann's in the early days of ESPN's *SportsCenter*. The NPR show *Car Talk* was also mentioned. Bob Ley paid us back for the live show we threw for him by providing a killer quote, describing the advice he had given ESPN's producers: "I said you basically just need to tell them how much time they have and turn them loose." When we walked into the ESPN compound the morning the article broke, the whole office rose to their feet and gave us a standing ovation from behind their desks. Many of these same people had mocked us the day we first arrived. It was all a little embarrassing, and I was relieved to be able to close myself into the sanctuary of our closet.

That article turned our brand into hyperdrive. Celebrities who were in Brazil started to call ESPN to find out if they could come and take photographs in the Panic Room. NFL defensive tackle Ndamukong Suh was the first to come in that night, a man so enormous we almost had to wedge him into our tiny studio. Television network executives flooded our agents with offers of television deals. We now had to fit a bewildering flurry of conference calls with ESPN, Fox, and NBC into an already packed schedule. Perhaps most rewardingly of all, the ESPN producer slithered into our little studio carrying a six-pack of beers and doing something I had never seen before: attempting to smile at us. "Lads, some hard-earned ice-cold brews," he said, in the watery tone of a man who knew he had been forced into a charm offensive. "Let's celebrate the success we are achieving *together*." Insert eye roll.

The rest of that World Cup was a blur of research, production, calls with agents, and commercial offers. In between, we thrilled at a multitude of exclamation-point moments. Many off the foot of James Rodríguez, an impossibly good-looking Colombian talent who blasted a tournament-leading six goals, dragging Colombia all the way to the quarterfinals and redefining the way we say the world pronounced James ("Ham-ez.") We were also paid witness to Luis Suárez, the skullduggery-soaked Uruguayan striker who had offended the entire African continent in 2010 by saving a goal-bound Ghanaian shot with his own hands, one-upping his heel status by biting an Italian opponent in the shoulder mid-game. All this action, from the sublime to the dentally ridiculous, was a gift for Davo and me, and our growing audience on *SportsCenter*.

My wife, Vanessa, flew over for the semifinals. She landed seconds before hosts Brazil faced up to a fearsome Germany in the World Cup semifinals. I was barely able to kiss her hello before finding a place for her in a packed green room, jamming her on the couch beside Gilberto Silva, the analyst who had won the World Cup with Brazil in 2002.

Even with Neymar out with injury, the Brazilians in the ESPN office were swaggering with confidence and expectation. They had not lost a competitive match at home since 1975, and the way their players bellowed the national anthem before the game reinforced the sense we were watching a team on a mission from God.

What followed turned out to be one of the most harrowing ninety minutes of football I have ever witnessed. Eleven minutes in, with the frenzy of the national anthem no doubt still crackling around their brains, Brazil defended with an adrenaline-filled recklessness, leaving the lethal Thomas Müller utterly unmarked to volley home. The room was silent, bar a suppressed cackle of delight from German analyst Michael Ballack, who had all the charm of *Conan the Barbarian*–era Schwarzenegger. Gilberto Silva glared at his colleague manspreading in an armchair to my right.

We would hear that Saxon cackle on repeat in the first half because what followed was Brazilian self-destruction bordering on national surrender. Two German goals flew in mercilessly from all angles within the course of just 179 seconds. After the fourth, a clinical move straight through the soft, disintegrating Brazilian gut, Ballack could no longer contain himself. "This is too easy," he boomed, drawing out the two syllables of the final word like Arnold in *The Terminator*. That was too much for a visibly distraught Gilberto Silva, who leapt across the coffee table with arms outstretched, hell-bent on throttling Ballack. It took the combined efforts of Ruud van Nistelrooy and former Argentinian midfielder Santiago Solari to hold him back.

Silva was ushered out of the room, and perhaps it was for the best. The Brazilian fans who had expected to watch a coronation were now forced to witness a national funeral. I was sure a handful of those Brazilians I had seen execute artful keepie-uppies on Copacabana beach along with their dogs could have mounted a sterner resistance. The yellow-and-gold-clad home fans in the stadium booed their team off at halftime and spent the second half ironically "olé"-ing every German pass in an attempt to vent their fury and disappointment, deriding the men who had been national icons less than ninety minutes earlier. Even for neutrals, the game was too emotionally distressing to watch. This was more than a loss. It was as if Brazil's entire football heritage was being dismantled goal by goal. The green room emptied out. Only a handful stayed, including my wife and Ballack. I pitied the Rio-born makeup artist who was obliged to remain at her station by the back wall and had to watch the entire annihilation. She sat slumped in a near-fetal position in her own makeup chair, head in hands, weeping.

Germany won 7–1. It honestly felt like they had scored 70 goals. Think of how harrowing it would be if America's best NFL stars faced another nation and were blown out. After the final whistle, I walked out into the streets of Rio with my wife, streets that were packed with dazed Brazilians who were completely silent. A national collective dream, shattered into a million pieces with the world watching. We walked to Shirley, a classic old Rio fish restaurant where I had begun to eat late every night. Outside of it, a car had been set on fire and burned quietly. The flames foreshadowing the return of civil unrest now that the football ceasefire had been broken.

Germany faced Lionel Messi's Argentina in the final. In the buildup to the game, the terrible prospect of the Argentines, the host-nation's archrival, winning on Brazilian turf became known as "Pesadelo" (Nightmare). Hundreds of thousands of Argentinians flooded across the border, making parts of Rio feel like Buenos Aires, filled with songs about Maradona's legend outstripping that of Pelé. No matter the outcome, this was a national nightmare for Brazil.

The game was a prolonged grind that went into extra time. Messi had been undeniable earlier in the tournament, but his World Cup was defined by the moment two minutes into the second half in which he was set free on goal, with only giant German keeper Manuel Neuer to beat. He proceeded to slip the ball agonizingly wide. The mischievous German Mario Götze made no such mistake when he was presented with a half-chance, 112 minutes into a shattering period of extra time. At the height of speed, he knocked a cross down with his chest, then dove to slap home an ethereal left-foot volley. A decisive, epochal moment in a night of wearied minds and limbs.

The end of a World Cup is always filled with sadness. It feels like an entire world is no more. There is also the instant awareness we must all have to wait four long years until we experience the global connection once again. But it is also accompanied by a sense of relief. To cover a World Cup is to give yourself over to its demands entirely. After a month in Rio, I was utterly shattered. My wife said I looked like Bruce Willis near the end of *Die Hard*, but without having lived out any of the heroic action scenes.

After the Brazil semifinal, Vanessa and I had taken a cog train up to see the Christ the Redeemer statue on Corcovado Mountain. When we reached the top and looked out at Rio, Vanessa turned and hugged me tightly, then started sobbing. She did not say anything, but I realized all of the stress she had felt over the past eight years as I had struggled to build a career as a football broadcaster in America was pouring out. All of the fear for our kids. All of the pent-up sense of frustration and occasional disappointment. I held her and then looked up at Christ on the rock with his art deco face and stared him right in the eye. At that moment, I was overcome by one feeling.

One day, the US men were going to win this thing.

Chapter 11

2018 World Cup, Russia

IN THE BRIGHT lights of a New York City studio, Bryant Gumbel, esteemed host of HBO's *Real Sports*, read the following words off a teleprompter, undoubtedly, for the very first time. "The World Cup conjures great passion in every country around the world, apart from this one," he began, before mustering every ounce of his veteran professionalism to mask his sense of surprise and disdain as he continued, "Americans have been aggressively blasé toward the game they call soccer. So how does one explain the success of two bald Englishmen *Men in Blazers* who have somehow gained fame and garnered an American following by talking about the beautiful game?"

What followed was a fifteen-minute behind-the-scenes documentary telling the story of *Men in Blazers*. It was helmed by veteran reporter Andrea Kremer, who was brave enough to leave the known world of the NFL sideline to travel with us on the opening leg of our first-ever tour across the nation for the duration of the 2018 World Cup. By that time *Men in Blazers* was popular enough to spend the entire tournament playing one sold-out theater after another, from Los Angeles to New

York City, night after night for a month. Kremer was with us in LA, St. Louis, and Seattle, and the scenes of football fever she shot cut together to make for remarkable viewing.

The more time Kremer spent with us, in theaters packed with young American football fans, the less she could mask her astonishment that these scenes—and this passion for football—could exist in America. "For decades, it has been the greatest riddle in sports. How to sell the world's most popular game to the United States?" she marveled breathlessly. "Somehow no one tried the obvious solution: take two balding Englishmen, shove them in a broom closet, and have them talk about whatever they have on their mind."

The scenes the documentary captured were indeed incredible, filled with football-loving Americans doing the Icelandic Viking Thunderclap, then pouring into a nearby bar after the show to meet us face-to-face and smash some beers, as was our custom. The HBO feature analyzed the success of our weekly television show on NBC, showing snippets of the guests we had welcomed, including John Oliver, Matthew McConaughey, and Will Ferrell (who deadpanned, "If you ever want tickets for LAFC, I got you . . . half price"), noting correctly that a lot of our popularity was grounded in our ability to "find a way to talk about soccer to a country that had not yet talked much about soccer." In one interview, she talked about how we had tapped into a massive fanbase by simply meeting their yearning to creatively connect to each other and the sport.

The night I watched that *Real Sports* piece debut felt very out of body. Yes, *Men in Blazers* had a television show covering the Premier League on NBC Sports. And yes, it was performing as strongly as the actual live games that came before it. But the ethos of the early Panic Room days had not changed. We were still a threadbare operation run by a tiny staff of three: me, producer Jordan Dalmedo, and showrunner Jonathan Williamson. So while we were hosting some of the biggest names in America as guests on our show—Eva Longoria, J.J. Watt, and McConaughey amongst them—and booking and marketing a monthlong national tour, we remained the size of a tiny cult restaurant in Brooklyn with a Michelin star and a chef who also worked as the maître d', waiter, and busboy.

That hit home when the *Real Sports* producer asked if his team could come in and film us on a show day. "We want to shoot some scenes in your writer's room," he said with the unbridled enthusiasm of a labradoodle let off its leash early in the morning at a dog park. I tried to dissuade them by explaining that there was not much to see, but he would not be deterred and so arrived with a four-camera team at 8 a.m. on the morning of a broadcast. That four-camera team then spent half a day crowding around the sight of JW and me sitting together in a cubicle with laptops on knees, as I blocked out my lines and JW wrote Michael's, silently bashing out the entire show in a joint Google Doc together. It took about an hour for the producer to realize that nothing more exciting was going to happen, and he turned to me and said, "You guys are like shadow puppet theater, casting a mighty shadow, but when you peek behind the screen, it's just one person's hand making little shapes right by a bright light."

This was humorous, a little hurtful, and an absolute truth. We were a tiny team, armed with an almost missionary zeal, a relentless work ethic, and a touch of deluded madness. If I had known how hard it was to book, market, and produce a national tour with three people, I would never have engaged in that march of folly. But not knowing what we were getting into made us fearless.

The motto of our podcast was stolen from a Philip Larkin poem, "We should be careful/Of each other, we should be kind/While there is still time." That sense of kindness was tested by the fact that the 2018 World Cup took place in Russia. Vladimir Putin's Russia. A rogue state.

This was not new terrain for FIFA, who had used past World Cups to serve up propaganda victories to Mussolini's fascist regime in 1934 (Surprise Winners: Italy!) and the Argentinian military junta in 1978 (Surprise Winners: Argentina!). The Russian football team, however, had historically been Cleveland Browns Bad. It would have shredded the modicum of sporting credibility commercial football still possessed if the hosts had channeled the Mighty Ducks and won the whole enchilada. Instead, the true victory Russia received lay in the political currency Putin's regime received from being given the gift of lording it over other world leaders in the presidential box for the oncoming thirty-two days of World Cup action.

Hosting duties had been awarded December 2, 2010, at a meeting of the FIFA Executive Committee in Zurich. The United States had actually arrived at the ceremony feeling swaggeringly confident that they would win the honors. Their representatives boasted about the viability of their bid, which had been centered around the noble ideas of our nation's diversity, the potential for record attendance and record profits for FIFA, and the fact that all stadiums and necessary infrastructure had already been built by NFL teams. How naive they were. The FIFA leadership of the day had little interest in existing stadiums. The construction process of new infrastructure enabled plenty of opportunity for kickbacks. We were offering the decision makers the exact opposite of what they were looking for. Silly Americans.

Yet, if the US bid team were blindsided, the English were left truly shamed as they had flown in Prince William, and that even more important royal David Beckham, to boost their bid. That's how confident they were of winning. The duo had to sit there ashen-faced as 2018 was awarded to Russia, and even more jaw-droppingly, 2022 was handed to the tiny Gulf state of Qatar, an oil-rich nation which had never even played in the World Cup.

Even FIFA's leaders seemed rattled by the strange hosting duo. "We go to new lands," declared a grim-lipped Sepp Blatter, the soon to be deposed president of FIFA, after reading the results out to the world. Both bids were colored by the individual corruption that was erupting amidst Blatter's executive committee at that moment. I watched the vote live on a laggy livestream in my office in New York City, keeling over with a sense of shock and impotence when the two winners were announced. There was such a brazenness to it all. How could Qatar, with 1.7 million people, only 300,000 of whom were citizens, whose football team had never previously qualified for the tournament, and where it is 104 degrees in the summer, be fit to host the biggest sporting event in the world? It felt like the far side of Mars had more self-evident strengths as a pragmatic destination.

So insane was the Qatar decision that the selection of Russia was overshadowed in the moment. But as the 2018 tournament charged toward us, Russia invaded and annexed Crimea, and the prospect felt more Kafka-esque. Indeed, a spigot of terrible stories rumbling into the tournament threatened to undermine Putin's dream of a global PR Coup as the world was rocked by a series of terrifying headlines. From the decision to legalize cocaine and heroin with a prescription within World Cup stadiums, to the construction of gigantic Soviet-style drunk tanks to counter English fans' beer-fueled antics, to the threat of an actual locust plague of biblical proportion descending upon the host city of Volgograd. British Prime Minister Boris Johnson spoke openly of his fear the tournament would serve Russia's propaganda interests in the same way the Olympic Games in Berlin had for Hitler in 1936. The drumbeat of sordid news stories leading into the tournament suggested this would be one World Cup best savored on television from the comfort of your own home.

Just as it seemed the darkness swirling around the tournament could not feel worse, the United States—our nation that had invented the automobile, space exploration, and the Cronut—somehow failed to qualify for the first time since 1986. I should preface the story of how this disaster unfolded by noting that, when it occurred, I felt an immense amount of guilt and personal responsibility. That remorse was located in the fact that while broadcasting the 2014 World Cup, I spontaneously announced live on television that if the US emerged intact from its opening-round Group of Death, I would become an American citizen. I made good on that vow, and the United States immediately failed to qualify for the next World Cup.

The truth was, the act of being sworn in as a citizen in a courtroom packed with 162 new Americans, hailing from 47 countries around the world, in front of my wife and kids was one of the most moving experiences of my life. While it was true that my youngest son, Oz, was a little disappointed the morning after that I did not immediately start talking like James Earl Jones, to fulfill my youthful dreams of moving here, dreams powered by John Hughes movies, the Super Bowl–winning Chicago Bears, and Tracy Chapman's debut album, was a personal ecstasy. Not to mention the power to vote, and I am not going to lie, the ability to sweep through passport control quicker. I had felt American for a long time. I had lived here for over half of my life. My wife was American, as were my four children. This moment truly cemented the sense of common destiny I felt for the US Men's and Women's Soccer teams. Then the very next time I could cheer for them, they crapped the bed, as if I was the latest sleeper cell secret agent dispatched by Moscow. (First rule of sleeper cells... don't tell anyone you are a sleeper cell. Unless it is a double bluff.)

How did this American Soccer Heart of Darkness journey go down? In a style reminiscent of that Francis Ford Coppola quote from the *Apocalypse Now* documentary, "We had access to too much money, too much equipment, and little by little, we went insane." The cycle began with Jürgen Klinsmann retaining his position as head coach for a second cycle, maintaining one hand on the reins, and the other on the forever stream of espresso cups. After the 2014 World Cup joy, I felt as buoyant and optimistic as Captain Edward Smith, commander of the *Titanic*. His words before that beauty set sail were "I cannot conceive of any vital disaster happening to this vessel." What happened to the US Men was essentially the American footballing version of that story.

The team's results began to nosedive. When we were shocked by Jamaica in the 2015 Gold Cup semifinal, our first loss to a Caribbean nation on American soil since 1969, Jürgen's leadership was showing visible signs of grating on many of the players, and worse, the fans. They were done with the difference between his big vision talk and the oft-insipid play of his squads. Klinsmann continued his penchant for auditioning any minor European-based player he could discover. He clearly did not trust the skill of any domestically based MLS talents. If you truly despised him, and many fans really seemed to, it was easy to make the case that it had been a mistake to keep him on for a second crack at the World Cup.

There was a fleeting respite in the summer of 2016 at the big South American international tournament, Copa América, which for unexplained reasons, other than the highly probable appetite for kickbacks by the organizers, had been agreed to be played on American soil. We cheered on our boys even as we braced for a car crash, but the US played just well enough to squeeze past mid-level threats Paraguay and Ecuador to reach the semifinal. This was the USA versus Lionel Messi's Argentina. A chance to prove we could hang. Instead, we were torn apart limb from limb. A 4–0 beatdown that could have been so much worse. The gulf in class was so evident, it was like watching an apex predator play with its food before gulping it down and devouring it whole.

Chastened, Klinsmann and his team attempted to refocus their attention on qualifying for the next World Cup. The final round of qualifying in our region is called the Hexagonal. The six best teams play each other at home and away with the top three qualifying immediately, and the fourth-placed team having a chance to do the same via a playoff against another mid-level continent. Was I worried going into the Hex? Not in the slightest. The US had last failed to qualify in 1986, and it was honestly considered a lock for us to emerge unscathed as one of three and a half teams out of six that included Trinidad and Tobago, population 1.4 million, about as big as Maine, and Panama, with 4.5 million people and Kentucky-sized.

The adage of the Hex is, win your home games, don't worry about the road games in which bags filled with urine could be flung at you by the crowd, and you will qualify. But then in our first game, we faced that forever dread rival, Mexico. The match was on home turf, in the mighty fortress of Columbus, Ohio. The score there is legally mandated to be Dos a Cero, but not this time, amigo. A horrific performance culminated in an 89th minute header from legendary rogue Rafa Márquez to deliver a 2–1 defeat. This was soon followed by a 4–0 road loss at Costa Rica, the first time we'd ever lost the opening two games of the Hex.

I had spent the afternoon with Jürgen Klinsmann in Washington, DC, shortly before the Ohio game and found him to be unusually subdued. A shadow of the man I had come to know during the 2014 cycle. Back then, his modus was fractious. No matter what he was supposed to be doing, he emitted the sense he was too busy for it. But when I filmed him in DC, he had all the time in the world for me. The entire camp felt different. The players wandering around the team hotel traditionally thrilled in the opportunity to be together. The culture was typically one of good-natured competition and mutual support. But on that day, with results faltering, the atmosphere was sullen and poisonous. Chatting to the players gave me the sense their brotherhood had been replaced by frustration bordering on mutiny. Against that backdrop, Jürgen was happy to hang with me, talking on and off the record. It felt like, at that moment, he needed a friend.

Jürgen, being Jürgen, tried to keep it upbeat. I asked him if he was sure the US would still qualify. "One thousand percent," he replied. He then told *The New York Times* he was "not afraid" about getting fired and that his critics "don't understand soccer or the team" before flying to Berlin and attempting to project positive vibes by hanging out with Barack Obama and German chancellor Angela Merkel at a state dinner. He gave Obama a German jersey with No. 44 on it, and Merkel a No. 1 USA jersey. Three days after flying home, he met with US Soccer president Sunil Gulati in Los Angeles and was fired. An era coming to an end, with the once swaggering Jürgen making a shocking exit mid-season, like Mischa Barton's character disappearing in the middle of *The OC*.

We had little time to mourn. This was a moment of chaos and fear. US Soccer sent up their version of a bat signal, and who answered but that old Dark Knight, sixty-five-year-old Bruce Arena, the lacrosse coach turned football manager who had led the US through the highs of 2002 and lows of 2006. The US team were on the precipice of the abyss and Bruce was the wily old riverman who could navigate them through treacherous rocky waters. Arena now had eight games left to salvage qualifying and perhaps a crack at atoning for his dreadful 2006 World Cup experience.

Bruce was a cultural sea change from Klinsmann. The sensible khaki dad Snagglepuss to replace Jürgen's Teutonic hippie-dippie. This was not a glamorous moment. This was like the US Soccer equivalent of having to call in Winston Wolf from *Pulp Fiction* to clean up a mess of our own making. This was the exact opposite of a rejuvenation.

A couple of days after his reappointment, I flew to Los Angeles to interview Arena. By that time in my career, I had filmed some of the best managers in the world, including Liverpool's Jürgen Klopp, Chelsea's Jose Mourinho, and Manchester City's Pep Guardiola. I had never spoken to anyone like Bruce before, though. He met every question with pursed lips, treating any query as if it was below him. At the same time, he appeared utterly unable to muster a single coherent answer. Exasperated,

I asked him to explain in simple language how he could take a hot mess of culture of a squad and turn it around. His eyes bulged, then he stared at me for a moment before quipping dismissively, "This is not my first rodeo, you know."

Arena's first move was to uptick optimism by matching thirty-three-year-old icon Clint Dempsey, the gent who had been pretty much the entirety of the US offense, and fusing him with our new great hope, eighteen-year-old Christian Pulisic. The next big thing from Hershey, Pennsylvania, who had become a teen sensation after moving to German powerhouse Dortmund aged just sixteen. The US had never had a prospect like him—a kid who could play with intense tactical precision and dribble with the touch of a poet. We had seen Dempsey smash the ball at goal whenever he could, and Landon Donovan destroyed all-comers in MLS, but we never had a player at world level who could compete.

I traveled to Dortmund to film Pulisic when he was eighteen. Back then, he was living with his dad who had moved over there to support him. He was still a kid in many ways, yet I watched him come on as a substitute against Real Madrid in the Champions League and change the game. He then burned off the excess adrenaline by reverting to being the kid he still was, staying up all night to play strangers on his Xbox. Pulisic was a record breaker. He scored his first goal for the US Men's National Team hours after his prom, became the youngest American to play in a World Cup qualifying game, and the youngest to score twice in a game. The team quickly became built around him, and the cultural mania that surrounded the player was unprecedented. Even LeBron James posted on Instagram while wearing a Pulisic jersey. At MiB, we had a meme created by one of our fans that used a medieval painting of an angel carrying a big baby up to heaven. The fan had put Pulisic's head on the angel and my big bald face on the baby. And it felt right. A reflection of the prevailing wisdom, that no matter what the problem was, Pulisic was going to save us all.

Bruce Arena cemented Christian as a starter, which led to a feel-good 6–0 stomp down over Honduras, a victory that bordered on a bloodletting. We even grabbed a point in the return road game against Mexico at the vaunted feared Azteca, courtesy of an inspired Michael Bradley chip from barely inside his opponent's half. The mood change suddenly felt delirious. World Cup qualifying was in our hands. Russia here we come. Bruce Arena was lording it up, carrying himself like Sting on the Police reunion tour. Yes, the entire band was back, but it was very clear to everyone, especially Sting, there was only one star in this show.

Yet, football is always unpredictable and a shock home loss to Costa Rica, in Harrison, New Jersey, wiped the smile off even Bruce's face. He started to remind people the team's predicament was Jürgen Klinsmann's fault, not his. Three straightaway draws left the US needing wins in the last window. Broadcaster and perpetual hot-taker Alexi Lalas called out the team, deriding them as "soft, underperforming, tattooed millionaires." Pulisic laughed the comment off: "I am not going to lose sleep about what Alexi Lalas has to say about us."

Amidst the chaos, the final pair of games began so positively. Pulisic tore Panama's backline apart in a 4–0 thrashing. The final match in which we just needed a draw against Trinidad and Tobago, or other teams to lose, felt like Bruce Arena's coronation. ESPN's Soccer Power Index gave us a 93 percent chance of making it. Trinidad had lost eight of its last nine games. Their population was roughly as large as the Greater

Hartford, Connecticut, metro area. As the worst team in the Hex, T&T had nothing to play for but pride. Our eighth straight World Cup qualification felt like a slam dunk.

But to misquote Chinatown, "This is CONCACAF, Jake." Our footballing region is a bizzarro-world in which startlingly unexpected outcomes have become normalized. The game was held in Couva, a small town thirty minutes outside the capital of the Caribbean country. Before the game, heavy rainfall left a moat in the track around the pitch. The US Soccer Twitter account mocked the conditions as the US players gave each other piggyback rides over it.

The game itself was an agony to witness. Throughout the night, the low hum of a generator on the far side of the stadium ground away like some kind of psyops torture technique. As bad as it felt, the United States performance was worse. In the 17th minute, an innocuous clearance ricocheted off the shin of defender Omar González and looped agonizingly over goalkeeper Tim Howard. A second goal then came out of nowhere, too, a 35-yard speculative long-range blast by Alvin Jones, an obscure defender, that caught Howard napping. Jones had never scored for the Soca Warriors before.

Pulisic pulled one back ninety seconds into the second half. The US proceeded to set siege to the Trinidadian in the second half but their goalkeeper, Adrian Foncette, who played for a local pro team, Police F.C. that represented the local police services, pulled off a series of brilliant saves, each one more stunning than the last, draining American belief with every feat of athleticism he accomplished. Watching at home in New York City was akin to being forced to experience someone you love flail, then drown, and be unable to do anything to save them.

Down the stretch in the 77th minute, Clint Dempsey hit the post. Yet, as bad as it was in Couva, the Hex's other games were going on simultaneously. Suddenly, miraculously, and cruelly, the worst outcome began to grip each of them. Honduras had twice been losing but somehow summoned the tenacity to clamber back from behind to beat Mexico 3–2, then Panama, who had first been awarded a phantom goal that never actually crossed the line, grabbed an 88th minute winner against Costa Rica. The odds of this were incalculable. To watch these goals fly in the box-within-box on live broadcast was to witness a Götterdämmerung situation in which the US did not even get the fourth-place playoff spot. At halftime, both Honduras and Panama had been losing, and the United States were through. With half an hour left, both results were still draws and we were safe. Indeed, we were still through as late as the 88th minute. Then came a denouement akin to the exquisitely choreographed climax of an early Guy Ritchie movie in which half a dozen rival gangs all take each other out.

Unlike a Guy Ritchie movie, though, the good guys were the ones being whacked. We fans had come to celebrate a wedding that had turned into a funeral. At the final whistle, Pulisic crouched on the field, ugly crying. He was still in his uniform, sobbing into his hands when his teammates put him in the shower. Arena sat there dumbfounded in his black suit with black polo, dressed for mourning. Tim Howard was asked if it was his last game with the US Men's National Team and he started crying. Tim Howard was thirty-eight. Christian Pulisic was nineteen. They were symbols of a team stuck between generations experiencing a result that bordered on arrogant self-destruction. The World Cup journey we had all dreamed of and expected had turned into shattered hope. All I could manage was to tweet out the chorus of Tracy Chapman's "Fast Car." The lines of longing that begin, "City lights lay out before us and your arm felt nice wrapped 'round my shoulder," hoping that the incomprehensible sense of sadness I experienced in the moment would be put into perspective by Tracy's unfathomable sorrow.

I watched the players' tears at home. I understood their pain. The true repercussions of sporting mistakes do not carry the same meaning as those made in real life. Football is often heralded as "the most important, least important thing." Yet, I can only compare the emotions that overwhelmed me in the moments after full-time to those you experience hearing news of an unexpected death, a sickening shock so profound it feels like you have been physically attacked.

This was more than the loss of one match. It felt like the US Soccer program had just taken the game they were responsible for growing and set it back a decade. I had always imagined America's football progress would occur in a straight line to glory. That truth was shattered, and it felt profoundly embarrassing. The scorn and mockery from those who still hated soccer was instant and resounding once news of crackled out over *SportsCenter*. It was also significantly louder than any bellow in a moment of glory. We were a punchline again. ESPN wrote: "No one still believes that we will win," mocking the once beloved fan chant. Fox host Rob Stone tweeted: "I need a drink. For a month straight." Piers Bloody Morgan tweeted: "RIP US 'soccer.'" With "soccer" in quotes, because he's an arsehole.

America hates losers. Our women's team were winners. Our men were hapless figures of shame and derision. I did not go to bed that night. I stayed up, accompanied by a large scotch, trying to imagine what my crew at *Men in Blazers* could possibly salvage from a tournament that did not feature the American men. It felt like we had just self-inflicted a catastrophic devastation upon our credibility as a soccer nation. One that would impact our business and livelihoods.

We did not know it at the time, but there would be a light in the darkness. Almost instantaneously, American players in their teens realized they could not stay home in MLS if they wanted to fulfill their potential and they moved, almost en masse, to European clubs to test themselves against the best quality of opponents they could find. Jürgen Klinsmann was gone, but the philosophy he had articulated became lived truth. But dark near term was reality. After qualifying for seven World Cups in a row, the United States did not make it to Russia 2018.

We now had to experience a World Cup without the United States in it. A baffling notion in the moment. *Men in Blazers* was about to partner with a large media company. That opportunity evaporated within days of the loss, the company reaching out via text to say that their data suggested football's profile would now go into freefall. That Americans would not care. Sponsors pulled out, unsure how to tell their stories to the American public. Landon Donovan, one of the greatest American players of his generation, was confused enough to appear in a commercial campaign for a bank, lifting a green scarf, proclaiming: "My other team is Mexico," pledging his allegiance to the United States' archrivals, a move for which he was instantly eviscerated. But besides the panic, and the true sense of doom that we all felt in the moment, I was most saddened by the set of memories new American soccer fans would be deprived of by missing the tournament. The memories we had made together in 2010 and 2014 had been the prime drivers for the growth of the game. As Dante's Francesca says in Canto V of *Inferno*:

"There is no greater sorrow than to recall happiness in times of misery."

When I am at my saddest, I crave action. We held a meeting of our staff the day after the debacle. There were four of us there. Me, producer JW, our technical brain in a bottle Jordan Dalmedo, and John Johnson, the Tony Award–winning theater producer who, despite sweeping all the awards for *Hello, Dolly!* with Bette Midler and *Three Tall Women* with Glenda Jackson, was still game to sully himself with us. Together, we racked our brains about how to cobble together a plan to still bring American fans together around this tournament.

The meeting began bleakly. We were all still stunned by the US National Team's ineptitude. But as we teased through the strengths and weaknesses of the moment, we talked our way into a plan born partly of rational confidence, and partially of magical thinking. We knew from the rise of our podcast that the audience here was still growing steadily and inexorably, World Cup to World Cup, rather than the overnight fad it was projected to be in 1994. The tortoise rather than the hare, but its roots had grown deeper and stronger as a result. A stunning 26.5 million Americans watched the 2014 World Cup final. A recent Gallup Poll among adults aged eighteen and thirty-four had uncovered that 11 percent cited soccer as their favorite sport, the exact same number as basketball. Both dwarfed baseball's measly 6 percent. Our audience was aged between twenty and thirty, the very listenership media analysts covetously refer to as "the Demo." We knew that their love for the English Premier League, the Champions League, the Mexican National Team, and the Mexican domestic league, Liga MX, had been propelled by a number of intertwining factors.

Global Soccer was the perfect sport for the internet era.

Just as baseball thrived in the golden age of radio, and the NFL boomed once television supplanted it, soccer had suddenly thrived in the United States because of the ubiquity of the internet, which for the first time empowered Americans to connect consistently to the ongoing storylines of the global game in real time. Fans in Manchester, New Hampshire, suddenly followed the soap opera that is Manchester United, and supporters in Madrid, New Mexico, could suddenly decode the goings-on in Real Madrid, as closely and with as much insight as those who live in the exact same zip codes as those two clubs' stadiums.

That blossoming love affair was not unrequited. Over the previous decade, the world's powerhouse teams like Barcelona, Real Madrid, Liverpool, Manchester United, and Bayern Munich had become obsessed with America, sensing the virgin terrain, audience size, and corporate sponsor-density as the perfect target at which to evangelize their brands. In the summer of 2014, 109,318 fans had packed Michigan's Big House to watch Manchester United and Real Madrid play a preseason game, a number that was eye-popping by European standards. A footballing arms race ensued as the clubs battled to win over American fans' hearts, minds, and fleshy wallets.

While those football colossi dreamed of taking over America, American sports owners took over the powerhouses. The dizzying global viewership numbers (an estimated 700 million people around the world tune in to watch Liverpool play Manchester United in regular season games. This number dwarfs the Super Bowl) and lack of the handcuffing revenue share prevalent in American Major Leagues attracted a phalanx of US entrepreneurs to charge headfirst into the game. By 2018, almost 40 percent of the Premier League teams had American owners, including Los Angeles Rams' Stan Kroenke at Arsenal,

Tampa Bay Buccaneers' Glazer Family at Manchester United, and Jacksonville Jaguars' owner Shahid Khan at Fulham. That year's Champions League semifinal featured Liverpool and Roma—two European legends, both owned by Bostonian-based businessmen John W. Henry and Jim Pallotta. The game should have been played at Fenway.

All of this was reinforced by the quiet explosion of the video-game maker EA Sports' juggernaut FIFA franchise as the silent hand that has grown the game in the United States. Unlike its NFL or NBA video game counterparts, whose popularity is an extension of its fans' preexisting love for those leagues, EA Sports had become a gateway drug for soccer in America, seeding a familiarity with the game, its nuanced playing styles, and stars across an entire generation of young, blue-blooded traditional American-balls sports-loving fans who previously discarded the sport as an adolescent rite of passage. The US had become the brand's second-biggest territory, eclipsing Germany and trailing only England.

In a way, we knew *Men in Blazers* was the living proof of all of this. Indeed, we had thrived because of it, and so, we sensed that even though the United States was out, and with Russia feeling like a less than desirable destination, there was an opportunity to still tour the nation and create a space for football fans to meet their kin again, and enjoy the global circus. We persuaded ourselves it might even feel freeing—to watch a World Cup when you were able to choose whom to follow with fresh eyes.

Still, the idea to go on tour and do nightly theater shows in which we would relive the day's action in the company of a live audience felt mad. But then Budweiser stepped in to give us the money they were no longer going to use for the failed US Soccer team, and suddenly John Johnson was taking a month off work to put a coast-to-coast tour into action—one that would take us from the West to the East, from sea to shining sea. A voyage of discovery that would ultimately teach us a heartwarming lesson: US Soccer may have failed us, but American Soccer was alive and well. As we traveled from city to city, we were able to explore and celebrate each fan culture's unique idiosyncrasies and broadcast them out to the nation.

We began in Budweiser's hometown of St. Louis, where we toured the brewery and learned that the proper way to pour a beer is to just dump it in the glass and create a massive foam head so that the carbon dioxide evaporates from the glass rather than bloats up your stomach. We pretended that drinking fresh Budweiser where it was brewed, like a Guinness in Dublin, just hit different. We then settled in to watch the tournament kick-off at a hotel bar in which we had to bribe the waiter $20 before he would deign to turn the sound on.

First, a subdued Robbie Williams sang with the look of a man who had been imprisoned in the Gulag for the last ten years and was playing for his freedom. No one seemed more surprised that Robbie Williams was playing the opening of the Russian World Cup than Robbie Williams. But his crooning was merely the supporting act for a UN-style address by Vladimir Putin, who attempted to refute accusations that his nation would be the worst hosts since James Franco at the Oscars by declaring his nation to be "an open, hospitable, and friendly country."

It all felt so deflating in comparison to the nipple-tingling electricity around the opening games of South Africa 2010 and Brazil 2014. The best thing you could say about Putin's display is that he showed a lot of restraint in resisting the urge to ride in on horseback, shirtless, with Alexander Ovechkin riding sidesaddle before doing the "wrestling a bear thing" at midfield.

As for the game, we had waited 1,432 long days since the 2014 World Cup final had ended for the 2018 tournament to kick off. For some reason, the opening game served up the two sides ranked the lowest in the competition, hosts Russia and Saudi Arabia. It's like kicking off the NFL Season by having the Cleveland Browns scrimmage against their practice squad, if both teams were just a bit more morally compromised. The game was an eyesore. It was Robbie Williams bad. The most intriguing action appeared to be in the presidential box, to which we were treated to constant cutaways in which Putin sat next to Crown Prince Mohammed bin Salman with FIFA president Gianni Infantino jammed in between them, beaming as if he knew the optics made him, a soccer bureaucrat, appear like the most powerful man in the world.

The football was so poor I spent most of the game wondering what the three were talking about. Putin perhaps mumbling, "Maybe I invade you, maybe I hack you, who knows . . . who knows . . . ? Life. It is full of, how do you say, Mr. Bond, 'Surprises'?" His Russia ran rampant, winning 5–0. It felt like we had just witnessed the first Russian victory in the modern period that did not involve Bots, fake Facebook accounts, or Troll Farms.

That night we marveled about it all in front of a sold-out crowd in St. Louis and also celebrated that city as one of the most fertile crescents of youth soccer development in the nation's history. From Harry Keough, the postman turned defender who held the mighty England team at bay at the 1950 World Cup, leading a team which had five players from The Lou to Tim Ream who would later become the captain of the

US Men, to Becky Sauerbrunn, who led the Women's National Team, and more. The crowd conveyed deep pride in their locality. When we welcomed Josh Sargent as a guest, the noise from the crowd that greeted the appearance of this eighteen-year-old local product, who was already plying his trade in the German Bundesliga, felt like we had brought Pelé himself onto the stage.

In the first week of the World Cup, we flew into Seattle to find a thronging packed house that was both knowledgeable and wildly passionate, then watched the games on a trip to Portland, Oregon, banging out scripts like a rock band who had to not only perform every night but also write a new album to perform every single day. Portland was the loudest audience we had ever encountered. The crowd drank the venue out of alcohol, then proceeded to shame-lecture me about my selection of Budweiser as a drink of choice, opposed to one of hundreds of local microbrews they had at their disposal.

Billy Beane joined us live onstage in San Francisco where, despite the absence of any kind of professional team in the vicinity, the high density of techies correlated perfectly with the early adopter mindset that drove the Premier League's rise to popularity. There was a line around the block to get into the theater and start drinking two hours before our show began. The US failed to qualify for the tournament. I wondered how large the crowd could be if they had?

The first week of a World Cup is always the best: three matches a day, one after the other, an experience which acts simultaneously like a monthlong football Christmas and a weeklong dip in global office productivity. The opening notes of this tournament were ones of surprise and cutthroat competition. World Cup newbie Iceland faced up to powerhouse Argentina.

I loved the Icelanders and had just traveled over there to make a documentary about their curious rise as a footballing micropower. The tiny nation of just 352,000 people—a population on par with Corpus Christi, Texas—was the smallest to ever qualify for World Cup play. Led by charming head coach Heimir Hallgrímsson, a dentist, they were a tenacious collective. Many of the players truly believed Viking blood ran through their veins. No matter who they were playing, they always believed that they would win.

I was fascinated by how pragmatic they were as a people. Yet they also believed everything was possible. A survey of that island discovered that 54.4 percent of Icelanders believed in elves and trolls. After witnessing the game, in which they felt like a pub team against Lionel Messi's elite football force, I ended up believing in elves and trolls, too. Sergio Agüero of Argentina opened the scoring. We had seen this man thrash many goals in the Premier League and keep his cool, and yet he suddenly lost control after scoring while wearing his national team's jersey.

Iceland, though, was undaunted and equalized, stinging the Argentinians in transition. Argentina was rocked, yet had a chance to restore order, drawing a penalty. Up stepped Messi, that divine footballer voted the world's best player five times by then. He faced goalkeeper Hannes Halldórsson, a gent who also moonlighted as a local videographer. Shockingly, it was Messi who crumbled under the pressure of the moment, firing the kick at a place where the giant Icelandic shot-stopper/cameraman could smother.

Messi's face was instantly wracked with pain. The soul-crushing burden weighing down a man who knew he had to lift his team to glory, and needed that glory to cement his own legend, had just failed himself, his teammates, and his nation. A stark contrast to the mood on Twitter, which exploded with a highlight clip of the save as broadcast on Icelandic television. The noise that came out of the local commentator's mouth sounded like a squirrel having tantric sex.

The surprises kept coming. Landon Donovan's newly beloved Mexico beat defending champion Germany 1-0 at the Luzhniki Stadium in Moscow. The Germans, usually the Darth Vader of global football, suddenly humbled. The world learned that the German language has a word for losing an opening game: *Auftaktniederlage*. They would not recover, and after sixteen consecutive World Cups, crashed out at the group stage for the first time. The defeat felt like an echo of history. Germany now 0-2 on Russian invasions.

So many of our fans, in the search for a rooting interest, pledged their allegiance to England as a natural outgrowth of their Premier League fandom. The familiarity of the stars of the league pulling on the English shirt made it an effortless transition. The squad was also shockingly likable. In stark contrast to superstar egotistical big names of yore, this version was packed with young, humble, relatable talents who were obsessed with table tennis, pool, and Fortnite like the fans who adored them. They were led by Tottenham's Harry Kane who came across as English in the same way a Spitfire squadron seems English in a 1960s war film. Personally, I felt circumspect, the result of being burned one too many times by England in my youth, and the fact that the team had just crashed out in back-to-back tournaments made my default setting "won't get fooled again" to quote the Who.

The English opened brightly in Volgograd, which World War II buffs might remember better as Stalingrad. A city that had become the hotbed of Putin's nationalism to the extent it was now policed by Cossacks on horseback armed with whips. The threatened locust infestation never materialized. Instead, a swarm of midges emerged from the Volga River, descending upon the England players during warmups, but they were not the greatest challenge of the night. Spitfire Squadron leader Kane opened the scoring, an achievement that caused the entire team to break out in an unabashed display of collective humping. Yet Tunisia was a plucky collective and they forced their way back into the game through a penalty. As the ball flew in, it felt like the sound of tabloid journalists sharpening their knives ready to gut their own team was audible.

England manager Gareth Southgate, who at the outset was known only as an innocuous character with the charisma of a regional bank manager, kept his composure on the sideline and at the last he was rewarded. In the 91st minute, off a corner, Harry Kane was left relatively unhindered, and he punished the Africans, like Tom Hardy in *Dunkirk*, shooting down the German Bomber just before his own fuel ran out. Watching that moment, I realized I had spent so many hours of my life watching England play football that I could summon very few happy ones. What Harry Kane did then as he snapped his neck muscles to head that ball home was an astonishing human act. He flipped an incredibly numbing, tedious script of national failure on its head. Gareth Southgate celebrating on the sideline, wearing just the waistcoat, which soon became his signature style, now looked like he was at a wedding and the DJ had just slapped on "It's Raining Men."

As England revealed themselves as a giddy, optimistic unit worthy of being happy about, France arrived with a squad as well equipped as Khaleesi disembarking in Westeros, with her

Unsullied and Dragons in tow, and similarly hell-bent on claiming the crown. The French squad was formed of a trout farm's worth of talent resembling a kind of Pro Bowl roster that was previously only seen on fantasy teams in EA Sports FIFA. Critics doubted whether their pragmatic coach, Didier Deschamps, could muster a tactical plan to harness their overabundance of potential. A challenge best embodied by his utilization of maverick Paul Pogba, an effervescently potent midfielder who could dominate games yet often seemed to save his best performances for social media. Pogba opened the group stage with disciplined intent and was decisive in key moments, sitting deep, then springing forward to smite all comers.

In the middle of the tournament, Budweiser invited us to travel with them to Russia as their guests for a couple of games. I flew over to Putin-ville with producer JW and the experience was much like going through The Looking Glass. Three generations after the Cossacks chased my family out of the country, I was back, because my love of football is just that powerful. The truth was, I had been to Moscow before, but this city we now walked around was unrecognizable to my previous visit. It was now a place gussied up by the best movie-set designers money could buy. Every wall had been whitewashed bright white. The bulbous onion domes on the hundreds of churches littered around Moscow gleamed with newly applied gold leaf. The hundreds of limbless war veterans I had previously encountered, begging on every corner, were now nowhere to be found. I shuddered to think what had happened to all the stray dogs that had once careened around unhindered. Indeed, it felt like anyone who was not model-esque in their beauty had been evacuated from the streets and replaced by a shoal of high-class prostitutes shipped in from regions across the country. The city was throbbing with beauty and sense of possibility. It also felt as inauthentic as the streets of Seahaven in *The Truman Show*.

JW and I got our steps in as we marched around a city packed with international tourists, all of whom appeared as charmed by Moscow as we were, unaware we were all dupes as we tweeted about its qualities, unwitting servants of Putin's propaganda dreams. The Russian locals attempted to be welcoming, whilst staying committed to their true air of menace. Their overall vibe was "Smile with a grimace that makes it very clear I am secreting a homemade shiv on my person." I gleaned from my rides on the palatially vaunted subway system that the male fashion trend for the summer appeared to be "enormous men carrying little manbags." The bigger the man, the smaller the bag. Most looked like they had just enough room to carry a wallet, some lip balm, and the severed finger of your enemy. It was always evident to me that I was, by some measure, the weakest man in Moscow. This was a city where every single piece of children's playground equipment appeared to be put in place solely to be used by small groups of swole men for makeshift MMA training. Many had Messi tops on. That little dude was on three out of five advertising billboards everywhere across the city, and it was only when walking around you truly appreciated the crushing level of pressure he was operating under.

We threw ourselves into this World Cup moment with the locals. On the first night, we watched Russia play their final group game against Uruguay in a bar built into a decommissioned 1950s nuclear shelter hundreds of feet underground. Russia lost but still emerged successfully to reach the knockout round. At the full time whistle the Russian fans sent a round of vodka shots for everyone at the bar, then proceeded to smash the bottles on the floor. It was both thrilling and intimidating to drink with the locals in their moment of national glory. They all eerily looked and acted like the gangster Paulie and Christopher chased across the frozen wastes of the Pine Barrens in *The Sopranos*.

We then went to watch a game live, snapping up tickets to witness Neymar's Brazil face Serbia. The atmosphere before the game was oddly silent and somber. Thousands of us walked through multiple security fences. The only sound was that of young female volunteers who had been positioned with bullhorns on lifeguard chairs spaced out every 100 yards and were instructed to shout "Welcome to Russia, beautiful Russia," which gave the pregame a cold, angsty vibe, like a scene from *The Handmaid's Tale* in which Gilead had been awarded World Cup hosting duties.

The stadium was packed. There were more Brazilians at the match in Moscow than I had encountered in Rio, where so many of the tickets had been corporate comps. We sat behind a lively, heavily tattooed duo who were utterly amped. The bigger one, wearing a Neymar shirt, looked like a Brazilian version of Ronnie from *Jersey Shore*. His friend, who was plumper and hairier, was super high and had the air of a gent looking for a fight. Once the game kicked off, the two stood up and proceeded to make their way through every single contact on their WhatsApp lists, video-calling one after another to boast that they were at the game. If the contact did not answer, they would quickly record a personal video message and dispatch it. I did not understand what they were saying but there was a liberal use of the word "Mano." Brazilian Ronnie's stamina was undimmable. It was fascinating to observe. Both men had traveled thousands of miles to be at the game, yet neither watched a second of it. However, their emoji creativity was indefatigable. Also impressive: The wireless cell service at the stadium was the best I had ever experienced. No expense had been spared to support Putin's propaganda desires.

The actual matchday experience may have been sterile, yet the memories of the games we watched in Moscow's local football bars were intoxicating. We quickly found a favorite, a shack boldly named Football Republic, which was a grand name for a bar that was essentially someone's backyard where you could down giant Belgian beers and watch the match on a couple of televisions that looked like they had been hauled straight out of a couple of locals' living rooms. This place was a veritable United Nations of sporting passions. Amidst the clink of beer steins, cigarette smoke, and fried cheese, we found a sliver of space to experience Portugal toil against Iran and a defensively vulnerable Spain struggle to impose themselves against Morocco, who came within minutes of stealing the game. Both games boiled down to late and prolonged refereeing decisions, Spain being awarded a 91st minute goal, which had initially been wrongly called offside, and Iran then being given a 93rd minute penalty to tie and shock the Portuguese and made the packed crowd of every nationality jackknife through a rollercoaster of emotion. To watch the Spaniards savor both decisions, enjoying their rival Portugal's comeuppance even more than their own team's achievement, was proof that spite is the rocket fuel of human motivation.

On the final night, Bud organized a boat ride down the Mosvka River during which we would partake in watching England's third and final opening-round clash via an enormous cinema screen, which swayed proudly after being set up on the deck. Bud bottlers from all over the world joined together to watch England, fresh off blasting six goals past a hapless Panama, their biggest-ever tournament victory. They now faced their first elite foe, Belgium. When the draw was initially made, this felt like one of the glamour matchups of the opening round. However, both teams had already qualified for the knockout round, so the spectacle was oddly diminished as both nations actually conspired to lose. They both knew the second-place team would earn a spot in what was perceived as the weaker side of the elimination bracket and be gifted an easier pathway to the final.

The game was akin to a faked orgasm, with both managers afterward making straight-faced attempts to convince the world that the aforementioned orgasm had been real. Both rested their key players. The football suffered, played without commitment or emotional investment. Yet, you would not have known from the deck of the Bud Boat. As the pleasure cruise passed the Peter the Great monument, St. Basil's, and the Kremlin, the noise was cacophonous, with beers going airborne at every opportunity, chucked into the murky waters as an emotional release. At the final whistle when Belgium had squeaked it 1–0 via a singular moment of excellence from Adnan Januzaj, it was the English fans on the Bud Boat who lost their minds. They felt like they had lost the battle but won the war. The game broadcast instantly cut out and a Russian DJ pumped up the volume on Pitbull's slightly nauseating World Cup song vaguely audible all over Moscow. A laser light show cut across the deck and two dozen balding middle-aged boozed up English guests cleared the dancefloor by cutting frenzied shapes they probably had not made since rave died.

I left Russia relieved to have survived intact, and as the proud owner of a tiny man bag of my very own, a trend I was now determined to import to the United States. But first: England versus Colombia in the Round of 16. A game I braced to watch with the *Men in Blazers* staff in a bar in Brooklyn where we had a show that night. I kept telling myself I did not care about the result, because I did not support England anymore, but I was insanely nervous. Even though I am now more American than Kenny Powers, watching England play World Cup football remains a uniquely powerful emotional experience. I knew just how much the team's success meant for my family back home in England, especially my dad. The optimism he experienced in the present coexisted in my heart alongside the throbbing open septic wound of countless self-sabotaging failures past. Living out the game, I was suspended between a bold confidence and a sickening, fearful, soul-crushing sense of doom.

To recap: England thus far had beaten two poor teams, and lost to one strong opponent, albeit in a game neither wanted to win. So, we had little idea going into this game exactly how good the English were. Thus, it was calming to witness Gareth Southgate's team assert themselves with a display of early confident, hungry football. Colombia, though shorn of their injured talisman James Rodríguez, sat back and fought hand to hand, a coiled fist ready to strike. The game was a knife fight, in which England took the lead when a Colombian defender acted out the first twelve pages of *The Joy of Sex* on Harry Kane in their own box. Even though the Colombian players took turns to scuff the penalty spot while icing Kane, he was unflappable, and his aim was true.

Cue one more set piece goal for England, which was just as well. They simply could not score in open play. Yet, a team whose creed was "live by the set piece" then died by the set piece. In the 93rd minute, off a corner, Colombian defender

Yerry Mina leapt up to thunder a ferocious header skidding off the bounce into the top corner of the net. England had been within seconds of victory but the instant the ball went in, it felt as debilitating as if we had lost. In extra time, the emotionally exhausted English could barely complete a pass, attempting to hold on in the thirty added minutes, which were a grinding sickener. The mood in the Brooklyn bar which had been so wired at kickoff was now deathly. The experience of watching became abject, savage misery. I wondered exactly why we all loved football anyway.

The game went to a penalty shoot-out. A poisoned chalice for the English nation. I would honestly have rather watched the movie *The Human Centipede* than experience all that was to come. England had lost five straight penalty shoot-outs in major tournaments. Each had felt less a sporting moment, more like making England fight the American War of Independence all over again.

Indeed, some of my most traumatic memories as a fan revolved around England penalty misery.

OUT in 1990

OUT in 1998

OUT in 2006

Worse, *this* young England National Team had just made the nation fall in love with watching them, which in a way, was an achievement worth more than victory. Now they had to face their national bête noire: A penalty shoot-out. I typed into my game notes: "Those who don't know history are doomed to repeat it by penalties."

The shoot-out turned out to be what Martin Scorsese would refer to as "Cinema." Colombia went first, Radamel Falcao firing down the middle. Harry Kane stepped up in his Spitfire to power home his second penalty of the night and tie it up 1–1. Juan Cuadrado sent a shot over a diving England goalkeeper Jordan Pickford, and Marcus Rashford kept apace by lashing low into the bottom left corner, 2–2. Luis Muriel sent Pickford the wrong way, 3–2. Up stepped English midfielder Jordan Henderson. He trudged to the spot, and it felt in that moment as if he were the last thing we needed to see. Henderson is the epitome of English bravery. A true lion of a leader. But a penalty shoot-out is about technique and mental focus as opposed to bravery and adrenaline-fueled passion. As he walked up, it was clear to everyone in the Brooklyn bar that we were about to witness the most English Englishness that ever Englished. If we could see it, how could manager Gareth Southgate not? Henderson tried to side-foot into the bottom right corner, but his shot was too careful, too tentative, too telegraphed, and goalkeeper David Ospina flung himself to parry. As he leapt up and pumped his crotch toward the crowd in a personal moment of triumph, it was as crushing as if the Beatles had just broken up all over again.

England's goalkeeper Pickford had not gotten close to a single Colombian shot all night. Yet suddenly we had respite. Mateus Uribe lashed a howitzer of a shot against the top of the bar, and England's master-archer, Kieran Trippier, was unwavering, going to the top right corner, and we had life again at 3–3.

Sudden death kicked in with the fifth round of kicks. Colombia's Carlos Bacca went first. Jordan Pickford was then a young keeper who had been maligned by pundits for being too short and for using his wrong hands in key moments. Here, though, he sought to take control of the situation, spending an age before returning to his line, a psychological ploy, making it clear he was in control of the situation, and the kick would be taken on his time. He then leapt up and banged the crossbar, an old trick that left the upright reverberating like a guitar string, reinforcing the enormity of the task ahead. Bacca attempted to clear his mind, taking deep breaths bordering on gasps of panic. He stepped up and fired centrally. Pickford had dived early and to his right, yet somehow, the Everton goalkeeper was able to trail his left hand behind him to swat the ball aside with the strong wrists of an onanist, like an English Dikembe Mutombo. A moment both anti-historical and borderline rapturous as if it had been ripped live from the Marvel Comic Universe. I was struck by a surging reminder that it is possible for humans to change who they are in life.

If England scored now, they would win. For the task, they dispatched Eric Dier. A defender with the doomed countenance of Job, who always tried hard in the face of constant calamity that seemed to dog him. In the list of English people I would have liked to have seen walk to the spot in that moment, Dier probably ranked about number 47,536,211, two places ahead of my own mother. My hopes for Charlie Brown kicking a field goal with Lucy holding are higher.

I am not a religious man, but in the seconds before a decisive penalty kick, I do find myself bargaining with God. Dier stepped up and dispatched a shot to the left. Ospina guessed right but the kick was so well placed he could not stop it. Dier did not seem to know how to celebrate as he wheeled away and the commentator blared four words I did not think I would ever hear in my lifetime, "ENGLAND WIN ON PENALTIES." As the England players charged downfield to mob Pickford, it felt like his achievement ranked up there with the Industrial Revolution, the works of Shakespeare, the development of the scientific method by Sir Isaac Newton, as great moments of English history.

I was watching in the bar with my wife and producer JW. I hugged her in a way I had when she told me she was pregnant with our first child. It was profoundly moving to witness Gareth Southgate in that moment. A man who, as a player, had missed an England penalty in a semifinal shoot-out during Euro 1996, and had turned that trauma into a life lesson to lead his nation to victory.

Until this moment, Southgate had seemed like a risk-averse leader. Suddenly he appeared as a waistcoated Moses who could lead his people to enter a Promised Land he could never access himself. As Dier delivered the win, Gareth sank halfway to his knees arching his back and pumping his fists into the Moscow night sky, like a footballing Freddie Mercury. Then, in an act of true empathy and nobility, he walked over to console Uribe, the Colombian who had hit the crossbar with his penalty as Southgate had once done.

Gareth's subsequent postmatch comments were empathetic human poetry. "I've learned a million things from [my own penalty miss] and the years that followed it," he said. "When something goes wrong in your life, it doesn't finish you and you should become braver, knowing that you've got to go for things in life and don't regret because you didn't try to be as good as you might be." Those are words of wisdom to live by, which transcend football. They sound like American ideals, but are actually refractions of Churchill's apocryphal quote, "Success is not final, failure is not fatal. It is the courage to continue that counts."

Watching the English nation rise in this moment made me

feel a distant echo of joy. If all it took was me becoming an American for England to experience victory, it felt like a win-win. England now believed in its footballers again. *The Guardian* journalist Hadley Freeman wrote that a friend of hers had compared England to "one of those crazy people who goes on a good date and immediately starts planning the wedding."

The phrase "Football's Coming Home" exploded over social media. A nostalgic and ironic line lifted from the official single from two comedians, David Baddiel and Frank Skinner, ahead of the Euro 1996 competition. The lyrics relive the serial heartbreaks that English fans had suffered over the decades, weaving itself into the fabric of the nation as an anthemic pub chant:

Three lions on a shirt!
Thirty years of hurt
Never stopped me dreaming.

It had now been over fifty years since England had won the World Cup in 1966, a date that seemed as distant as William the Conqueror invading Britain in 1066. This song reflected the eternal and defiant sense that somehow persevered but now, with England winning, and via a penalty shoot-out no less, its meaning resounded. The phrase "It's Coming Home" had for so long been self-mocking. Suddenly it felt cocksure. The tune was edited into a phalanx of memes, celebrities posted themselves singing it on Instagram, even Prince William tweeted it after the win. This sense of hope all felt so un-English.

The England narrative dominated the tournament, but other storylines crackled alongside it. Hosts Russia faced Spain, unbeaten in twenty-three games, in Moscow. I pitied the referee, Björn Kuipers from the Netherlands, who was undoubtedly shown his version of the peepee tapes by a Putin operative before kickoff. Spain outpassed Russia 1091 passes to 272, but they could not pull their relentless opponents out of shape. Throughout the tournament there had been an abundance of rumors of Russian doping. Watching their players shuttle around, chasing shadows, without tiring or showing signs of being mentally worn down made those rumors appear real. The Spaniards thought they had won a penalty late on—the decision not to award one remained controversial to some—but you could just see the terror in the poor referee's eyes as he instantly had to balance making the right decision against his ability to touch car door handles with confidence for the rest of his life.

When the game went to a penalty shoot-out, few neutrals watching doubted who would win. If the Russians could weather Sean Connery's Russian accent in *The Hunt for Red October*, they could survive anything. Their goalkeeper Akinfeev, who had been irredeemably bad throughout his entire career, transformed himself into the Kremlin Wall, saving twice to catalyze Spanish tears. It was both shocking and strangely unsurprising to watch. Like a Russian election in which Putin was the candidate. Burger King elected to celebrate by launching the offer of a lifetime supply of Whoppers to Russian women who got pregnant by World Cup players, to develop "the best football genes" and "ensure the success of the Russian team for generations to come." A campaign that was quickly canceled after a global outcry. McDonald's marketers would never.

France clipped Argentina 4–3. The ongoing "Ralph Wiggumizing" of Lionel Messi was hard to witness. The Argentines had been leading 2–1 until French defender Benjamin Pavard unleashed an airbender of a long-range blast to level the score. It was immediately clear to all watching that we had all just witnessed the finest moment in Pavard's life. Even if he proceeded to become the first man to walk on Mars, cured cancer, or wrote epic poems of Homer or Virgil quality, nothing he could do would compare to that goal's foot shape, strike, spin, and placement.

Cometh the hour, Cometh L'Homme. Electric young French star Kylian Mbappé then took over the game, scoring twice at the tender age of nineteen. An age at which all I cared about was beer, mixtapes, and football. He single-handedly torched Argentina in a World Cup game with the entire planet watching. His second goal was an exhilarating 80-yard dash in which he must have experienced more adrenaline than I had in my entire life. Messi looked overwhelmed with grief as he staggered off the field. Aged thirty-one, it felt as if we may have just witnessed him play his final World Cup ever. The broadcasters immediately wondered if Messi could be considered a great if he had never won the tournament, despite the record haul of silverware he had amassed with Barcelona in the club game. I scribbled a Fyodor Dostoevsky quote in my game notes, "Pain and suffering are inevitable for persons of broad awareness and depth of heart. The truly great are . . . always bound to feel a great sense of sadness during their time upon earth."

Within hours, Ronaldo would also crash out as Portugal's aging backline was savaged 2-1 by Uruguay's fearsome strikeforce Edinson Cavani and Luis Suárez. The duo was a study in contrast. Cavani, with his defined cheekbones, looked like Tommy Wiseau's younger, more athletically gifted brother. Luis Suárez, with his impossibly white teeth and by all means necessary mindset. The duo embodied the collective spirit and fight of their tiny nation, who played with true garra charrúa, or warrior spirit. Both men had been born within a month of each other in Salto, population just 114,000 and it was their interplay that did it for Portugal. Two kids from the same hood dazzling together on the world's greatest stage. Ronaldo scored four times in this tournament and forced the world to stare at his crotch and thighs, while having Drake namecheck him in a song, but he was out of the World Cup. Upon reflection, there are a lot of my life bucket list goals he achieved in there.

England made light work of Sweden in the quarterfinal. They were calm, clinical, and the result was never in doubt. Another goal from a set piece, many of which had been inspired by NBA inbound pass set plays, did the trick. With their screens, pick-and-rolls, and continuous movement, Gareth Southgate's team were like watching the Boston Celtics or Miami Heat play World Cup football. But who cared about how they won? They had now ridden this tactic all the way to a World Cup semifinal, defining themselves as something unique—an England team who was young, confident, and having a great time, which for an English footballer is a revolutionary idea. For decades, England's finest athletes had toiled like Sisyphus, pushing a rock up a hill only to be crushed by it. This time, the England squad had arrived with modest goals—as humans not gods—fully aware of their own strengths and weaknesses, just hoping to "enjoy" the experience. With this mindset, they had excelled. The football had not been pretty, but the results had been beautiful. A testament about another secret in life: You should enjoy what you do.

England would now face Croatia in the semifinal—a team who had audaciously outlasted Russia on penalty kicks after passing around them for 120 minutes yet still being held to a

2–2 draw by Russia's suspicious ability to never stop running. The Russian penalty takers crumbled in the shoot-out, however, no doubt caught between the specter of glory or the Gulag. I watched along with a crowd in Philadelphia and realized, if soccer just went straight to penalty shoot-outs, the sport would be bigger than NFL within a few months. The way the crowd cheered every miss despite having mouths full of cheesesteak was a reminder of how American sports fans live for the savage cruelty of the spectacle.

Reaching a World Cup semifinal felt like England's equivalent of Benjamin Franklin discovering lightning is a form of electricity. My brother sent me photos he had taken in London. The St. George Cross flag fluttered everywhere. A booze-sodden euphoria gripped the streets. A nation worn down by the Brexit referendum looked great again. Gareth Southgate had achieved demigod status, his signature waistcoat right up there in the pantheon of great vests alongside John Travolta in *Saturday Night Fever* and Diane Keaton in *Annie Hall*.

That semifinal was sensory overload. I truly cannot remember being gripped with such a level of heightened excitement ahead of a game of football. The English felt like they were on the cusp of violating the very laws of nature by achieving the one act deemed impossible for them: winning. The power of hope present multiplied by open wounds of countless prior failures made sleep an impossibility. I traveled up to Boston, scene of that night's live show, early in the morning and realized that the concept of England winning was as incomprehensible to me as the number infinity or the idea that space goes on forever. My tiny mind could not conceive of such a thing.

I watched the game in a hotel bar that was packed with

American England fans. They were ready to party, but it was clear to me, Croatia was a phenomenal collective, capable of pissing in the punch. So, in the fifth minute, when Kieran Trippier stepped up to arc a free kick over the wall and into the top right-hand corner of the net, I did not scream. I did not move. I was paralyzed by shock in apparent contrast to England goalkeeper Jordan Pickford, who ran around in glee like the most athletic hobbit in the Shire. After all those years of failure. Where there was once darkness, could it be that now there was only light?

For a second I let myself dream of a final between England and France, aka Battle of Hastings 2: Electric Boogaloo. But then all the memories of old games lost snapped back to the front of my mind. I thought of that unwritten rule that you should not score too early. To do so gives a team a false sense of security and throws them off their game plan. The other team almost have too much time to respond. Croatia were truly tenacious, propelled by the great midfielder Luka Modrić, a diminutive man who looked like a medieval cowherd but capable of orchestrating unparalleled midfield poetry. At first, England knew they had the game by the throat and tried to finish it by creating missing chances. Then Modrić began to influence the game as the English elected to grit out the victory, sitting deeper and deeper and daring Croatia to break them down. It became nervy fare. One England defender saved a goal by taking a crushing shot to the testicles, which the broadcasters showed from multiple angles as if impressed by this act of sacrifice. I never previously understood why some people on Instagram elect to have the word "breathe" tattooed onto their wrists. As the game clock ticked by slowly, I gained a sudden appreciation for their wisdom.

England ultimately broke in the 68th minute. Ivan Perišić raised his foot high to knock the ball home as if he was an expert in Croatian capoeira. England was suddenly rocked, like a boxer out on their feet. Croatia just worked all the pressure points, moving the ball like a clan of East European ninjas. Everything English seemed to melt. The team's cohesion, shape, and sense of belief and composure. I asked Twitter what else felt like this feeling other than sports. Every woman follower I had instantly tweeted back a single word: "childbirth." I was seven Budweisers in and found myself screaming, "What are you doing?" at the television, at young footballers who were at the peak of their game and trying their hardest.

I felt for these young men, coming together from towns scattered all over England, especially in the North, the more hardscrabble part of the country, who had grown up watching England teams do what England teams do, which is lose. Remember, we are not trained to think differently in England. We are stoic people. We take our lumps and suffer our lot. But these boys had been on the brink of defying history. And now, as the game went into extra time, they were helplessly overrun. Croatia's passing pressure was relentless and it felt almost like a mercy killing when the English backline switched off and Mario Mandžukić, a true footballing sniper who grew up in Slavonski Brod at the crossroads of Europe, punished them to deliver a decisive winner. In that moment, my mind again turned to another Churchill quote, "To build may have to be the slow and laborious task of years. To destroy can be the thoughtless act of a single day."

England was defeated, and still I took to the stage that night in Boston clad in a waistcoat in homage to Gareth Southgate, the man who had done the impossible and made an English nation come together and believe. There was no shame in being beaten by Croatia. They had defined themselves as the masters of extra time in this tournament. This nation of just 4.1 million people—roughly the same population size as Oregon, the twenty-seventh biggest US state—had developed enough talent and tenacity to reach a World Cup final where they would ultimately be mauled by the dominant French, who won their second title.

For me, this Russia World Cup was over the moment England crashed out. I was honestly stunned by how much I cared. As I watched the semifinal, my mind was flooded with the memories of humiliations past—of Maradona torching us in 1986, Gazza's tears in 1990, Beckham's Red Card in 1998, David Seaman's flailing arms in 2002, Wayne Rooney's stamp in 2006. This England journey was different, and it was so healing to experience noble English joy that as I sat at the bar, even in defeat, my eleven-year-old self, fifteen-year-old self, and nineteen-year-old self were watching alongside me.

In life, it is impossible to shed the sense of where you come from, and football has a great power to remind you of that by enabling your deepest memories to well up and overwhelm you even when you think they lie dormant. I pretended I did not care about the England team, but as we relived the game onstage that night, I found it difficult not to tear up talking about the reality that had played out against the backdrop of Brexit and government collapse. Amidst that chaos, as the nation tore itself apart, football had felt like a lone uniter. Now it was gone.

At the end of the game, English fans had serenaded their defeated team by chanting the chorus of Oasis's "Don't Look Back in Anger." Watching that moment again with a live audience, I started sobbing. The idea of an English team who departed a World Cup with dignity was that powerful. The nation was still the best in the world at having massed groups of fans throw their beers in the air. No one could take that away from us, but the knowledge these young footballers had given English kids a glimmer of a different possibility for England broke my cold heart.

That night, postshow in a Boston bar, was a turning point for another reason. It was the first time an investor approached me to talk about the vision I had for *Men in Blazers*. He had seen the segment on *Real Sports* and tried to capture my attention by telling me he believed I was running, in his words, "a hundred-million-dollar business."

By that time, I was so ground down both physically and emotionally I did not process a word. The man's mouth kept moving, but all I heard in my head was the sound of the summer.

Three lions on a shirt!
Thirty years of hurt
Never stopped me dreaming.

Chapter 12

2022 World Cup, Qatar

MATTHEW McCONAUGHEY IS staring at me as we prepare to watch a World Cup game together. Our heads float side by side on the split screen. Ever the Hollywood A-lister, Matthew has rigged some kind of elite high-def shooting setup, which accentuates the ravishing handsomeness of his features. He wastes little time before leaning into the camera and delivers the kind of testament to the game that felt like it should have instantly been awarded the Pulitzer Prize for Poetry. "Football is the greatest invitation," he began. "Around the world . . . if someone has a soccer ball, you can walk up, you don't even have to introduce yourself. They will kick the ball to you and all of a sudden you're in the game. The soccer ball is a great equalizer. It's a peacemaker."

This is no dream. Only football can do this. McConaughey had joined us for a US group stage game against England live on Twitch. Eight hundred thousand people were tuning in just to watch us watch the match on a livestream. For the record, I rooted for the United States at Bruce Springsteen–esque levels that surpassed even McConaughey's. How we got here is a reflection of how popular football, *Men in Blazers*, and Matthew McConaughey had become.

To be truthful, it was a miracle we had made it here at all. In 2020, the pandemic knocked global football out of action for three months at its height, threatening to strip my life of its purpose. The moment lockdown began, our community of listeners flooded our mailbag with messages that made it clear they felt the same. On the second day I was cooped up at home, I had a call with my production partner, Jonathan Williamson. A few weeks earlier, the two of us had made a film about our visit to the Churchill War Rooms in London. A historic underground complex that served as the prime minister's government command center through the most desperate days of the Battle of Britain, when it felt like the nation was on the brink of German invasion. At the end of the film, I talked about the power of the place and the lesson it teaches you—that human beings reveal their truth and are ultimately remembered for how they function in times of challenge and duress. In this moment, we agreed to try and channel the spirit of the War Rooms. Rather than stand dormant during this lockdown, we would double down our output and go on what we jokingly referred to as "war footing."

What this boiled down to was simple. Whereas we had previously released a single show and accompanying newsletter every week, we would immediately begin to do so on a daily basis. It sounded counterintuitive, expanding our output at the very time we had been deprived of actual football to talk about. But our mission became one of attempting to bring a spark of joy and connection with our audience. The emergence of Zoom technology allowed us to beam-in interviews with some of the world's biggest footballers, who were grateful for something to do as they too were locked down in their own homes. I moved my wife and four kids out of our New York City apartment where it was impossible to find the silence needed for broadcasting and into a home with a studio in Westchester and began to run happy hour livestreams, attempting to bring respite to audiences of doctors, teachers, and frontline workers. They joined us by the thousands to talk about mundane football memories with a sense of hungry wonder. It was relentless work, yet it was exhilarating, and the size of our audience soared in response.

After sixty-seven long days of lockdown, football finally returned, and the game instantly took on new levels of meaning and depth of connection for all of us. The first matches, played in Germany, were known as "Geisterspiele" (ghost games) as they were played without fans. The opening fixture was Schalke 04 battling archrival Borussia Dortmund in the famed Ruhr "Revierderby." I had rarely been more eager to watch a game of football outside of a World Cup, and after weeks of sporting famine, I craved the sense of normalcy the game can bring. It was in truth a bizarre thing to witness. The players were not allowed to shake hands or even spit on the field. A weird hush descended right before kickoff. Where you normally would have a surging roar of crowd anticipation, we were left with only the emptiness of a fanless stadium.

There was prevailing concern before the game began, that stripped of its audience and noise, football would be shorn of its ecstatic magic. We need not have worried. The instant Dortmund opened the scoring with a sweeping team move that was finished clinically by the relentless Erling Haaland, social media crackled in awe and appreciation. A heartfelt moment in which the millions of us watching around the world were bonded in that positive, human way that only sports can conjure. Following the game at home, I exhaled with relief and swore I would never take this precious sense of connection for granted again. Indeed, the legacy of the pandemic was the extent to which we committed our energy to it, building out a vision to turn our single show into an entire network, with multiple voices covering every aspect of the game—men's and women's, club and international, domestic and global. The loneliness and tragedy of lockdown had twisted lives around the planet. All that mattered to me now was devoting every ounce of energy I had to adding to the sense of optimism and joy in the world by endeavoring to do good things with great people.

That sense of positivity was severely tested by the fact that twelve years after FIFA's surreal decision to confer hosting duties upon Qatar, the reality of a World Cup in the tiny desert nation was now thrust upon us. With temperatures burning over 106 degrees throughout the summer, FIFA made the unprecedented choice to shift its crown jewel tournament from June to November, requiring the entire global club calendar to contort, pausing midseason for its purpose. The world of football suddenly felt like it had been relegated to the status of a plaything. A geopolitical pawn serving the needs of a wealthy gulf state's desire to flex its muscles in the face of its regional rivals.

For its part, Qatar lavished over $260 billion to create new infrastructure and build eight fantastical new stadia, jamming them within its four and a half thousand square miles. Their construction cost more than money. In the process of their creation, 6,500 migrant workers had lost their lives in unexplained circumstances. A grotesque contortion of beauty, which beats at the heart of the game. Irish journalist Miguel Delaney wrote the haunting thought "There's an old line that people measure their lives in World Cups. This World Cup can instead be measured in lives." Why was all of this happening? In the week running up to the tournament, we gained a sense of the prime driver when it was announced the monthlong festival would generate $7.5 billion in revenue. A startling number that was a billion dollars more than Russia four years earlier.

Many of the footballers found themselves in a difficult moral position, caught between their childhood dreams of playing in a World Cup and the sense of outrage they felt after learning about the migrant deaths. The Norwegian team warmed up for a qualifying game wearing T-shirts that proclaimed, "Human rights—on and off the pitch." The Danish squad elected to wear a muted jersey with logos and markings toned down, declaring, "We don't wish to be visible during a tournament that has cost thousands of people their lives." Seven European teams announced they would sport rainbow armbands as a sign of inclusion and anti-discrimination, an idea that was hastily abandoned once FIFA threatened to impose sporting sanctions on those who partook in the protest. As the activism flickered, it felt as if this was a tournament that would have to be watched on a split screen between the action on the field and the geopolitical battles off it. But such is the power of football, that the second a ball was kicked, the sense of outrage and talk of protest was muted, a phenomenon that could be summed up in football terms as Cognitive Dissonance 1, Morality 0.

At *Men in Blazers*, we watched all of this while girding our loins to repeat the national tour experience we had patented at the previous World Cup, going coast to coast to play theaters for the month of the tournament. The star wattage emanating from our guests had grown in correlation to the size of our platform. John Oliver came on to talk about England, Parisian band Phoenix jumped aboard to discuss France, Eva Longoria to talk Mexico. The Manning brothers had made their "Manningcast" a phenomenon, and we also built out a footballing version of their watch-alongs, bringing on celebrity guests like Will Arnett, Tony Hawk, and McConaughey to revel game-by-game on Twitch on a near-daily basis.

Again, we found ourselves in St. Louis for the opening day. An occasion that set the phantasmagorical tone for all that was to come. Host Qatar had never played a World Cup game before, but they'd had over twelve years to plan for this moment. The story of their team was, like nearly everything else in their tournament, one of throwing money at something to stimulate it artificially. Qatar has roughly 300,000 citizens (on par with Iceland) but roughly 6,000 registered soccer players. So, they flung over a billion dollars to build a state-of-the-art development academy, dispatching a phalanx of scouts across the developing world. In turn they harvested a mercenary army of talent from across Europe, Africa, and Asia, bringing them back to Qatar to be part of a squad of which ten of the players were born outside of the kingdom, but were given "socio-economic citizenship" as opposed to full citizenship, a status protected defiantly in Qatar. After all that, could the hosts now deliver a performance to prove their nation's footballing legitimacy to the watching world?

We only had to wait for the opening game to discover the answer. It was held after a lavish welcome ceremony, put on in the shiny new Al Bayt Stadium, constructed to resemble a tent to reflect the nomadic roots of the Qatari hosts. The pregame choreography involved a mélange of cultures. Dua Lipa and Shakira were among the many world-renowned artists who were reported to have turned down Qatar's gilded offers to perform, so we were treated to a lot of drumming, a dozy camel, a smattering of K-Pop, and a spoken-word performance by a rather befuddled Morgan Freeman whose presence only seemed to serve as a reminder that everyone has their price. From his box, FIFA president Gianni Infantino beamed away, proudly sandwiched between Qatar's Emir Sheikh Tamim bin Hamad Al Thani and Saudi Arabia's Crown Prince Mohammed bin Salman Al Thani. Two fraught regional rivals, brought together by football. The trio looked on expectantly, hoping for a home-team performance twelve years in the making, which could mute the deafening noise of controversy around this tournament.

The Qatari team took to the field and were welcomed by an ecstatic maroon-clad ultra-group who bounced and bellowed to cheer them on. That welcome was perhaps the most impressive moment of the game from a Qatari perspective, because their team's performance proved to be as calamitous an opening showing as any host nation had ever shown. Perhaps overawed, our hosts were slapstick and self-harming. Their opponents, the far more experienced Ecuadorians, ran rampant, humiliating their opponents physically and tactically, scoring twice with ease in the first half. It could honestly have been five- or six-nil if the South Americans had not elected, for reasons unknown, to restrict themselves to only attempting bicycle-kick circus trick shots on goal. The Qatari fans that remained by halftime in a fast-emptying stadium appeared to have hung around only to boo their team off. The Ecuadorian fans were delirious, chanting, "Queremos cerveza, queremos cerveza" (We want beer, we want beer), a devious dig at the late and unprecedented decision to ban alcohol from the World Cup, which reduced Qatar's big day to feeling like a crowd scene from a *Simpsons* episode.

The artificial tone of the entire tournament was set by the fact that even the Qatari "ultras" were ersatz. Terrified that their nation's lack of authentic football culture would expose their hosting bona fides, the tournament organizers had rented hundreds of fans from a Lebanese team, taught them a handful of new chants and the Qatari national anthem, and imported them wholesale. A story that underscored both how many Arab nations had truly passionate fan cultures and could have authentically hosted the tournament, while reinforcing the synthetic soulless tone of the entire enterprise. One journalist quipped, "Qatar feels like a country that's being unboxed for a World Cup." A German newspaper wrote that their writers en route to games "would probably drive past more World Cup stadia than fans."

The United States entered the fray on day two. This was a relief after their catastrophic failure to qualify in 2018. A glut of ambitious young American talents had replaced Landon Donovan and Clint Dempsey's generation wholesale. They had all found footholds at clubs across Europe at an unprecedented scale. Midfield terrier Tyler Adams played for Leeds in England. Weston McKennie, a footballing bowling ball, plied his trade at Juventus in Italy. The young prince Christian Pulisic had flickered then floundered at Chelsea.

Yet, their individual achievements at club level had not transferred to any significant impact as a national collective. The team were now led by player turned middling MLS coach Gregg Berhalter. Still threatened and burned by the big ideas of foreign coach Jürgen Klinsmann, the Federation had gone for his polar opposite. A bland American-born manager who could possibly rebuild the brotherhood of the squad, Berhalter was tactically suspect and had the charisma of Dunder Mifflin's HR rep Toby Flenderson.

To compensate for Berhalter's glaring deficiencies, the team's PR team spent years valiantly attempting to paper them over by pitching personal tidbits they hoped might make the coach sound interesting. Relentless stories about his vast Starbucks city mug collection or sneaker obsessions had the opposite effect. The only thing that fans cared about was the team's results. When the US lost, and the team's official account thought it was still important to tweet out the news that their manager had been wearing Air Jordan 1 High in the "Lost & Found" colorway, it was not well received. The numbers turning out to watch the team dwindled as it stumbled from one sad performance to another, devoid of a pragmatic tactical vision and a coherent depth chart. News that Berhalter had arrived in Qatar equipped with seven pairs of sneakers, one for each possible game through to the final, was met with a shrug. All that mattered was whether the team could finally go that deep into the tournament. Most fans were sure Berhalter had overpacked.

I will admit I took delight from the fact that the team were back in the World Cup. This was the first time they had qualified since I had become an American citizen. Even though Berhalter's squad had struggled through qualifying, once you reach the World Cup, magical thinking propelled by yearning quickly swamps and overwhelms reality and rational truth. I made myself believe that Christian Pulisic, freed from the misery of his club experience, would be hungry for redemption and ball out in a US jersey, enabling us to reassert as a force to be reckoned with. I was not alone in this desire. Pulisic remained the one name only vaguely known by American non-soccer fans. A reality television show, *Pawn Stars*, inadvertently and hilariously coined for him the nickname "LeBron James of Soccer." Thousands of diehard soccer fans in this nation knew that one incredible moment akin to Landon Donovan's 2010 wonder goal against Algeria could turn his career around and give the team the TikTok highlight they craved and, frankly, needed.

The US had been drawn into an opening group that included echoes of World Cups past in opponents England and Iran. We opened though with Wales, who had made it to their first World Cup in sixty-four years. A tiny footballing overachiever propelled by their own sense of national destiny, replete with Welsh-born actor Michael Sheen dropping pre-match pump-up speeches in which he roared, "A victory song that floats through the valleys, like a red mist, rolls over the mountaintops, like crimson thunder. A red storm is coming to the gates of Qatar!"

I had waited 3,065 days to watch the US men play a World Cup game. I marked the occasion live on Twitch with thousands of fellow Americans, Scott Galloway, and US Women's Captain Lindsey Horan. In the run-up to kickoff, I was more nervous for this game than I had been for any previous World Cup tilt. So many of these US players were now regulars on my show, coming on to tell their stories to the American audience, that their success or failure felt personal to me. Tyler Adams, the captain, had a monthly show with me on our network. I was well versed in the price he and his family had paid to reach this moment. The three-and-a-half-hour round-trip car rides he had taken on a near daily basis for seven years to train at the New York Red Bulls Youth Academy. He had first swaggered into my studio at age seventeen and told me his dream was to captain the United States at the World Cup. As he took the field now wearing the captain's armband and sang the national anthem, I was deeply aware of all the moment meant to him.

Despite this, even I had to admit the Welsh fans won the singing of the national anthems. I am not Welsh, but as they roared "Land of My Fathers," I welled up. My hometown of Liverpool butts right up against North Wales. I have many Welsh friends in my life and knew how proud they are. After sixty-four years of longing, of being bullied by the English, they had shucked the haters, asserting themselves, and were now on the precipice of launching their own World Cup journey. It was magnificent to behold.

Once the game kicked off, though, the United States tore into the Welsh with fury, confidence, and all the fearlessness that Tyler Adams had promised me for months. Wales were barely able to cock a fist before the 35th minute when Christian Pulisic bolted forward like liquid mercury, as if he knew the second he took possession what he was going to do with the ball. He was going to hurt a man, just as he had countless times on the playing fields of Hershey, Pennsylvania, back when he was a kid. Pulisic stabbed a straight pass to a diagonal-running Tim Weah, that New York–reared son of Liberian footballing icon George Weah, a striker so potent, he had leveraged his playing career into a spell as Liberian president. Being the son of a legend is no easy feat. See Chet Hanks. But Tim Weah rose to the moment using the outside of his right foot to stab the ball past the keeper, to do something his dad never did—putting the Weah name on a World Cup scoresheet.

For all of the American dominance over the Welsh, many of the traits and strains that had long dogged the Berhalter era remained evident. This team did not know how to turn possession into chances. Their set pieces were woeful. Their mentality lacked ruthlessness. Cobra Kai's John Kreese would say they did not know how to "sweep the leg." This weakness inevitably bit us in the ass as the Welsh came out to attack in the second half with sixty-four years of pent-up energy. The US wilted, losing control of the midfield, then limply conceded a penalty to aging Welsh superstar and quasi-full-time golf aficionado Gareth Bale. Bale converted it himself, instantly etching his name amidst the Richard Burtons, Catherine Zeta-Joneses, and that Julia Roberts's roommate sidekick from *Notting Hill* in the Mount Rushmore of Welsh all-time greats.

At the final whistle, the game was a draw but felt like a loss. A game we should have won was thrown away, with our own cockiness playing a lead role in why. Yet, I could not be angry. Welsh actor Ioan Gruffudd joined us on Twitch to articulate his emotions, and he talked with passion about how we had witnessed his team live out their national anthem on the field. The ethos of "Land of My Fathers" is "even though we were conquered, you will not silence us." That is what we had just experienced and who could resent that? A plucky nation roaring back inside ninety minutes on a football field. Even though I felt the sadness of another massive chance missed for the US, the knowledge of the sheer volume of joyful beers being sunk across Wales tempered that frustration.

That night we took the stage with Tom Brady's nemesis Nikki Glaser, who was the exact person we needed to make a despondent postmatch audience roar with laughter. As we broke down the game, Glaser theorized that football had not quite caught on in the Midwest because American women don't like short guys and the sport had too great a preponderance of them. Even as the mood lightened, I could not shake the sour mood born of wasted opportunity. We had seen glimpses of how good this young US team could play football, but how much they still had to learn about the game mentally. In truth, though, if you had offered me a draw before kickoff, I would have taken that offer, or as they say in football parlance, "bitten your arm off." Rationally, I remained aware that not losing the opening game of the tournament is the cardinal rule, and we had avoided that fate.

We now had to wait four days to face Euro 2020 finalist and 2018 World Cup semifinalist England. Still under the management of Gareth Southgate, who had by now abandoned the waistcoat, England had just obliterated Iran in their first game. A 6–2 win in which the players' only mistake was to sing the word "Queen" out of habit during the national anthem, now named "God Save the King."

This was the game every American fan had circled in their calendar since the draw. A seismic clash between the two sides of what Churchill referred to as the "Special Relationship" and a test of our boys' ability against a team stuffed from top to bottom with globally renowned Premier League names. I drew a modicum of strength from the fact the US had never lost to the English in World Cup play. Our 1950 team of semi-pros shocked one of the most vaunted English teams of all time in Brazil. That 1–0 win remains one of the greatest upsets the tournament has ever seen. In 2010, Clint Dempsey's speculative drive delivered a 1–1 tie. We watched with Matthew McConaughey as this game in Qatar continued that seventy-two-year run. A 0–0 stalemate battled between two deadlocked midfields. The highlight of the match occurred when Christian Pulisic dropped his shoulders in the first half and unleashed a stunning drive, only to hit the bar. McConaughey reeled away in agony, proclaiming, "The Wheaties box was waiting!"

England had been cautious throughout, yet our Berhalter-led team remained constipated, unable to create chances and lacking composure in key moments. By the end of the game, even Matthew McConaughey appeared to run out of energy. He left the livestream by promising that "Soccer's Coming Home." The US had avoided my greatest fear—an English beatdown with the whole nation watching. Yet, they still had work to do. We now faced Iran in the final group stage game needing a win to progress. As we approached matchday, I experienced a sense of excited possibility coupled with a grating sense of fear. I knew this was the most talented group of individuals the US has ever assembled at a Men's World Cup, yet, as a collective, their play had been so much less than it should have been. I also knew that if we could not beat one of the three teams in the opening round, we did not deserve to emerge into the knockout stage of the World Cup.

World Cup games are almost always layered with history. This clash evoked memories of the previous in 1998, when the US faced Ayatollah Khomeini's Iran in the shadow of the hostage crisis and soiled themselves in the eyes of the nation, losing 2–1 and triggering rapturous scenes on the streets of Tehran. This game also became politically toxic, but for self-sabotaging reasons. US Soccer elected to post an image of the Iranian flag with the Islamic Republic logo airbrushed out of its social media platforms. Their spokesperson confirmed the removal was intended to be a show of support for women in Iran fighting for basic human rights. This poorly thought-out idea set off a political firestorm. The Iranian government waded in, accusing US Soccer of removing the name of God from the national flag, demanding the Americans be expelled from the tournament. Suddenly, the State Department had to issue a statement making it clear this was not the official position of the US government.

The posts were quickly deleted, but the damage had been done. Things began to go very, very *Argo* in the run-up to the game. Gregg Berhalter was subjected to questions about the strategic placement of US warships near Iranian waters. The players had to answer a glut of geopolitically loaded mind-bending questions, which was the opposite of how footballers want to approach the most pressure-filled game in eight years.

The issue came to a head in the pregame press conference when a hostile Iranian reporter ambushed Tyler Adams, first chastising his pronunciation of the country's name, then asking the US captain if he was comfortable representing the United States as a "country that has so much discrimination against Black people in its own borders." Adams was gloriously diplomatic in his answer. "There's discrimination everywhere you go," he began. "One thing that I've learned, especially from living abroad in the past years and having to fit in in different cultures and kind of assimilate into different cultures, is that in the US, we're continuing to make progress every single day."

Tyler grew up in Wappingers Falls, New York, with a remarkable family I had come to know well. I felt so much pride as his answer continued. "I grew up in a white family, and with an African American heritage and background. So, I had a little bit of different cultures, and I was very easily able to assimilate. Not everyone has that ease and the ability to do that, and obviously, it takes longer to understand, and through education, I think it's super important. Like you just educated me now on the pronunciation of your country. So, yeah, it's a process. I think as long as you see progress, that's the most important thing."

I can't think of many modern-day politicians who could have handled that situation with more intelligent graciousness than Tyler in that moment. He agreed to join me on *Morning Joe* right after the incident and joked that after he had spent the last year answering my questions on our podcast, the Iranian journalist's gotcha attempts were child's play in comparison. I felt incredibly proud of my friend.

The game itself was what I would call a "three pair of underpants affair." A true grudge match during which, I am not too proud to admit, I soiled myself a little, watching live on Twitch again, along with novelist John Green, who began our broadcast so stressed out he was crouching behind his couch. Iran opened aggressively, hoping to deliver an early knockout punch. The US repelled them but were nervy and wasteful in possession. Then it happened. In the 38th minute. A great American moment up there with the moon landing, the Wright Brothers' first flight, or Season 1 of *White Lotus*.

Dutch American free spirit Sergiño Dest nodded the ball intelligently back across the area, into a vulnerable spot Kenny Loggins would refer to as "The Danger Zone." Talking about vulnerable spots, as Christian Pulisic swooped in to finish, the Iranian goalkeeper Alireza Beiranvand smacked clean through him like an Iranian drone strike straight to Pulisic's down belows. Somehow the American still had the guile to sacrifice his body by propelling the ball home with his crotch region, before falling to the turf in agony. John Green exclaimed that he was "drenched in sweat watching Christian Pulisic be separated from his testicles." I was so overjoyed, I would honestly have donated one of my own to our nation's goal-scoring hero had he asked for it.

In the second half, the United States ran out of gas in their customary style. It was hard to watch the way we ceded all momentum, initiative, and possession and were simply staring into the abyss. John was reduced to quoting Ulysses's declaration that "history is a nightmare from which I am trying to awake." We both nearly died when the referee decided there would be nine minutes fifty-three seconds added on for extra time. That 593 seconds felt like it took about two years. Iranian players flailing away in the area, handling the ball themselves then claiming a penalty. As our players dropped back ever deeper, we were Bon Jovi-ing it and "Livin' on a Prayer." John offered "a finger or two" in exchange for the game ending. I actually started to feel a stabbing pain in my chest as the clock ticked on. It was as if the whole team had seen the white light and decided to move toward it, but then, the salvation of the final whistle, which sounded to me like the words of the poet Philip Larkin, "On me your voice falls as they say love should, like an enormous yes."

The American players fell to the turf in astonished exhaustion such was the relief of qualifying for the knockout round for the first time in eight long years. More than that, they had exorcized the trauma of the past with that shocking 1998 World Cup loss to Iran avenged. In the moment of victory, there was a beautiful display of sportsmanship as US left back Antonee Robinson took time to console a sobbing Iranian opponent. There had been dreadful reports of the pressure the Iranians had experienced, with their families being threatened by the regime if they elected to signify political protest by failing to sing the national anthem before the game. Losing the game likely triggered all kinds of fear. In this moment, Robinson hugged Ramin Rezaeian, a powerful example of empathy that I greatly admired. Watching Americans navigate the football world in victory, but also humility was a healing balm after the needless strife that had led into the game.

The US were now in the wide-open waters of the knockout round's Last Sixteen, where anything was possible. We would next face a true contender in the talent-soaked Netherlands. A team with their own sense of destiny in this World Cup as their legendary, gruff coach Louis van Gaal was battling prostate cancer. His team were yet to be defeated in the eighteen games since he had taken over, and this was likely to be his last tournament. Thankfully, Pulisic's scrotal region had healed sufficiently for him to lead our young boys into battle as they set out to win a men's knockout game for only the second time ever—and two of those had been in the first World Cup way back in 1930. I can't describe my relief as somehow US Soccer restrained themselves from accidentally unleashing some poorly doctored version of the Dutch flag in the run-up to the game.

The Netherlands, that land of Eddie Van Halen, Van Gogh, and Anne Frank, is hard to despise, but the way the match went made me think deeply about that classic Austin Powers quip, "There's only two things I hate in this world: people who are intolerant of other people's cultures and the Dutch." It was a one-sided trauma. A 3–1 thrashing like a scene in an old war movie where one adversary has suddenly discovered gunpowder and the other fights futilely with heavy swords and crossbows. The Dutch stormed forward with telepathic cohesion, kinetic passing, and emphatic finishing. The US were clearly shattered after their exertions against Iran, but that did not excuse the way we were carved apart on repeat. It was honestly hard to believe we had liberated Eindhoven on *Band of Brothers* for this.

We watched the game on Twitch with the chef and humanitarian José Andrés, who tried to calm viewers down, specifically me, by taking us on a tour of his kitchen. He had so much on the go: turkey in the oven, oysters, lobsters, Hawaiian shrimp, razor clams, lamb stew on the stove, cheese out for snacking. For large stretches of the game, I just let him zoom in on each element as a distraction from the football carnage occurring. When the game was lost, Chef Andrés departed, but not before lamenting, "This is a life lesson, we as individuals are only as good as the people around us, we need to work together and help each other, and that is true in the spirit of football as well."

After the game, the Dutch manager Van Gaal went out of his way to mock Berhalter's tactical naivete, laughing in his press conference that "the US didn't adapt, they didn't adjust." An unusually public critique that meant the aftertaste of our exit was one of wasted opportunity and failure. The US were out in the Round of 16 for the third-straight World Cup appearance. There is no doubt this nation that considers itself to be the world's lone superpower and has achieved dynastic levels in the women's game can and should aspire to be more than the sixteenth-best team in the world. So numbed, I ended the broadcast with the Ralph Ellison quote from *Invisible Man*, "Life is to be lived, not controlled; and humanity is won by continuing to play in face of certain defeat."

The US departure from the tournament hurt all the more because the general tenor of the rest of the play was one of wide-open opportunity. Germany lost to Japan and Morocco shocked Belgium in the group stages. Most of the action, however, was taking place not off the field, but around it. Iranian fans brought banners into the stadia promoting women's rights, rainbow flags were banned by Qatari security, a German minister then wore a LGBTQ+ armband in the presidential box.

Serbian players hung a controversial banner depicting the outline of Kosovo filled with the Serbia flag in their locker room. Perhaps most macabre of all, Croatian fans taunted Canadian goalkeeper Milan Borjan, who was born a Serb in Croatia, unveiling a banner with the name of the village his family had been forced to flee. By selecting Qatar as the host, the genie was out of the sports and politics bottle, and everyone was now using the tournament to protest and lay political body blows on everybody else. Global football was acting as a mirror reflecting the world in all of its light *and* darkness.

The bizarreness of the tournament, and its collection of chaotic microaggressions, cried out for a hero and a cohesive narrative. Enter Lionel Andrés Messi Cuccittini. Aged thirty-five, Messi was in his fifth World Cup and under intense pressure to deliver glory. In Argentina they revere no man more than the creative playmaker. The Number 10 is El Diez, a role romanticized by Diego Maradona, who leveraged it to gain the status of national mythical hero. Win and the 10 is beloved. Lose and it is always his fault. That was a pressure so great that Messi had threatened to retire due to the weight of the shirt after lashing his penalty kick over the bar during the loss of 2016 Copa América to Chile, admitting sadly, "It's been four finals, I tried. It was the thing I wanted the most, but I couldn't get it, so I think it's over." That retirement lasted exactly two months before he returned, explaining, "I love this country and this shirt too much," and so he rolled into Qatar to try to win the World Cup again like a footballing Captain Ahab.

Watching Messi was to see a man you rooted for, because so much about him screamed the opposite of an elite athlete. In a world of genetic freaks, of chiseled abs and sculpted legs, not to mention the post-Beckham era of the Uncannily Handsome

Footballer, the Argentinian was conspicuously nonconforming. Standing a diminutive 5'7", squat and thick-necked and illogically pale, sporting a scruffy beard that went only so far toward obscuring the softness of his jawline and a hairstyle that can only be described as Supercuts, Lionel Messi gave off normal guy blessed with the football skills of god. Maradona himself once quipped that it looked like Messi was "playing a kickabout with Jesus."

Messi's narrative was known around the world as if it were a biblical story. A kid from Rosario, the son of a steelworker who signed the boy over to Barcelona on the back of a napkin at age thirteen. Nurtured in their famed academy, he was given growth hormones due to his short stature and became a kind of phenomenon that the fabled club had never seen. With Messi as their talisman they won ten Spanish league titles, four Champions League trophies. He scored a club record 474 goals, many of them sublime. He was still scoring at an outrageous rate in what should've been the autumn of his career, and it seemed like he might go on forever.

And then, suddenly, it was over; the club, teetering toward insolvency, had to sell their favorite son. He was shunted off to Paris Saint-Germain, the superclub bankrolled by the Qatari royal family, a place where insolvency would never be a concern, and there, for perhaps the first time in his adult life, he floundered. In his first season playing in Paris alongside fellow megastars Kylian Mbappé and Neymar, his former teammate, he showed flashes of genius, but by his celestial standards it had been a barren, soul-destroying experience. The World Cup offered a sense of redemption within redemption. Here was a man battling to define himself as the greatest ever. He was most often compared with that other diminutive left-footed Argentine genius, Maradona, and in almost every metric, for both club and country, he'd surpassed his predecessor. Except at the World Cup, which he had never won. Now was his chance.

There was one enormous snag for Messi. This was a very different Argentinian team to the truly great ones that line our imagination. A squad caught in the process of a generational transition, led by a young, inexperienced manager, Lionel Scaloni, a forty-four-year-old from Messi's hometown of Rosario. Scaloni had been appointed after the team's lackluster 2018 World Cup. Fans were underwhelmed by his arrival as his previous experience had been limited to that of assistant coach. Even Diego Maradona spoke openly about what a random choice he was, yet the Argentine Football Association, like the nation itself, was financially bereft and could not afford to appoint a big-name leader. Scaloni proceeded to go about his work, embracing his outsider status, lack of experience, and vulnerabilities. He set about creating a squad culture built on honesty, brotherhood, and trust, which had been so absent in Russia, where rumors abounded that the players themselves picked the starting eleven. The tactical style of the team became about defensively committed counterattacking football. A commitment forged over barbecues and cumbia music.

It worked. Scaloni's Argentinians fought their way to regional glory in the 2021 Copa América in Brazil, ending a twenty-eight-year title drought. After a win in the quarterfinals, a meme went viral on social media picturing Scaloni driving an old bus, with Messi at his side in the front seat with the rest of the team jammed in behind him. The vehicle was decorated in the national team's colors, and the affectionate phrase "La Scaloneta" was emblazoned across the front, combining the coach's name with the suffix connoting small size, or collective group. As the Argentinian team won one game after another on the way to the Cup, the nickname stuck in the hearts and minds of the nation. A hype train of sorts, or modest hype bus at least. This was their team. The manager may not be a genius, but he could drive the bus and keep people on board, and with Messi alongside him, everything felt possible.

This is how Argentina arrived in Qatar, along with a reported two thousand pounds of meat to barbecue. Here was a squad forged without ego, a factor that stood out as much as their football ahead of the tournament. They began against 1000–1 tournament outsiders Saudi Arabia, a team of globally unknown talent who played in the nation's domestic league that had only won one game at a World Cup since 1998 and were widely expected to be cannon fodder.

What ensued was one of the most eye-popping shocks in tournament history. Messi opened the scoring with a penalty inside ten minutes. But that proved to be a mere misdirection. Saudi Arabia turned out to be a well-drilled squad, under the stern coaching eye of Hervé Renard, a Frenchman who stood on the sideline with shirt buttons gaping open like a Harlequin Romance cover come alive. His team had an advantage. They had trained together for a solid two months in which Renard had drilled them to snap to life on the counter, and it paid off as they caught an oddly disjointed Argentina cold. The Saudis scored two astonishing goals inside five minutes. The first began with Messi being dispossessed after a loose touch. The second, a sidewinding crack of thunder that instantly earned its place in the pantheon of great opening game goals.

Messi appeared shellshocked and unable to summon any kind of response to Saudi Arabia's Miracle on Ice moment. The Saudis immediately declared a day of national holiday to celebrate their sporting glory with autocratic undertones that was inarguably one of biggest World Cup upsets in tournament history. As the game clock wound down, the Emir of Qatar was seen to wrap a Saudi flag around his neck, an astonishing symbolic display. For years, Qatar and Saudi Arabia had been ensnared in a vicious regional rivalry. Ahead of the tournament, that friction had toned down, and now the Emir, fresh off watching his own team soil themselves, was going all in on the Saudis.

Watching Messi slump off in defeat is truly to understand what Prince meant when he sang about the sound of doves crying. The creaking ache of World Cup failure felt like it was happening for our hero once again. A delirious Saudi fan interrupted a Korean reporter's broadcast to press his face against the camera and cackle "Where is Messi?," a phrase that gave the tournament its first and most astonishing global meme. Sad Messi is the most heartbreaking Messi.

This was fight or flight time for Lionel Scaloni. The mood in Argentina was somber but unusually calm. In 1990, Maradona's Argentina had been similarly shocked by Cameroon in their opening game, then shrugged the defeat off and made it all the way to the final. So, the team and the coach were given grace by a nation beset by economic woes and frenzied inflation. Footballing success felt like a national mission in a time of austerity and fear. One government minister articulated the priorities, saying: "Inflation can wait, first we need to win the World Cup." Scaloni understood the depth of his nation's need and set to work, overhauling his starting lineup with a suddenly unsentimental eye. Iconic veterans with big reputations and tired legs, like Papu Gómez, were dropped. Young guns Julián Álvarez, Alexis Mac Allister, and Enzo Fernández were eased in, bringing with them a vitality and spark that transformed the team.

Mexico were Argentina's second foe. A game that was not technically a must-win, but it certainly felt like one. I remember tuning in and knowing a draw would mean Argentina could survive by beating Poland by two goals or more, but there was also a looming sense of darkness. The fear of mortality. Of having to watch Messi, a man who had given the world so much pleasure, slowly fade away like an Argentinian Bing Bong tragically disappearing in the memory dump in *Inside Out*.

The game was a cage match from the off. Both teams demonstrated a taste for the dark arts. Eyes were poked by fingers. Faces were clutched. Bodies flung themselves to the ground. The Mexicans attempted to nullify the actual play with their shithousery and turn it into a hand-to-hand battle, forcing the Argentinians to feel both the sharpness of their elbows and the weight of their own anxiety. The fear gripping the Argentinian team was palpable. Messi kept dropping deeper and deeper, and in a game that witnessed more yellow cards than shots on goal, he initially cut a frustrated figure, his team bereft of ideas other than to match foul with foul.

Mexico began that second half by adopting a formation reminiscent of that ancient Roman battle tactic testudo, in which the fighting force would drop back, lock arms, and raise their shields up to create an impenetrable wall. Argentina attempted to raise their intensity to little avail. The stadium became a crucible as the clock ticked on the 64th minute. Then Messi took possession of the ball on the edge of the area. The commentator reflected that the thirty-five-year-old had "barely had a sniff." The position felt nonmenacing, until the little Argentinian filled it with menace. He took one touch, then rifled a low drive with precision and seething ruthlessness. The goalkeeper was not expecting the shot. No one was. The moment felt cosmic, and the release globally cathartic. Messi charged away, arms spread, and was embraced by his entire team as the commentator popped, "That's what they came for." He was right. We had come to watch Messi seize destiny in the style of Achilles slaying Hector in Homer's *Iliad* or the Geatish warrior slaying the monster Grendel in *Beowulf*.

Late on, one of Scaloni's newly empowered youngsters, Enzo Fernández, killed the game off with his first international goal after a burst of speed finished off by an arcing drive cut of dreams and rainbows. A surging strike eclipsed only by the sight of veteran Messi running over and nestling head into his young teammate's chest like an Argentinian Care Bear. An Argentinian Care Bear that was really, really good at football. To watch it felt celestial, a feeling of deep global emotional connectivity, which after the profound loneliness and separation of the pandemic felt truly purifying.

Scaloni now felt empowered to cast a new young core of Fernández, twenty-two-year-old Julián Álvarez, and twenty-three-year-old Alexis Mac Allister around Messi. A flurry of young, fearless, talented legs around the otherworldly old man. In the final group game, Álvarez and Mac Allister rewarded their selections by scoring as Argentina clipped Poland 2–0, completing the rebound from the ugliest of first game losses by winning the group. La Scaloneta was rolling into the knockout rounds as thousands of Argentinians flooded Qatar to witness their team's journey with their own eyes, turning the formerly sterile and overtly political tournament into the equivalent of a home affair.

In the Round of 16, Argentina faced plucky, disciplined,

ferocious Australia, who played with intensity but switched off twice and were punished both times. First by Messi, who notched his 789th goal in his 1,000th game, and then by Álvarez. It was striking to watch the Argentinians experience victory. Ever since that Saudi wake-up call, they marked the final whistle with the kind of grand celebration that would be more fitting of a final. The fans met the players' tone, creating a cacophony that bordered on rapture. I had rarely seen a team and its supporters so in tune with each other but also wondered whether living life at that extreme emotional setting created a pressure of its own that would prove to be mentally exhausting.

Argentina's quarterfinal with the Netherlands was a game that the streets will never forget. It was the sixth time these two giant powers had met in the tournament, and the layers of history conspired to manifest this bar brawl. It was to be a thunderous exchange that felt like Messi versus history, and the country of Argentina against the brain of Dutch coach Louis van Gaal, a brain that was only slightly smaller than the manager's legendarily giant ego. It did not disappoint. We witnessed four goals, eleven penalties, sixteen yellow cards, and one red. Lionel Messi was asked postgame what had happened out there, and he answered honestly, "A bit of everything,"

We would never have known from the beginning. The opening exchanges were insipid. Two teams dug into their own trenches without either truly willing to commit and go over the top. It felt like the Dutch game plan was to hold Argentina at bay and let them start to fail in the mire of throat-constricting pressure. It would have worked if they were not playing against Lionel Messi. In this late phase of his career, no longer the Messi of total domination, more the Messi of moments. And so, it came to pass in the 35th minute, in which he burst into the Dutch half, rolling left, and then somehow managed to dispense a no-look pass in the opposite direction that cut through six Dutch defenders to free young Nahuel Molina in to poke home his first-ever national team goal. Messi's pass looked like a Hollywood CGI special effect. How did he see the space? How did he intuit his teammates' run? How did he compute the physics of execution? It was magic.

The Netherlands had not trailed all tournament but with seventeen minutes to go, they were two behind. Messi attacked again, this time finishing emphatically from the penalty spot. A strike that appeared to reinforce the sense of a Hero's journey unfurling before the eyes of the world. Messi's teammates hugged him in a relaxed way that was the footballing equivalent of a banner spread across the cockpit of the USS *Abraham Lincoln* proclaiming mission accomplished.

But the game was only beginning. We did not know it at the time, but there was so much football, and even more human emotion still to come. We had merely peaked one mountain and still had a crest line of further peaks to emotionally ascend, because, in the 78th minute, Louis van Gaal unleashed his substitute, Wout Weghorst, a lumbering journeyman 6'6" striker. Think of him as Dutch for "Plan B." His teammates began to fling long balls forward, a strategy that paid off within five minutes as Wout snapped his neck to flick a header home.

Weghorst, though, was just getting started. In the 90th minute plus ELEVEN (yes, eleven!), the Dutch won a free kick on the edge of the area. They did not have much of an angle to work with. Cue a masterful van Gaal flourish. With seconds to play, the wily old Dutch fox unleashed a moment born of equal part creativity and testicular fortitude. He drew up a set play that felt like it was ripped from the NBA. A reverse pass rolled into the big man with the soft hands. Instead of taking the free kick in the expected traditional fashion—blasting the ball on goal with venom—the Dutch rolled it short and softly toward Weghorst, that long veil of a man whose stretched body you would imagine had the steering wheel of a crude oil tanker. He then pivoted like a Jet Ski, shaking his hips like a Dutch Shakira, then rolling the ball home past a stunned Argentinian backline. The shock of this moment was so supreme. Like the rest of the watching world, I was utterly lost in this game. I did not know who I supported, I no longer knew what I cared for or even what was a good outcome. This goal was so jarring, I felt unmoored from my emotional center, and I know I was not alone. Suddenly, the narratives of Lionel Messi's legacy and Van Gaal's last dance—a coach battling cancer—were pitched against each other in a battle royale. Both teams had lived every single one of the human emotions, in some combination, and were not going to stop.

The game went to a penalty shoot-out. As I have made abundantly clear, they remain the cruelest way to end a game. An individual pursuit only loosely connected to the collective endeavor of the 120 minutes that preceded them. Rock, Paper, Scissors would arguably be a fairer way to choose a winner, or a breakdance battle at the very least. In this one Argentinian goalkeeper Emi Martínez, a man who lives for chaos and hijinks, stepped up and made two saves to deliver victory with a roar and end a game that Argentina had won three times. They had been 2–0 up. They had been 2–0 up in the penalty shoot-outs. They survived, but only just, in a game whose malicious side tone was perfectly captured by a photograph taken seconds after Argentina hit the winning penalty. Traditionally, the victors celebrate with relief and joy. On this occasion the Argentinian players' instant reaction was to storm toward their opponents and bark mocking taunts to their faces. Defender Nicolás Otamendi led the charge, putting his hands to his ears, as if saying "I can't hear you now" as the defeated Dutch slumped over in the anguished fatigue of defeat.

I felt for the Netherlands. Yes, maybe this was punishment for giving the world Tiësto, but they had fought so bravely, hand to hand, eye to eye, in the support of their beloved coach. They were shattered in defeat, and Argentina were the team that lived on. The Saudi debacle felt like it had occurred a year ago. This was now a different team thriving under unfathomable pressure, capable of tapping into seemingly inexhaustible levels of exertion and emotion, led by Lionel Messi, the tiny, tattooed Odysseus.

Even though I was neutral in my support, I was breathless by the end of the game, soaked in sweat, beer, and piss, some of it my own. What we had experienced felt inconceivable. I talked onstage that night about how it stung me when Dana White, the head of UFC, had said earlier in the week, "I can't stand soccer. I think that it's the least talented sport on Earth. There's a reason three-year-olds can play soccer. You run around and kick a ball." If Dana White had watched this game, I'd like to believe he would have been enlightened. Dana White would have witnessed the entire human experience.

I would also like to believe Dana White would also have savored one last moment of Messi magic, which felt like it had been ripped from UFC weigh-in culture, during the postmatch interviews in the tunnel. Messi was giving his immediate reactions, an experience in which he traditionally specialized in the art of saying very little. Not on this day. Messi spied Weghorst lingering at a distance in his peripheral vision. Mid-interview, he stopped, stared, and hollered, "¿Qué miras, bobo?" (What are you looking at, fool?), giving the planet an instant meme in his thick Argentinian accent and also offering us a glimpse of a different Messi, one stripped of the handlers and commercial sheen that made him seem like a little Ewok. Was this the real unvarnished Messi? A deeply competitive, aggressive shit talker? Or was this a different Messi, a man in his fifth World Cup who knew it was now or never, channeling the spirit of Maradona, no more Mr. Nice Guy, just win at all costs? A man who had become the perfect embodiment of the classic Argentinian ideal of football in which beauty and the dark arts are appreciated in equal measure? It was a pleasure to ponder.

That night, we were about to take the stage in Los Angeles with Will Arnett when the darkest news broke from Qatar. In the last minutes of Argentina's victory, the American journalist Grant Wahl had collapsed in the press box and had passed away in a local hospital. Grant was a kind human being who only strove to do good. He had been a pathfinder as a journalist. One of the first to cover football in the United States, and as such had made others realize it was possible to build a career in the field in this nation. We took the stage with heavy legs and heavier hearts the night. The show itself felt like a wake shared with an audience who were also stunned by the news. The suddenness, location, and context of Grant's passing made it feel unfathomable. I ached for his wife and family, as well as the journalists who had been seated alongside their colleague in this darkest of moments. Far from our families, we all had to return to the game and think about the press box. One in which he was not.

But the tournament goes on, and the Argentine journey

continued. By now it had its own anthem that fans would bellow before, during, and after the games. Named simply "Muchachos" or "Guys," it included the lines:

> *I was born in Argentina*
> *Land of Diego (Maradona) and Lionel (Messi)*
> *and Diego, in heaven, we can see him . . . cheering on Lionel.*

A beautiful and poetic framing for all we were witnessing. Here was a father-son vision quest, with Messi attempting to carry the entire team as his patriarch Maradona had in 1986 and lift his nation in the style of a son who knew destiny did not wait, it loomed. As he "boboed" his fallen foe Wout Weghorst, Messi appeared ready to deliver and become the subject of ill-advised tattoos all over the bodies of his fellow Argentinians.

Croatia awaited in the semifinal, pitching Messi against fellow aging midfield grandmaster Luka Modrić. At this point, Argentina was a team surfing on the edge of an awesome tidal wave of emotion. We could only hope that the wave would sweep them to glory and not crush them with its power.

Croatia played with experience and indefatigable grit. They had survived their previous two games on penalty shoot-outs, like a team of Rafael Nadals in tie-breaks hoping to drag their opponents into a world of pain knowing that they can suffer more than anyone. A mentality born out of their nation's turbulent modern history. However, this game against Argentina proved to be one too far for their shattered backline. Messi stepped up to the penalty spot to open the scoring. In the moment, I was suddenly filled with fear for him. His career conversion rate of just 77 percent from the spot is the one slight weakness in his sublime skillset. He was facing a Croatian keeper, Dominik Livaković, who had been so dominant in two previous penalty shoot-outs. As Messi prepared his run-up, I thought about the intense pressure on his shoulders, the weight of the jersey, and wondered how he was even able to breathe as the rest of the world hyperventilated. Messi demonstrated unwavering confidence, smashing the ball home. I thought back to the two thousand pounds of meat the Argentians had schlepped to Qatar. I swear that shot was hit with the force of all two thousand pounds.

The goal broke the Croatians. They now had to chase the game. It was quickly clear they did not have the legs to do so after back-to-back marathons. Pushing for a goal, they left themselves comically open to Argentinian counters and the clinical precision of Julián Álvarez, who netted twice. The second strike was created by another Messi run for the ages. The little maestro was scurrying down the right, with giant defender Joško Gvardiol smothering him. Gvardiol had been dominant the entire tournament, but suddenly the Argentinian wriggled like a conger in shallow waters, vaporizing his opponent. I once interviewed the Uruguayan poet Eduardo Galeano and he told me, "Maradona dribbled as if the ball was stuck to his shoe, but Messi dribbled as if the ball was worn inside his very sock," and watching him eviscerate Gvardiol before cutting back deliciously for Álvarez to rifle home was a moment that made the heart sing. At the final whistle, it was beautiful to watch Messi and the hugs he shared with his team, and with Ángel Di Maria in particular. The thin-faced teammate who looked like a Giacometti sculpture of a footballer and had played by Messi's side for fourteen long years. Di Maria lifted his friend up as if he himself were the trophy.

And in a way, he was. A human ark of the covenant, guaranteeing victory to whoever he rode with.

Argentina had reached the World Cup final for the sixth time. A second final for Messi. His shot at redemption for the 2014 final loss and that extra time bumble in Brazil against Germany. There were amazing scenes at the Plaza de la República in the center of Buenos Aires. Millions of proud Argentinians communing as far as the eye could see, yearning for their nation to be champions, for themselves yes, but even more so, to witness Lionel deliver the glory. Their nation was in a ragged state with a shattered economy, and inflation poised to hit nearly 100 percent on the year. Poverty was widespread as was political corruption, but if Scaloneta's team could deliver victory, his country could project the illusion of how they wanted to be seen, as a courageous winner on the global stage through the work of one man. Messi. A demigod to his people now, and even though they had grown used to watching him deliver such brilliance on a regular basis, they were not taking a second of paying witness to his greatness for granted.

In the final they would play France, the defending champions, who had seen off the English 2–1 in the quarterfinal. A game in which poor England captain Harry Kane had both equaled England's all-time goal-scoring record and then dispatched a late, potential equalizing penalty soaring over the bar and into orbit like a prototype for English SpaceX. In the agony of the moment, it was clear that in the most British way possible, none of his countrymen would remember his record goal haul for their nation and would harbor only the agonies of that single cruel miss. Hell always overshadows heaven.

In the semifinal the French had faced the Cinderellas of the tournament, Morocco, a magical squad who mixed the passion of Arab football with the tactical discipline of the European game. They had played fierce and disciplined football, soaring underdog football to clip Canada and Belgium, outlast Spain on penalties in the Round of 16, and then shock Ronaldo's Portugal in the quarterfinals. Perhaps unsurprisingly, Ronaldo did not take tumbling out of his fifth World Cup well, charging straight off the field without his team, leaving a vapor of vanity and human agony behind him as he laugh-cried like a Portuguese Claire Danes. It remained unclear if he was crying because his tournament had ended in failure yet again, or because his nemesis Messi remained in it. Regardless, Morocco had made history. Eighty-eight years after Egypt became the first African representative nation in the World Cup, fifty-two years after Morocco themselves first participated in the tournament in Mexico, and thirty-two years after the magnificent Cameroon reached the last eight, the continent of Africa had its first semifinalists, an achievement that was celebrated across both Africa and the Arab World.

The final was the perfect matchup. Messi attempting to cement his status as Greatest of All Time. Standing in his way was his club teammate Kylian Mbappé, the young Parisian icon who was striving to become the first player since Pelé to win two World Cups by the age of twenty-three. Here was a clash akin to the De Niro–Pacino restaurant scene in *Heat*. A team desperate to deliver glory for their hero and their beleaguered nation, against the defending champions hoping to become the first country to go back-to-back since Brazil 1962. This was football romanticism meeting football pragmatism. Bookmakers deemed it too close to call. All we knew, we were guaranteed to witness Messi tears at the end, either from joy or profound sorrow. To make the individual head-to-head even spicier, Messi and Mbappé were tied in the race to be the tournament's top scorer, with five goals each.

We watched this game on Twitch with famed skateboarding icon Tony Hawk. We talked about how this was meant to be Messi's moment, but Mbappé was the kind of guy who lives to steal another's spotlight and make it his own. His football was a mix of scorching pace, clinical potency, and nonchalant cool. Thomas Mars, the lead singer of the French band Phoenix, had watched him with us and compared the way Mbappé played football to the way Marvin Gaye innovated music.

What followed has been hailed as the single greatest World Cup final of all time. It felt ironic that a tournament at which beer had been banned was witness to the drunkest finale in tournament history. The pregame narrative had focused on the Argentinian emotionalism and whether the team could harness its rawness into a power of good, or whether it would overwhelm and bury them alive. Yet, it was France, the team who had made four World Cup finals in the past seven tournaments, who seemed like they were daunted by the occasion. Di María stormed into the penalty area and was clipped from behind in a reckless piece of adrenaline-filled decision making by French striker Ousmane Dembele. There was no doubt who would step up to take the penalty kick that followed. Lionel Messi, by now, playing raw, emotional football akin to witnessing Kurt Cobain with Nirvana stripped down to his essence on *MTV Unplugged*, stutter stepped then side-footed home.

In the 36th minute, Argentina found a second, a goal born of a stunning team move, less a collection of passes and more a constellation being shot into the heavens in real time. Messi of course played the pass that unlocked the French defense, drawing three defenders and then evading them with an avant-garde outside of the boot flick. It was his old companion Ángel Di María who capped off the move with a clipped angled drive, like a Rosario Scottie Pippen supporting Messi's tiny Michael Jordan. After celebrating with his teammates, Di María sobbed as he walked back to the halfway line. The tears looked born of both relief and ecstasy. The Argentinians were so dominant, it felt like the entirety of the pressure of the occasion was now lifted. France was wilting, forced into two panicked substitutions before halftime—a first for the World Cup. Nothing worked. The French not only failed to conjure a shot on goal in the opening forty-five minutes, they did not have a single touch in the Argentinian penalty area.

The second half saw little evidence that Di María's tears were misplaced. Mbappé appeared to have been silenced, his threat defanged. But the notion of routine wins was anathema to this Argentinian team whose currency was drama and chaos. So perhaps it should have been no surprise in the 80th minute when Mbappé came to life and became unplayable. First, he corkscrewed a penalty into the corner, causing the cameras to cut to an anguished Emmanuel Macron leaping from his seat in the dignitaries' box like a normal fan. The French president would do the same again just ninety-four seconds later as Mbappé casually yet viciously lashed a side-on volley from distance, a staggering moment of sporting violence and emotional juxtaposition. As Mbappé wheeled away euphorically, a one-man declaration of "Liberte, Égalité, Mbappé," the cameras cut to Messi, who almost dropped to his knees for a second as if the very life-force had been sucked out of him. This was a devastating sporting turn. If the French had not previously given the world the word "Renaissance," it would have been coined in that instant. One minute, the Argentinians were imagining all the celebratory Malbec they were about to sip, the steaks that would be barbecued asado in their honor, and the dizzying tangos that would be danced around them. The next, they were dragged back in a knife fight with France, this courageous team of moments, for whom Mbappé was on a one-man mission to wield the fatal jab.

Suddenly this World Cup final felt like an NBA Finals game in the last minute when there is no holding back. Both teams just charging end to end, shot for shot, with shattered legs and spent minds. Twenty-two men bonded by fate and the knowledge that glory and infamy were the spoils for the victors. No quarter could be given. Both teams had soared, both teams felt the drip of their wax wings melting.

Into extra time, Messi stabbed Argentina back into the lead, only for Mbappé to equalize from the penalty spot yet again, becoming just the second man ever to score a hat trick in the final. This was euphoric, breathless fare. Surreal and grand and moving, which is what modern football is at its best. Messi and Mbappé trading moments like they were playing football—real, honest to God, *Plato's Cave* football—and everything else was just shadows.

The game went to penalties. Argentinian goalkeeper Emi Martínez was born to take charge of this drama, with his athleticism and his black belt in dark arts. Martínez had just single-handedly, or single-footedly, kept Argentina alive in the last minute, executing a spread-eagled kick save at full stretch to shut down young French attacker Randal Kolo Muani and preserve the draw. In the shoot-out, he unveiled every move from his *Big Book of Shithousery*, throwing the ball away to unnerve French kicker Aurélien Tchouaméni, who then had to fetch it and subsequently missed. The second Argentinian substitute Gonzalo Montiel converted the winning penalty, Messi sank to his knees in the center circle and was engulfed by the entire squad. In that moment he was a man transformed. It was as if he had become Messianic Messi. An immortal, joining Maradona, all the while remaining himself. The two Argentinian greats stylistically representing a duality of rapturous emotions standing opposite each other like brilliant bookends, both glorious in their own right.

The trophy celebration was, befitting for a tournament that had been overbearingly artificial, bizarre. Salt Bae, the narcissist turned salt-sprinkling Turkish steak famewhore, somehow inserted himself into proceedings. Qatar's Emir Sheikh Tamim bin Hamad Al Thani then wrapped Messi in a traditional cloak, or bisht, before the trophy lift to reinforce his nation's link to this moment of glory. Underneath it all, though, there was still a beating heart sense of the soulful story at play. The most synthetic of World Cups ended with a superstar stripped bare and expressing his emotions to the world, the weight and burden of his country lifted off his shoulders. Messi had fulfilled his destiny, like Odysseus at the end of the *Odyssey*. I thought of my old Latin teacher barking, "Prosperity is restored to Ithaca, and Odysseus is home at last," and understood what he meant for the first time.

Across Argentina, mobs of fans flooded the streets. In Buenos Aires, over four million men and women of all ages swamped the area around the iconic Obelisco monument. Drone cameras filmed the blissful scenes as supporters climbed fences and buildings, singing their anthem, carrying banners paying tribute to both Messi and Maradona. The fans would ultimately embrace their returning players not only as sporting victors, but as significant figures in their nation's history and lore. The great sportswriter Hugh McIlvanney articulated this phenomenon best when he wrote, "There is a beautiful self-contained quality about a World Cup final. All the other matches, whatever their own vivid excitement, can only nourish the expectations of that last collision. Earlier days offer sudden death but this is the only one that offers instant immortality."

When I finished my final broadcast, my dominant emotion was one of an enormous relief and pride that an American audience of soccer-curious, NFL-reared sports fans had just been exposed to this footballing miracle—one which words could not do justice but was all the more powerful for being so emotional and indescribable. I was also suddenly aware of just how deeply shattered I was. Over the course of the month, we had traveled coast to coast across ten cities, unleashing seventeen live shows, and over one hundred podcasts, which had been listened to over thirty million times. But above all, the memories that we had made together were beyond number.

After my final broadcast, I dragged myself back to the hotel where I was staying and just summoned the energy to check in. As I waited by the elevator, slumped over my bags, I ached to find my room and fling myself to bed. The elevator doors slid open, and to my surprise, my eldest son, Samson, bolted out of them, hugging me, accompanied by a gaggle of mates. They had all flown in from New Orleans to be with me in this moment. That night, we ended up at a bar, feasting on chicken wings and beers. Battered but propelled with the exhausted delirium that only a World Cup can bring, we spent time calculating on a napkin that it was a mere 1,271 days until the next World Cup kicked off on North American shores. I was honestly too tired to say much, but I know I have rarely felt more content in my life. I was hyperaware of the conveyor belt of life we are all moving along as individuals, coupled with a precious sense of just how fast life moves. Above all, still buzzing in the embers of Messi's glory, I realized that the experience of World Cups that felt vast and infinite when I was a kid is actually so limited. Each of us has but a handful of World Cup experiences in our lifetime. What matters is how we use them. I looked at Samson and remembered that I had experienced my first tournament when I was twelve years younger than he was at that moment. I raised my beer and toasted my son with the silent wish that as fans, we should find a way to savor each and every minute of football and life, and never waste a single opportunity for memory-making together.

Afterword

Soccer's Coming Home

AND NOW THE 2026 World Cup is upon us. The tournament will thunder onto American shores with its forty-eight teams and thirty-nine days as the biggest ever. While we know that opportunity will forever change the profile of the game in this nation, everything else on and off the field is an unknown, still to be lived out and written.

The run-up to this tournament has been chaotic. A reflection of the complex state of our world. While the World Cup has never been bigger, it has also never been more in thrall of the political and cultural wars that grip and distort everything else. Football is, at the end of the day, just a mirror to the societies which surround it. It always tells you things.

So, I will leave you with this last thought, which sounds like a warning, but is really a wish. In truth, modern football has long felt under threat. The game itself is so simple, yet in the current period, it has often seemed in danger of eating itself alive because of the unchecked amount of money awash in the sport, the self-interest of the bureaucrats meant to safeguard it, and the obsessive interest it has drawn from strongman autocracies. Better writers than me have warned how these elements would kill the game, like the Grimm Brothers' fairytale "The Golden Goose."

However, the older I become, rather than becoming disenchanted with football because of the growing ugliness which often swamps it, I have come to love it more. Simply because the pure joy at the heart of the game remains alive despite it all. And so, the feelings I experience from watching it have become all the more powerful because their emotional weight and the sense of electric connection it provides to the rest of the world are ever more precious in today's world.

I wish that on you. When the whistle goes, and the ball is kicked, may you experience that sense of anticipation, hope, and possibility. The feelings of being alive, of your heartbeat syncing with the rest of the world, watching transcendent, pure moments that can drive out darkness and let in light. I don't ask for too much. Just that, and may the American Men also win a World Cup in my lifetime. . . .

All the teams we support may be different, but right now, whether your team is considered a superpower, dark horse, or fairytale outsider, all we can do is pray, raise a glass, and know . . . there is No Sleep 'Til MetLife for the Final.

Courage,
ROG

Acknowledgments

THE STORY OF the rise of football in the United States has been my honor to witness and experience. It is powerful and unstoppable, and it has shaped my life. There could be no better partner to sharpen its telling than the team at Harper/Dey Street, who are the Brazil 1970 of publishing. My editor, Carrie Thornton, is one of the most remarkable human beings I have had as a creative partner. She inherited my first book, *Bar Mitzvah Disco*, when the bloke who acquired it upped and went off to Canada. Chance encounters can change your career, and Carrie has changed mine with her intelligence, patience, wit, and love. I am also grateful to Ben Steinberg, associate publisher, and Carrie's team—Drew Henry; Brian Moore, art director; Rachel Meyers, managing editorial; Meghan Wilson, publicity; Kasey Feather, marketing; Patrick Barry, interior design—and Liate Stehlik, president and publisher.

The designer Roberto Parada is the Baggio of book covers. I met Roberto when he painted a stunning image of my American influences (Tracy Chapman, *Miami Vice*, Walter Payton, and more) for a *Wall Street Journal* article about my last book, *(Re)Born in the USA*. I reached out to him to express my admiration, and we became friends. I am so grateful to him for leaping into action on this beauty. To paint in oils in our AI age of 2025 is to keep it real. Not to be hyperbolic, but it felt like I was working with Rembrandt himself.

George Milkov is the Marcelo Bielsa of fact-checkers. An obsessive, detailed genius who managed to immerse himself in the minutiae of 1978's Top Trumps cards and the David Beckham story arc with equal relish. George, your mind works so differently to mine. I admire you greatly.

My agent David Larabell is a human old-school wonder, like a character from *Mad Men* made real. David, I am grateful to you and all at CAA. That includes my agents Matt Chazen and Matt Olsen. I am also grateful to my manager, the inimitable Steve Herz, who is a mensch.

This book is also a story about the rise of the Men in Blazers Media Network, which has been the work of my lifetime. My production partner, Jonathan Williamson, has been the greatest companion in this epic journey that has shaped both of us. He is the brilliant ying to my chaotic yang, and I am so honored to have seen fire and rain with him. It is mad what we have done together. Scott Debson has been the third element in our trio. The Earth to JW's Fire and all that Wind that I contribute. To more, much more together.

There are so many staff I am grateful to for choosing to walk alongside us. I always say we are on a journey together and that it is not for everyone. But, my lord, there are so many good people doing great things who have fused their energy with ours, and we are all the better for it: Jordan Dalmedo, you are a genius. Jelissa Castrodale, you are one of the funniest humans I know. You too, Zac Lee Rigg. Max Jaffe, you are so annoyingly and effortlessly talented. Max Bonem, you are a soulful king. Polly Rose, you slay. Tom Dragisics and Craig McCarthy, we are so lucky to have you lead our live work. John Johnson, you invented it all and we stand on your shoulders. Charlie Kipp, Randy Kim, Evan Raimist, and Kenny Crocker, your creative brains are so harmonious. Ian Hutchison, your aesthetics give us all life, as does your personal journey to work with us. Tyler Litwinn and Gabi Palacio, you are mad talented. Steve Ellis, we are so lucky to have met you and grown with you. Bennett Jones, Gavin Faucette, Ryan Catanese, Burke Cherrie, and Chris Dean, you are all giants. Jen Samples, thanks for building The Women's Game, and Juan Castro for pioneering our Hispanic platform, Vamos. Jen Proctor and your team have smashed our booking production. Sophie Morrison learned more about the World Cup than she would have liked on this project. Above all, Joy Hampton, you are such a rock. Thank you for working with me on every project. You are such a thoughtful human being. Empathy is your superpower.

On the talent side, I have learned so much from so many of our cohosts. My OG Michael Davies; the Crown Prince of Harrogate, Rory Smith; Herculez Gomez; Brendan Hunt; Sam Mewis; Becky Sauerbrunn; Tyler Adams; Fabrizio Romano; and the mighty Larry Nance Jr. I am also grateful to Jonathan Hock, Jonathan Perelman, Remy Cherin, Pierre Moosa, and all at NBC; Shaw Brown, Steve Horowitz, and Rob Tillis and all at Inner Circle; Courtney Holt; John Green; JJ Watt; Noah Kahan; and the incredible John Oliver.

Thanks to so many people who have helped shape Men in Blazers more than they know: Matt Davis, John Seiler, Nick Kelly, John Deschner, Ricky Engelberg, Rob Stone, Chase Woodfin, Brittney Polka, Bob Ley, Connor Schell, Jürgen Klinsmann, Michael Kammarman and Neil Buethe, Brad Ross, John Kristick, Tim MacLehose, and Jon Tuck have all been game changers at different times. We are lucky to live at a time when Rebecca Lowe and the Two Robbies are broadcasting the Premier League into our homes. They have changed the game. Joe Scarborough and Mika Brzenzinski, Willy Geist, Alex Korson, and all at *Morning Joe* gave me the chance to learn how to do live television in the most nourishing and supportive setting. Our explosive growth would not have been possible without the support and counsel of Marc Lasry, David Blitzer, Greg Bettinelli, Brent Montgomery, Ryan Reynolds, Rob Mac, and all at Maximum Effort and More Better.

Two writers shaped the way I think about football: the legendary Uruguayan poet Eduardo Galeano, whom I was blessed to interview before he passed away, and Simon Kuper, whom I have been lucky enough to get to know well, after reading his book *Football Against the Enemy*. Both men saw football as a mirror that reflects the entirety of human experience. I always felt it did, but they were the first who committed it to word and validated those feelings. Rory Smith is better at expressing all of that than I am. I am so incredibly grateful to unpack the global narrative in that style, a couple of times a week. Philip Larkin, Primo Levi, Studs Terkel, and Tracy Chapman, you are also poets who have shaped my understanding of what I do more than I can say.

There is an old English saying that football is, at its heart, a story about parents and children. I truly believe that is its greatest truth—a vehicle of cross-generational memory. In that regard, I am so grateful to my grandfather Sam and my dad, Ivor, for inculcating a love of football deep in my soul, and for making me an Everton fan. The memories I have made around the club with you both are some of the most profound and vivid of my life. Being an Evertonian is about 97 percent of my identity. I like to joke that the other 3 percent is mere human being.

I am grateful to all at the club, especially Scott McLeod, who have given us the chance to work deep inside the club with Men in Blazers. When I am on the stage, live with Everton managers and players, it feels like my dad and grandpa are alive and sitting alongside me. That is football's power and I am so grateful for it. COYB, UTFT.

Also, I am blessed to be a fan of the Chicago Bears, Chicago White Sox, and Tulane Green Wave, all of whom have combined to provide me with sporting narratives that propel my life. I always believe if your sports teams are the most painful parts of your existence, then you are doing pretty bloody well.

Thanks to all my friends who have been part of the journey. Especially Amanda Epstein, James Kay, David Katznelson, Rachel Levin, and my greatest lifelong friend Jamie Glassman, a fellow Blue, without whom my life would be bereft and empty.

I am grateful to be from the city of Liverpool. That great bawdy hometown which has the most romantics and storytellers per acre of any in the world. I am also blessed to have been adopted by New York City. A magical kingdom I had painted on my wall as a kid and now experience in real life.

Finally, I want to thank my family. First, my in-laws, Jules and Lynn Kroll, for their constant support and interest. You have taught me the power of always showing up by coming to our live shows, especially the early ones that lasted about three hours longer than they should have. I am indebted to my late father, Ivor, and my beautiful mum, Valerie, for having me and filling my life with love and support. My dad died on July 4, 2024. I miss him every day. I am so grateful for the discipline and work ethic he exemplified and drilled into me. My brother, Nigel, and sister, Amy, are both wonderful despite being Liverpool fans.

My dog, Martin Scorsese, is the greatest hiking companion and an even better writing companion. My kids tell me it is you who keeps me sane. That is a lot to put on one hound, but you make that burden appear effortless. My kids, Samson, Ber, Zion, and Oz are a Back Four at the levels of Bixente Lizarazu, Laurent Blanc, Marcel Desailly, and Lilian Thuram. Each of you loves football and Everton FC, which are perhaps my greatest contributions as a parent. Remember that what is ultimately most important about playing football are the lessons about human nature it teaches you that you can use off the field in real life. My wife, Vanessa, is the single greatest human being I know. I wake up every morning and feel so lucky you are by my side. The only way I could be happier is if you and I could watch Everton win something together in our lifetimes.

About the Men in Blazers Media Network

THE MEN IN BLAZERS Media Network is North America's largest dedicated soccer-obsessed media company. Born of a passion for the global game—from the Premier League to the Champions League to the US Men's National Team—MIBMN has grown over the last decade from a single podcast to a network offering 360-degree coverage wherever a ball is kicked. Our speciality is a deep connection to the fans, authentic storytelling, and analysis, including dedicated platforms covering the women's game and the hyperpassionate Hispanic American soccer community.

So many of the biggest and most popular voices in the game have shows on the network, including Clint Dempsey, US Men's leader Tyler Adams, Vamos king Herculez Gomez, US Women's captain Lindsey Heaps, global newsbreaker Fabrizio Romano, and more, a chorus of voices producing weekly digital shows, podcasts, newsletters, livestreams, and a full lineup of national live events, as well as TV episodes and more.

At our core, we believe football is more than just a game; it's a lens to understand the world, feel human emotion, experience a sense of global connection, and make memories together. That is what makes it the most important, least important thing.

Courage.

@Meninblazers @WomensGameMIB @VamosMIB